Southern Decadence in NEW ORLEANS

Louisiana State University Press Baton Rouge

Southern Decadence in New Orleans

HOWARD PHILIPS SMITH
&
FRANK PEREZ

Foreword by Robert Laurent | Afterword by Maureen Block

Published by Louisiana State University Press

Manufactured in the United States of America
First printing

Designer: Michelle A. Neustrom
Typeface: Sentinel
Printer and binder: Sheridan Books, Inc.

Library of Congress Cataloging-in-Publication Data

Names: Smith, Howard Philips, author. | Perez, Frank, 1968– author.
Title: Southern Decadence in New Orleans / Howard Philips Smith and Frank Perez ; foreword by Robert Laurent ; afterword by Maureen Block.
Description: Baton Rouge : Louisiana State University Press, [2018] | Includes bibliographical references and index.
Identifiers: LCCN 2018001241 | ISBN 9780807169537 (cloth : alk. paper)
Subjects: LCSH: Southern Decadence (Festival)—History. | Gay pride celebrations—Louisiana—New Orleans—History. | Gay pride parades—Louisiana—New Orleans—History. | Festivals—Louisiana—New Orleans—History.
Classification: LCC HQ76.965.G38 S65 2019 | DDC 306.76/60976335—dc23
LC record available at https://lccn.loc.gov/2018001241

The paper in this book meets the guidelines for permanence and durability of the Committee on Production Guidelines for Book Longevity of the Council on Library Resources. ♾

For Frederick Douglas Wright,
the first Southern Decadence grand marshal,
and to all the most decadent grand marshals
who followed in his footsteps.

Real Southern Decadence is Boss Finley slapping the piss out of Miss Lucy in *Sweet Bird of Youth.*

—Jon Newlin

Contents

Foreword, by Robert Laurent xi
A Note on Numbering and Sources xiii

Introduction: The Quest for the Pleasure-Dome 1
1. Decadence Takes the World, 2016: Part 1 21
2. The Birth of Southern Decadence, 1972–1980 41
3. The French Quarter Gay Community 67
4. The Gaying of Decadence, 1981–1996 79
5. Southern Decadence and Carnival 98
6. Bar Culture and the Rise of Decadence 104
7. The AIDS Crisis and Community Building 115
8. The Juggernaut, 1997–2015 119
9. Decadence Takes the World, 2016: Part 2 143
10. The Future of Southern Decadence 159
Afterword, by Maureen Block 171

Acknowledgments 173
Appendixes 177
Putting on the Parade: Interviews with Southern Decadence Participants 179
Edward "Blanche" Norton 179
Robert Laurent 185
Lou Bernard Jr. 194
Errol Rizzuto 200
Greg Manogue (Miss Love) 206
Rip and Marsha Naquin-Delain 218
Early Southern Decadence Invitations 223
The Super 8mm Films 235
Master List of Parades and Grand Marshals 237
In Memoriam 243
Notes 245
Index 255

FOREWORD

To all the decadent, departed spirits that have gathered here tonight in celebration of Southern Decadence and its forces of Gaiety, Frivolity and riotous Cross-Dressing, we summon one particular Deity, one Prime Mover, to usher forth and join our gathered hearts. O True Spirit of Southern Decadence, O Original Cause of Jollity and Inebriation, return to this hallowed soil that you stumbled across in years previous. Sashay into our hood once more. As descendants and followers of your Decadent Ways, we beseech you, Michael Lloyd Evers, to bless us, gladden our hearts (and other portions of our anatomy), and allow us to revel in True Southern Decadence, Now and Forever. Amen.

—An incantation read in Armstrong Park by Southern Decadence Grand Marshal Edward "Blanche" Norton, 1995

The origin of Southern Decadence is very simple: it began with a party. In celebration of new and old friends meeting during some hot late August days in 1972, we decided to get together for one last summer revel before work and school began again. With Mardi Gras ingrained in New Orleans as a template, there was never a doubt that it would be a costume party. We added a theme emphasizing our Tennessee Williams intoxication and unwittingly began a tradition.

As a graphic designer, I volunteered to create an invitation for the event to make it more fun and "official." The only thing on our minds then was having a good time. When the second year rolled around, we decided to repeat the revelry but added the twist of meeting in costume at our favorite French Quarter bar before parading back to the house party. Successive years evolved into the bar crawl becoming the party itself. Our original group of participants eventually lost interest and faded away, but the festivity was evidently too good to be abandoned: it was continued by new blood. And it goes on to this day.

Kudos to Howard Philips Smith and Frank Perez for sussing out the truth of the origins of Southern Decadence and definitively correcting the misinformation that has accumulated over the years. Southern Decadence began as a gay, straight, and ethnically diverse celebration of friendship. The Original Belle Rêve Southern Decadents salute their descendants for the continuation of fun and festivity and the spirit of Laissez les Bon Temps Rouler!

Robert Laurent
New Orleans

A NOTE ON NUMBERING AND SOURCES

Discrepancies have arisen regarding the numbering of the annual Southern Decadence events, its grand marshals, and parades. For example, the 1974 invitation declares that it is the "Third Annual Southern Decadent Party," while the 1975 invitation announces the "Third Annual Belle Rêve Southern Decadent Parade," as the focus shifted to the parade rather than the party. The 1977 invitation refers to the "Fifth Annual Belle Rêve Southern Decadent Costume Parade," while the 1978 invitation refers to "Belle Rêve Southern Decadent Costume Parade," and then 1979 announces the "Sixth Annual Belle Rêve Southern Decadent Costume Parade," apparently skipping 1978 in the numbering sequence. In addition, in 1978, two grand marshals were chosen: Robert King, grand marshal no. 5; and Kathleen Kavanaugh, grand marshal no. 6. Hurricanes also caused several years to be canceled, thus obfuscating the tally even more: grand marshals were obliged to serve two years in a row. To avoid confusion, therefore, this book refers to Southern Decadence events and grand marshals by year rather than by number.

Unless otherwise noted, all quotations in the text are taken from the authors' interviews with the person being quoted. Interviews are listed at the back of the book.

Southern Decadence in New Orleans

“Elegy for Moss Land,” 1940. Double-exposure photograph by Clarence John Laughlin, capturing the slow decline of the Old South. This ruin and destruction became part of our collective consciousness. Courtesy of the Clarence John Laughlin Archive at The Historic New Orleans Collection, accession no. 1981.247.1.888.

INTRODUCTION

The Quest for the Pleasure-Dome

In Xanadu did Kubla Khan
A stately pleasure-dome decree:
Where Alph, the sacred river, ran
Through caverns measureless to man
Down to a sunless sea.
. . . .
I would build that dome in air,
That sunny dome! those caves of ice!
And all who heard should see them there,
And all should cry, Beware! Beware!
His flashing eyes, his floating hair!
Weave a circle round him thrice,
And close your eyes with holy dread
For he on honey-dew hath fed,
And drunk the milk of Paradise.

—Samuel Taylor Coleridge, "Kubla Khan:
Or, A Vision in a Dream"

The summer celebration in New Orleans known as Southern Decadence ostensibly appeared out of nowhere, opposite the grand festival of Carnival, a distorted reflection in a hot, steamed-up looking glass on the other side of the calendar. What began in 1972 as a simple party thrown by a group of close friends was repeated the following year and continued to gain momentum until it became one of the city's largest festivals. Southern Decadence now stretches across a whole week, with a formal coronation and press parties, and climaxes with a parade through the French Quarter. Multiple grand marshals reign over the festivities, which feature official colors, songs, themes, and charities. Crowds exceed two hundred thousand people, and the economic impact on the city is estimated at $250 million, perhaps more. Attracting mostly gay men, the event is a communal festival that takes place in and around the French Quarter and is characterized by street parties, drag contests, dancing, drinking, bead tosses, and very little clothing.

But it was not always massively popular, internationally known, or gay-centric. On the contrary, the original party was a smallish affair with both straight and gay participants who were seeking to stave off the restlessness of the summer of 1972, one of the hottest on record, as well as to celebrate their own good fortune, their friendships, and, most important, their love of this unique city. But the occasion developed into a quest for the mythical pleasure-dome—described by Samuel Taylor Coleridge in a drugged stupor and now rendered a trope of the collective unconscious—amid delirium and swoon and ultimately release from a shadowy, vagabond existence.[1] The unassuming party became an annual tradition among the founders and steadily grew larger until it overtook and consumed the hard-core devotees who religiously schedule their lives around Labor Day Weekend.

In New Orleans, the summer months are hot and sultry, filled with equal doses of unbearable heat and suffocating humidity. By the end of the summer, many inhabitants have either left town or been defeated by the heat. Around the city, especially in the old neighborhoods such as the French Quarter, Faubourg Marigny, and Faubourg Tremé, the only way to soothe the spirit in the late afternoon heat was a bottle or two of strong drink. By August, *ennui* had settled in for good, that terrible malady and half-brother of *melancholia,* whose other guise was terminal *boredom.* Yet *boredom* was simply one of the many symptoms of *ennui,* an almost lethal disdain for life itself and a doomed sense of fate coupled with decadence and destruction.

This seething sultriness of the air was long blamed for pestilence and insanity. Such was the case in 1853, when yellow fever attacked the city for months. After three weeks of unfavorable cold, the final days of July turned into an intense inferno, with the atmosphere so heavy and oppressive that breathing was nearly impossible. City officials, in an act of desperation, ignited barrels of tar and fired strategically placed cannons to purify the air, believing that this would solve the problem, but it was all for naught. In *The Diary of a Samaritan,* physician William Robinson described the city: "Not a breath of air disturbed the dense smoke, which slowly ascended in curling columns until it reached the height of about five hundred feet. Here it seemed equipoised, festooning over our doomed city like a funeral pall, and there remaining until the shades of night disputed with it the reign of darkness."[2] By the beginning of the fall, the pestilence suddenly disappeared, as if the equinox had, with its celestial conjurations, banished the demon it had unwittingly summoned. Though yellow fever no longer plagues the city, the heat, the terrible heat, remains.

In the late 1870s, Lafcadio Hearn began writing about the Creole culture of New Orleans. Working for the *Daily City Item* and then the *Times-Democrat,* he documented the strange and the unusual and endeared himself to the locals with quaint woodcuts and vignettes of daily life.[3] Hearn described the texture of the city's atmospheres in summer to an extraordinary degree in *Chita,* a novella set in 1867:

> Midsummer in the pest-smitten city of New Orleans. Heat motionless and ponderous. The steel-blue of the sky bleached from the furnace-circle of the horizon;—the lukewarm river ran yellow and noiseless as a torrent of fluid wax. Even sounds seemed blunted by the heaviness of the air;—the rumbling of wheels, the reverberation of footsteps, fell half-toned upon the ear, like sounds that visit a dozing brain. Daily, almost at the same hour, the continuous sense

> of atmospheric oppression became thickened;—a packed herd of low-bellying clouds lumbered up from the Gulf; crowded blackly against the sun; flickered, thundered, and burst in torrential rain—tepid, perpendicular—and vanished utterly away. Then, more furiously than before, the sun flamed down—roofs and pavements steamed; the streets seemed to smoke; the air grew suffocating with vapor; and the luminous city filled with a faint, sickly odor—a stale smell, as of dead leaves suddenly disinterred from wet mould,—as of grasses decomposing after a flood. Something saffron speckled the slimy water of the gutters; sulphur some called it; others feared even to give it a name. Was it only the wind-blown pollen of some innocuous plant? I do not know; but to many it seemed as if the Invisible Destruction were scattering visible seed![4]

In the American South, hot and sultry July and August are known as the dog days, a period of "stagnation, inactivity, and sluggishness," according to the *Old Farmer's Almanac.*[5] Legend directly linked the rise of Sirius, the dog star, in the constellation Canis Major, with the hottest and most humid weather of the year, an evil time when, as John Brady wrote in 1812, "the sea boiled, wine turned sour, dogs grew mad, and all other creatures including humankind became languid, causing diseases such as hysterics, frenzies and burning fevers."[6] But along with the languor, the hothouse air, stifling and close, there also bred a lurid and contagious form of decadence.

The New Century Dictionary defines *decadence* as a "falling off from a state of excellence and prosperity into ruin or decay."[7] In the eighteenth century, Edward Gibbon wrote that Rome fell because of its decadence, a line of pseudohistory that became part of the mystique and dire consequences associated with the term.[8] Something decadent was also seen as tantalizing, pleasurable, and ultimately deadly. To be decadent was to risk a great fall from grace. In the late nineteenth century, a group of French and English writers and artists became known as the Decadents. Their work featured unconventional and artificial subjects and a very subtle style, and they were characterized as appealing to luxurious self-indulgence and pleasures and as having low morals and a great love of delectation, money, and fame.

The term *Southern Decadence* entered the American lexicon at around the same time. The South and its old aristocracy remained firmly entrenched in their antebellum ways, seeking to return to those halcyon days but merely ushering in a period of even greater decline. The phrase eventually came to describe the South, with its strange sense of place and history, of progressive ruin and longing for the past.

Geographically and historically, New Orleans has always been simultaneously part of the Deep South and an odd outsider, an isolated island of hedonists carefully crafted and cared for by European settlers, or Creoles, especially the French and their Old World affectations. The city was already populated by pleasure seekers at the time of the Louisiana Purchase in 1803, and it continued to celebrate life to the fullest. Residents remained devoted to the illusive and ephemeral things that made life in the swamps not only bearable but even preferable. After becoming part of the United States, New Orleans became one of the country's largest cities, and lavish Mississippi River steamboats brought travelers who demanded entertainment. Rachel Jackson, the wife of President Andrew Jackson, recognized the city's sensual appeal, noting that New Babylon, as she called it, was both enticing and repellent.[9] When the summer heat became so unbearable, when the body refused to move amid such oppressive indolence, the only thing left was a desire for release and pleasure.

The Catholic Church had a strong hold on the city, bringing not only religious strictures but also the grand tradition of European Carnival. The city developed a love of masking, festivals, street parades, costuming, and lavish parties before the months of atonement during Lent. Carnival season began every year on the Eve of Epiphany, January 6, when New Orleans took on an air of otherworldliness and exoticism, and lasted until the dawn of Ash Wednesday, culminating in the pagan celebrations of Shrove Tuesday, a much-anticipated day for a city filled with sybarites. The traditions and rituals of the Carnival season have become as powerful as any religion, with parades, masked balls, Kings' Cake parties, and social gatherings embedded in the general psyche, a voyage to fantastic lands filled with mythical creatures.

In his macabre masterpiece, *Ghosts along the Mississippi,* Clarence John Laughlin not only documented the faltering and ruinous plantations from a bygone era but also waxed poetic and romantic about the architecture of the South and lost antebellum times. His often mysterious and provocative, and at times camp and lush, descriptions reveal a stereotypical and ingrained definition of *Southern Decadence*: the slow destruction of time and longing for the Old South. Many of his double-exposure prints bear such names as *Elegy for the Old South* and *Farewell to the Past.* The book's first plate shows a columned plantation mirrored in the seeping waters of the vast swamps around New Orleans, hovering above the reflection lodged strangely within the Spanish moss of one of Louisiana's ubiquitous old cypress trees. A lone woman rises out of the marsh, a dark figure beckoning to the past or pointing to what had been. Titled *Elegy for Moss Land,* this multilayered photograph, so evocative and surreal, became an iconic symbol of decay and destruction and a literal interpretation of *Southern Decadence.* Laughlin wrote eloquently about the South and its slow submersion into this realm of supposed decadence:

> Such are some of the histories of Louisiana's houses, too long to tell here in complete detail; too tragic for words alone to capture, since it has been expressed so well, so completely in great crumbling masses of wood and brick and stone; in walls cracked by the resistless and feverish searchings of plant roots; in stains from the hot caresses of the rain; the melancholia of great oaks, draped in their mourning gowns of grey moss; the smell of the magnolia whose scent is nearly tangible, summoning up a richness that seems, at times, to cling to the walls like a materialized memory; the violence of decay that produces in these surfaces colors as though from a sinister fairyland—in all these things the grandeur and decay of plantation culture is written in a language wholly integral with the things it describes.
>
> And these, but a few of the little-known, and tragic, chronicles of the shadow, which is time; and of the light, which is life—tales set in a land where the Mississippi, immense and heavy, shoulders the levees; a land where the earth melts imperceptibly into river and marsh; where moss reigns over un-

moving and menacing water; where time, light, and the river have formed an intricate and fateful web whose conformations have never found a duplicate elsewhere.

Herein, too, is conveyed some part of the strange and difficult beauty of Louisiana, for which we, who have loved her, can only cry: Louisiana, ruin-haunted land; land of the writhing, ever-coiling bayous, whose passages are lined with the grey dolorous membranes of moss; land of the magnolia whose wild sweetness becomes almost visible because of its heavy burden of remembrance; land of broken white columns struggling amid fierce green hordes of foliage; land of shadow-haunted and shadow-silent waters, mirroring a brooding that knows no bounds—a feeling of being lost forever in the savage and magical wilderness of time, where the past and the present have become one, and are forever and inextricably mingled! Louisiana: to thy moist and teeming earth; to thy flat dark mirrors overhung with the grey clouds of moss, and the green clouds of willows; to thy lush vestments of sugar cane and rice; to thy great sails of banana trees; to thy palms, which are quivering fountains of light; to thy heavily scented and moon-amorous flowers; to thy iron growths of balconies and cemetery ornamentation; to thy simple, naive, and earth-loving buildings of brick and plaster; to thee, whose very name is music, do our hearts turn, Louisiana![10]

Hearn summed up this interpretation of *Southern Decadence* in an 1878 letter:

I have spoken with enthusiasm of the beauty of New Orleans; I must speak with pain of her decay. The city is fading, mouldering, crumbling—slowly but certainly. As moulders and crumbles some quaint pleasure-house in the midst of weed-grown gardens once luxuriantly romantic as those which form a background for the warm pictures of the *Decameron,* so moulders this fair, quaint city in the midst of the ruined paradise of Louisiana. So, also, are mouldering all the old cities of the South, for their prosperity had its root of nourishment in the enormous wealth of the planters of cotton and rice and sugar, and that wealth is gone. I suppose that when the hatreds of the war have burnt themselves out; when the descendants of the ruined planters remember the family

> misfortunes only as traditions are remembered; when a new social system shall have arisen from the ashes of the old, like the new world of the Scandinavian Edda from the fires of Ragnarok—then shall the old plantations be again made fertile, and the cottonwood cleared away, and the life of the old Southern cities be resurrected. But the new South shall never be as the old. Those once grand residences that are being devoured by mossy decay can never be rebuilt; the old plantations, which extended over whole parishes will be parceled out to a hundred farmers from States that are not Southern; and the foreign beauties of New Orleans will never be restored. It is the picturesqueness of the South, the poetry, the traditions, the legends, the superstitions, the quaint faiths, the family prides, the luxuriousness, the splendid indolence and the splendid sins of the old social system which has passed, or which is now passing away forever. It is all this which is dead or dying in New Orleans, and which can hope for no trumpet-call to resurrection.[11]

New Orleans stubbornly retained its allure, its opulence amid decay, while the rest of the South remained populated with puritanical Southern Baptists, pursuing a life not of passion and make-believe, dancing and drinking, but of temperance, hard work, and moderation. Yet even today, many people from other parts of the South make pilgrimages to New Orleans to experience the hedonistic side of life, drinking, carousing, eating exotic foods, and watching the grand festivals and processions. At least in the early 1970s, most of these visitors were not pleasure seekers in a decadent sense but rather conservative and inflexible, with an insular view of the world, and the celebration that echoed the excesses of Carnival took on the name *Southern Decadence* to describe the response to fits of *ennui* during those slow, sultry summers.[12]

ᔓ

For many people, the social upheavals of the 1960s and early 1970s—sometimes violent protests against the unpopular war in Vietnam and in support of civil rights, women's rights, and the budding environmental movement, as well as the summer 1969 riots at New York City's Stonewall Inn—culminated in a re-evaluation of the self and one's place in a larger society, leading to new ways of thinking and living. Defining the zeitgeist of the new decade in terms of the decadent South became a touchstone for those seeking places of refuge from this larger society, those whom Jack Kerouac had dubbed the subterraneans: "They are hip without being slick, they are intelligent without being corny, they are intellectual as hell and know all about Pound without being pretentious or talking too much about it, they are very quiet, they are very Christlike."[13] Kerouac captured perfectly this sense of being below the surface, of belonging to another world, out of sight and secretly hidden away from the banalities of the quotidian. By the early 1970s, gender roles were becoming more fluid, with the line between masculine and feminine rendered less distinct, blurry, and at times superfluous. Clothing reflected this new mind-set, and the rise of the glam-rock movement and men confident enough to wear makeup and dresses signaled a drastic shift in consciousness and expression. Though such androgyny arguably had always existed among gay men and lesbians, it now spread to straight men and women, who sought new modes of expression within this underground. Charles Maniaci, a young transplant from Biloxi, Mississippi, in the late 1960s captured the spirit of this period of transition. Like many young men at the time from rural southern areas who were experimenting with and discovering their sexuality, he gravitated to the freedom of the French Quarter.

> I never felt comfortable in Biloxi. I loved my parents, siblings, extended family and friends, but I just didn't fit in. I knew that one day I'd break away somehow and live a freer life. Some of my Gulf Coast friends—all straight as far as I knew—and I would head to the Quarter to break free of the small town, rural mentality of our home cities and participate in the *joie de vivre* that the Big Easy offered. We would first hit the gay bars where men were very eager to buy us drinks, hoping to liquor us up and score.
>
> Early on we frequented Regent's Row, owned by John Emerold, the original Finale, and Café Lafitte in Exile. Usually at Lafitte's we would secure a place to stay with a gay man, who was willing to house a few hot boys. After my friends

were sufficiently drunk they would wander off to other locations on Bourbon Street leaving me with the host, and we would rendezvous sometime during the night or in the morning at the host's house. Regent's Row was a bit on the elegant side and had a piano bar. I was first introduced to Ruthie, the Duck Lady, there. Ruthie was a fixture in the gay bars and I spent many times sitting next to her at a bar, buying her a "beer for now and one for later." One night at Regents Row I met John Emerold, the owner, who took an interest in me as he did with many young guys. We became friends and had a relationship for a while. Life wasn't always easy in the Big Easy and Johnny helped me through many rough patches.

The original Finale was a dance bar that had a live band, Paul Varisco and the Milestones. Daisy Mae, the notorious French Quarter queen and her court, which included Foxy, Numa, and Miss Ella, would sit at a table near the door so they could scrutinize anyone entering the bar. If someone unknown to Daisy Mae or her court entered they were interviewed, camped around with by the queens and if not offended, welcomed and introduced around. Most of the patrons at the Finale seemed to know each other but were always on the lookout for the vice cops, who arrested anyone showing any form of physical contact between men. Men dancing with men was also illegal. The bartender would caution anyone who became too friendly with another man. There was always a bunch of fag hags in attendance, providing cover, especially if the alert went out that a suspicious character had entered the bar. If someone didn't pass Daisy Mae's scrutiny or the doorman's instinct, there was some sort of code between the doorman, Daisy Mae, and the bartender to alert the clients of danger, like a whistle or a special light flashing on the dance floor. Usually, the bar management would know of an impending "raid" by the vice as they had a paid informant on the inside and we were signaled to leave before they came. Over time, straight followers of the band started to infiltrate the bar and it became very mixed. Many of the gay patrons moved on to frequent other bars.

Café Lafitte's was more of a cruise bar. You went there if you wanted to get laid. There were always a lot of horny locals and transient visitors to the city up for grabs. Many early mornings after an evening at the bars we would go to the strip bars where the local musicians would congregate for jam sessions after the shows were over.

As for food, you could get a plate of red beans and rice at Buster Holmes for nineteen cents. The Coffee Pot was an early morning meeting place for many of the gays and drag queens. The waitress, Pearl, was like our mother and we lingered over countless cups of coffee. Alton was a black effeminate waiter who would camp it up with us. It was a fun place to be. Other favorite places were Café du Monde and Morning Call near Jackson Square.

Sometimes if we wanted to slum we would go to the Greek sailor bars on Decatur Street near Canal. This was a very dangerous and dirty area. My friends Angel, a playboy bunny, and her dyke lover, Harriet, would frequent these bars and give hand jobs to Greek sailors for money. The bars were interesting because the Greek men danced with each other and there was an atmosphere of "anything goes." The local vice seemed to ignore this seedy area.

There was a bar called the Safari, which was located near the bar that burned, the Up Stairs Lounge. There were black female strippers and we would go and watch them. The one we liked, Miss Jasmin, would frequently squat down near us during her show and ask us to buy her a pickle from a large jar, which was on the bar. We usually did for five cents.

If we—the young guys—weren't getting any more free drinks at Lafitte's, we would go to the Galley House, or as we called it, the Wrinkle Room. The older patrons were always nice to us and would gladly buy us drinks for our company. Mardi Gras was a sex free-for-all. On Bourbon Street in front of Lafitte's, people would form *daisy chains* and within the circle people would have sex. Fear of the vice cops seemed to disappear at Carnival.

The quarter wasn't very gentrified at the time. Beer cans were legal on the street and, in the early mornings during Carnival Season, Bourbon Street was at least ankle deep in empty beer cans and trash. The smell of stale beer, urine, and the remains of Lucky Dogs permeated the air. There were dangerous areas of the quarter and we didn't venture there after dark, like the area near Rampart Street and the park.

Of course jazz and the blues were the predominant music one heard floating out of most French Quarter bars onto the streets. However, we witnessed the changing music and drug scene at some of the bars, especially the gay ones. The movement seemed to flow from folk music to Beatles to Motown to psychedelics to disco or an overlapping of genres. As the hippie movement took root in the Quarter, the drugs moved from abuse of alcohol and prescription drugs (black mollies were very popular) to marijuana and LSD. Poppers (amyl nitrate) were popular on the dance floor as well as in the bedroom. Most bars were segregated during that period. With the influx of the free-love, anything-goes "flower children," my generation's involvement in the civil rights movement, and the Broadway hit *Hair* in 1968, those racial lines began to slowly crumble. It seemed the motto for the '60s was from Bob Dylan's 1964 hit, "The Times They Are A-Changin'." And we felt it.

Gay Carnival krewes were popular and getting an invitation to one of the balls was coveted. Membership was by invitation only and I was invited by a friend to be a member of Ganymede. It was one of the lesser-known krewes and didn't survive very long. We also knew many of the younger drag queens, who competed in pageants and preformed in bars as well as the gay balls. Drag was very popular across the South. Some of guys I knew who did drag later transitioned to beautiful, sexy women and performed as women in the straight strip clubs on Bourbon Street. Sadly, the gay community didn't understand transgender issues at the time and many shunned those who transitioned.

Sex was so available at the time. There was still a cultural taboo on good girls having sex, so boys would go out with their girlfriends and when they didn't put out, they would head for the quarter and a gay bar for a drink and perhaps more, depending on how drunk they were. And there were so many tourists who came to New Orleans at that time just for the sex. It was abundant and easy. Even if you asked a lone male stranger on the street in the French Quarter if he wanted to have sex, the answer was frequently yes. There were so many drunks and willing participants.

John Emerold who owned the Regent's Row bar also owned Canal Baths. In the late 1960s the locals I knew didn't frequent the baths, as they were considered dirty and because sex was so available elsewhere. Europeans and tourists

> frequented them for the most part. This changed as time went on and by the '70s more people were talking about going to the bath houses.
>
> After hanging out there on weekends, I moved to New Orleans in late 1968, after establishing some friends. I stayed with Daisy Mae and his lover Timmy for a short time until I found a roommate. After a while my group frequented the Caverns (affectionately called the "dildo room" because of the fake stalactites) and Pete's bar which was the first real disco in the Quarter.
>
> Many of my friends and I enjoyed the liberation from social taboos and the finding of self that the Quarter provided. We also knew that at some point it would be the time to take what we had learned and move on to a more stable environment. I moved in 1970 although I would spend some weekends there for several years. Most of us went on to college and began careers in other cities. Many of my friends moved to San Francisco. We all had a great love of New Orleans and were grateful for the personal growth afforded us there. There is no place on earth like the French Quarter, and I visit every opportunity I get.
>
> It was this curious and exciting mix of locals who understood the freedom that the Quarter offered, tourists looking for an escape from their normal routines, individuals not comfortable in their small towns, artists and intellectuals attracted to the bohemian lifestyle and the real unusual characters that found acceptance and made living in the French Quarter exciting.
>
> That would go on to be the essence of the 1970s.[14]

In this context, a group of transplants from Chicago, Manhattan, Lafayette, Baton Rouge, and other far-flung locales came together to create a powerful New Orleans tradition. Southern Decadence was given birth not as a consequence of these trends, but as a result of this sense of experimentation.

Although the early years of Southern Decadence appeared disorganized and even frivolous, certain parallels existed between its original outright and unbridled celebration and a similar consciousness permeating cinema and literature. In 1953, Anaïs Nin attended a masquerade party thrown by Paul Mathieson and Renata Druks. In keeping with the party's theme, "Come as Your Madness," revelers sported a variety of incredible costumes—Cleopatra, a

Spanish pirate Don Juan, the somnambulist from *The Cabinet of Dr. Caligari,* and a bejeweled Eastern potentate. Others carried death masks on sticks, painted themselves half-black and half-white, or twirled scarf-laden umbrellas above their heads. According to Nin, one of those in attendance was filmmaker Kenneth Anger, who "was waiting in the bedroom with a lighted candle and had asked Renate to let him know the propitious moment to make his entrance. He was dressed as Hecate, goddess of the moon, earth, and infernal regions, sorcery, and witchcraft. Only one heavily made-up eye was visible. His long black fingernails were made of black quills. The rest was all a towering figure of lace, veils, beads, and feathers."[15]

Anger used the characters from the party in his 1954 film, *Inauguration of the Pleasure Dome,* revealing sacred and profane archetypes as represented by demons and gods. Anger populated his insular universe with an array of pseudo-royals with pretensions of grandeur whose pastimes included ingesting jewels and transforming themselves into strange costumed creatures. A camp sensibility reigned, and his characters depicted this type of conjoining and reconfiguring as primal, subconscious. The denizens of Anger's pleasure dome included both straights and gays as well as people who were bisexual and transgender.[16] These characters served as the symbolic precursors of the Southern Decadence founders.

This disassociation from and criticism of so-called normative society were exemplified in a suite of films released around the time of Southern Decadence's founding. *Fellini Satyricon* (1969) offered director Federico Fellini's modern-day interpretation of a classic tale from the acerbic pen of Roman author Petronius Arbiter. The main characters, Encolpius and Ascyltus, came to vivid life as they navigated the labyrinths of the ancient Roman Empire, two randy and homosexual friends who exemplified the so-called decadence and decline of ancient Rome about which Gibbon had written. They explored the underground cultural fringe, making forays into decadence and extravagance as the empire tumbled into decline. Fellini integrated the experiments of the 1960s into his film, adding pansexuality to a panorama of existing sexualities. Decadence's founders were themselves fraying the fabric of New Orleans so-

Film still from Federico Fellini's *Fellini Satyricon* (1969), which embellished Petronius Arbiter's glorious portrayal of the decadence of ancient Rome. Courtesy of Produzioni Europee Associati/Album/Art Resource, New York. For editorial use only.

ciety as they navigated the streets in their gaudy costumes with their pagan pretentions, exploring and exposing these new excesses and tendencies in ways previously unheard of. Even in the city of voodoo and crackpots, subculture had always been just that—*sub*culture, hidden beneath—except for Mardi Gras, the one day of the year when all costuming was allowed. Southern Decadence was blasphemy, bringing into the street revelers all dolled-up in drag or dressed in phantasmagorical costumes outside the protective bubble of Carnival.

Many of the friends who founded Southern Decadence lived or frequented the ersatz salon at Belle Rêve,[17] located at 2110 Barracks Street adjacent to the French Quarter in the Faubourg Tremé, where they all came together in this, at the time, secret haven and flophouse. That community was reminiscent of the odd assortment of friends and lovers depicted in Jack Smith's *Flaming Creatures* (1963).[18] These ambiguous creatures, as Smith called them, freely donned women's clothes, at times appearing in full drag and at other times simply wrapping themselves in diaphanous fabrics. They exuded decadence and the exotic, like ghosts from a long-ago Hollywood set, a group of subterraneans hell-bent on self-absorption, illusory glory, and irony. In Smith's depiction, they were both innocent and sophisticated, although some of them were nude and the sex act was relegated to the *comique*. Andy Warhol's *Chelsea Girls* (1966) inherited Smith's aesthetic, portraying a similar group of creatures living at Manhattan's run-down Chelsea Hotel. The film featured drag superstar Mario Montez, who also had appeared in *Flaming Creatures*. Warhol's project involved the simultaneous projection of two filmstrips side by side, creating a dual narrative that rarely came together as a single story but nonetheless presented a disjointed and at times disassociated glimpse of reality.[19]

But the closest parallel to the coterie of friends who established Decadence lies in the outrageous characters of *Pink Flamingos* (1972), John Waters's underground film that particularly resonated with the gay community.[20] Made on a shoestring budget in the run-down areas of Baltimore, the film features a birthday-party sequence that exemplifies the period's antisocial and madcap sensibility, with camp reigning at every turn and no sacred cows. The party, held at a trailer in a secluded wooded area, is attended by bearded men wearing dresses and lipstick, a group that includes Divine, the consummate terror-drag revolutionary who may have taken her name from a character in Jean Genet's *Notre-Dame-des-Fleurs*. Waters used his troupe of transgressive actors in many other productions, but Divine always symbolized the ultimate drag persona, full of rage and compassion alongside a sense of high fashion and makeup

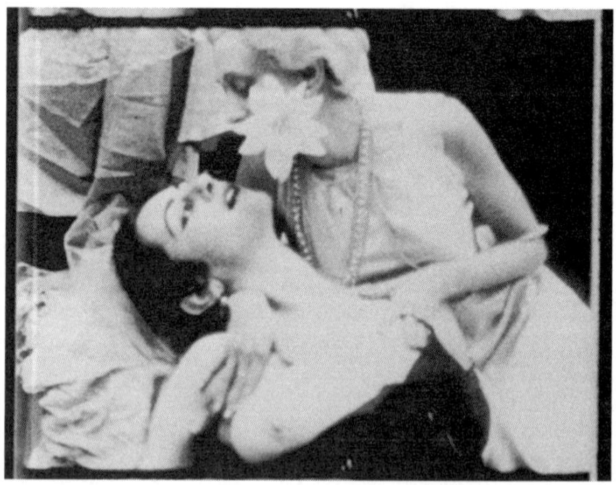

Film still from Jack Smith's *Flaming Creatures* (1962–63). Channeling an underground reservoir of Old Hollywood films and gay cultural references, Smith's film epitomizes decadence at its most camp. Copyright by Jack Smith Archive. Courtesy of Gladstone Gallery, New York and Brussels.

Film still from John Waters's *Pink Flamingos* (1972). Waters's transgressive film illustrates an underground group of misfits who continually challenged preconceived notions of gender and sexuality. Courtesy of New Line Cinema/Album/Art Resource, New York. For editorial use only.

artifice that harkened back to the golden age of Hollywood. Although Divine and her fellow creatures lived a mostly subterranean existence, when they did appear for public viewing, it was a spectacle to behold and more often than not a complete outrage. As Southern Decadence morphed into a grand display of parading characters and glamour-pusses, they, too, added a certain shock value to their escapades, which in retrospect were subversive, iconoclastic, and most certainly provocative.

Divine also joined the San Francisco theater group known as the Cockettes. Formed by George Edgerly Harris II (Hibiscus), who was living in a commune in the Haight-Ashbury, from a group of hippies in 1969, this mixed bag of men and women was influenced by the novel and the absurd, harkening back to the Cabaret Voltaire crossed with off-Broadway. The Cockettes handcrafted all their costumes themselves out of whatever was on hand with lots of glitter and other sorts of outrageous paragons. They "blithely mocked sexual stereotypes in clever numbers that featured outrageously androgynous costumes stitched together from thrift-store scraps and Dumpster castaways," wrote Pam Tent in her book about the group."[21] Shows referenced Old Hollywood glamour and paid homage to the screen goddesses of the past, such as Greta Garbo and Maria Montez. Men appeared in drag with their beards full of glittery and over-the-top make-up. Mostly improvised, their act mainly consisted of old show tunes, reconfigured in the moment to suit their bohemian and off-kilter style. At the Kaliflower commune, Hibiscus set up a room full of found costumes and clothing for creative activities. Costuming and then performing in public became a common goal with these groups, and they found it exciting to think that their lives were part of the show.

Stranded in Canton, William Eggleston's documentary shot partly on the streets of New Orleans in the early 1970s, captures the milieu in which Southern Decadence was born. Many of the film's main characters are simply drunken carousers and pistol-packing buddies, spouting off at the mouth in redneck bars, while others include jazz musicians and effete homosexuals lurking in the shadows. As Roberta Smith wrote in a 2004 *New York Times* article, "Shot in 1974 with a Sony Porta-pak, the crazily careering *Stranded in Canton* documents a cast of hard-drinking Southerners with the intimacy, ease and instability of a seasoned participant. In one sequence, a man with peroxide hair, makeup and a sequined T-shirt sings old love songs, swanning around with a toilet-paper boa. In others, shots are fired; good old boys decapitate chick-

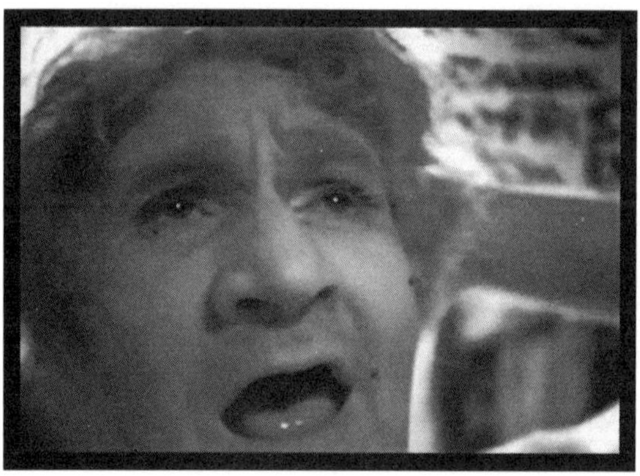

above: Film still from William Eggleston's *Stranded in Canton* (1974), showing Lady Russell. Copyright by Eggleston Artistic Trust. Courtesy of David Zwirner, New York/London.

right: John Kennedy Toole's masterpiece, *A Confederacy of Dunces* (1980), reveals the unique and at times outlandish culture simmering below the surface in New Orleans. Courtesy of Louisiana State University Press.

ens; and a young bearded man with an angelic face raves about being stranded in Canton, a colloquialism for being out of one's mind on drugs or alcohol. Whiffs of Southern Gothic . . . rise to the surface—fierce, tragic and proud."[22]

These types of characters are also evident in John Kennedy Toole's *A Confederacy of Dunces,* written in the late 1960s. Toole captures the grit and grime of the underside of the city in his depictions of the outré residents lurking in the corners of some of New Orleans's forgotten wards. His characters are formed from an odd mix of the eccentric and the exotic and may have been based on real people, highlighting another side of life in the hothouse of New Orleans.[23]

Other authors positioned their work in an explicitly gay New Orleans universe. For example, a Tennessee Williams play from the late 1950s—*And Tell Sad Stories of the Deaths of Queens*—focuses on an aging queen and her attempts to find love.[24] William Talsman's *The Gaudy Image* (1958) follows a New Orleans transplant's quest for the ultimate male figure, the "gaudy image."[25] A decade later, William Tressner used real characters from the French Quarter to populate *Queens of the Quarter,* an extraordinary tale of two young men searching for love.[26] Along for the ride were drag queens, hustlers, and young acolytes, struggling on a day-to-day basis to exist and find a certain legitimacy within their own small universe. Although many of these works were never part of the mainstream, they nevertheless reflected real cultural currents flowing through New Orleans that influenced the founding of Southern Decadence. These pariahs and misfits were kin to the group of friends who decided to parade around the French Quarter on the last official weekend of summer.

But the founders had no idea that their procession would expand and ultimately overwhelm the streets, taking on a new and dazzling form. The first few incarnations of Southern Decadence attracted little notice as revelers traipsed from bar to bar, waving fans, scarves, and cocktails. By the end of the first decade, however, hundreds had joined in, sashaying along as Decadence swarmed unsuspecting tourist bars. On one occasion, the procession ended up in the lobby of the Fairmont Hotel (now the restored Roosevelt Hotel) in the Central Business District, much to the consternation of the doorman, who tried in vain to prevent the mob from entering.

But enter they did, and with mazy motion reached their own caverns measureless to man. Samuel Taylor Coleridge's "Kubla Khan"—and especially its hallucinatory visions of a meandering river and a palace made solely for pleasure—struck a chord with many decadents and subterraneans. In Xanadu/Tremé, with its sacred muddy river flowing nearby, the originators of Southern Decadence, drunk on the milk of paradise, found their own pleasure-dome in a savage place, and all who heard should see them there, and all should cry, Beware! Beware!

1

Decadence Takes the World, 2016

PART 1

This is no longer the little bar stroll a few friends did all those years ago. It has morphed into something larger, and with that comes new responsibilities. We can never go back to what it was; we can only move forward and hopefully still keep some of the distinctive flavor that made it what it was.

—Southern Decadence Grand Marshal Tony Leggio, 2016

Southern Decadence 2016 featured more than one hundred events spread over an entire week and attracted more than 216,000 revelers. The handful of misfits and coconspirators who launched the party during the summer of 1972 could not have envisioned what it would become. But change is inevitable, an immutable truth embraced by some and bemoaned by others. It is as applicable to Southern Decadence as to anything else.

There is no debate about the fact that Southern Decadence began with a group of friends who simply wanted to have a good time. At base, the festival started as a celebration of friendship, and that idea remains at its core almost fifty years later. However, some of the founders now believe that Decadence has become too big, too expansive, and too commercialized, that it has lost the intimacy and camaraderie that characterized the early years. Instead of just one

Official Southern Decadence poster depicting the 2016 grand marshals: *left to right*, Tony Leggio, Felicia Phillips, Jeffrey Palmquist, and Derek Penton-Robicheaux. Design by Barrett DeLong-Church. Courtesy of Southern Decadence, 2016.

group of friends having a good time, hundreds of groups of friends now descend on New Orleans for Labor Day Weekend, enjoying themselves at various events.

Parade Day, Sunday, September 4

Sunday is always the most important day of Southern Decadence. Each of the four grand marshals—Philip Anthony (Felicia Phillips), Anthony Leggio, Jeffrey Palmquist, and Derek Penton-Robicheaux—woke early, eager with excitement and anticipation and perhaps slightly hung over. At some point that morning, Palmquist opened and read a letter from Miss Love, Southern Decadence grand marshal 1997, that he had received weeks earlier. Each current grand marshal had spent more than four months working toward this day. Indeed, for much of the time since the Grand Marshal Announcement Party in April, the grand marshals had been occupied with thoughts of fund-raising and preparation, event planning and attention to detail, creating costumes and navigating the city bureaucracy necessary to stage a parade.

Between 8:30 and 9:00 a.m., members of Palmquist's entourage arrived at Café Lafitte in Exile on Bourbon Street for an eye-opener or two. Several revelers, continuing the previous night's debauchery, dotted the bar-scape at Café Lafitte and other gay bars in the French Quarter. The members of Palmquist's entourage were easily recognized by the glittering *Quistadors* pins they were wearing. Each of the grand marshals had chosen a variation on the official theme of Southern Decadence 2016, "Decadence Takes the World," and Palmquist had adopted the historical figure of the Conquistador, combining the theme and his last name. Each Quistador would dress in the typical garb of a nation Palmquist had "conquered." After a few cocktails, the group of friends crossed the street to Palmquist's home, a 175-year-old Creole Cottage once owned by the legendary Jean Lafitte, for a pre-parade brunch in the rear courtyard. In addition to a pastry-and-fruit table, longtime French Quarter bartender Wilhemina Bennet staffed an omelet station. A well-stocked bar kept everyone lubricated, with mimosas frequently the drink of choice. After everyone had eaten, Palmquist welcomed his friends and announced, "This is

Southern Decadence 2016 grand marshal Jeffrey Palmquist and his Quistadors: *left to right*, Errol Rizzuto, Marsha Delain, Jeffrey Palmquist, Rip Naquin, Will Antill, Cam Zimmerman, Frank Perez, Samuel Colby Danna, Coca Mesa, Leslie Blackwell, Tim Kinzel, and Jake Stout. Copyright by Larry Graham. Courtesy of Southern Decadence, 2016.

the day we have been working so hard for." As he declaimed on the significance of the day and provided logistical instructions, the Quistadors smiled with familiarity and appreciation and satisfaction. Theirs had been a long journey.

Grand Marshals Announcement Party, Thursday, April 28

For the Quistadors, the journey began on Thursday, April 28, 2016, at the Grand Marshal Announcement Party. For Palmquist and the other grand marshals, it began a month earlier when he and Leggio, Penton-Robicheaux, and Felicia Phillips had been summoned by 2015 Grand Marshals Rip and Marsha Naquin-Delain to the *Ambush Magazine* headquarters, less than a block down Bourbon Street from Palmquist's home, for a meeting. As the would-be 2016 grand marshals entered the second-floor parlor overlooking Bourbon Street, they were greeted by all of the 2015 grand marshals: the Naquin-Delains as well as Misti Ates, Frankie Fierce, and Steven Mora. Everyone in attendance knew everyone else, and because grand marshals have sole discretion to select their successors, the purpose of the meeting was happily obvious. Fierce matter-of-factly declared, "Well, you know why you're here." But no one else would know for another month—everyone present was sworn to secrecy. Highly anticipated, the Southern Decadence Grand Marshal Announcement Party usually takes place shortly after Easter at a bar and features a drag show as well as the big reveal. The 2016 announcement party was held at the Four Seasons in Metairie, a bar then owned by two former grand marshals, Tittie Toulouse and Electra City.

As the patio area of the Four Seasons started filling up, a shuttle bus was winding its way through the French Quarter and Marigny, picking up the new grand marshals. They arrived near the end of the drag show and were secretly shepherded along the rear of the outdoor patio bar onto a stage, where they were introduced by their predecessors. When the festivities came to an end, the performers and patrons, including a handful of former grand marshals, boarded the party bus and headed back to the Quarter for a bar crawl to herald the arrival of a new Southern Decadence "season." The next four months would see a flurry of parties and bar hopping and fund-raising and parade planning. The announcement party was also the first official fund-raiser of the Southern Decadence season, with the drag show bringing in a total of $750.

One of the stops after the announcement party was the Double Play in the Upper French Quarter. As the group began loading onto the bus for the next stop, an interloper, a young man nicknamed Train Wreck, attempted to board the bus. Leggio was about to deny him entry when Palmquist drunkenly exclaimed, "Train Wreck!" A grand marshal's recognition was enough to allow Train Wreck aboard, but he disappeared at the next stop.

At Café Lafitte in Exile, Palmquist's home bar, drunken revelers received an enthusiastic welcome. Palmquist began chatting with a regular patron in the street. Another regular, on the edge of the conversation, exhorted his friend, "Blow him! He's a Southern Decadence grand marshal. You have to blow him! Blow him right here in the street!" Palmquist and the patron continued their conversation, which later devolved into flirtatious slurring and finally an embrace. Later at GrandPre's bar, they stumbled into a display case mounted on the wall, shattering the glass, first startling the crowd and subsequently eliciting a round of applause.

Crawfish Boil Fund-Raiser, Friday, May 13, Café Lafitte in Exile

Palmquist is a longtime bartender and assistant manager at Café Lafitte in Exile, the longest continually operating gay bar in the United States. Each of the grand marshals' home bars, along with a variety of other bars, hosted Southern Decadence fund-raisers. Here at Café Lafitte, dozens crowded the intersection of Bourbon and Dumaine streets and feasted on spicy crawfish and cold beer.

Many of those in attendance were Palmquist's friends and bar regulars. They were genuinely happy for him and wished him a successful reign. Many in the crowd reminisced fondly about Southern Decadence, while others anticipated this year's festivities, speculating on the theme and colors and the official poster. The total raised was $575.

Photo Shoot for the Official Poster and Press Party Fund-Raiser, Tuesday, May 17, Jeffrey Palmquist's Home

For many years, the grand marshals have designed a poster to showcase the year's theme and colors, which are revealed at the press party. This year, the poster photo shoot took place around the pool at Palmquist's home by noted French Quarter photographer and designer Barrett DeLong-Church. Not long after the press party, the poster adorned the walls of most of the city's gay bars and businesses owned by members of the city's LGBT+ community.

Press Party Fund-Raiser, Saturday, June 4, Bourbon Pub and Parade Discothèque

Much of the crowd, lubricated with booze, nibbled on food provided by Southern Decadence grand marshal 2011 Misael Rubio, owner of the Quartermaster Deli. After a number of drag performances, the four grand marshals revealed the official poster, designed by Barrett Delong-Church, one of the city's premier photographers. Dressed in white tops, the four grand marshals relaxed poolside alongside four shirtless men, each representing an ethnic group from around the world. Each grand marshal had selected a color: Leggio chose amethyst purple; Phillips chose ruby red; Palmquist chose sapphire blue; and Penton-Robicheaux chose pearl white. The official song was a creative remix of Ariana Grande's "Break Free" by DJ of the Year JRB, and the official charities were New Orleans Advocates of GLBT Elders (NOAGE) and Animal Rescue New Orleans (ARNO). Then the grand marshals introduced their lieutenants and entourage, who would assist the grand marshals with the logistics of producing Southern Decadence and provided emotional support and encouragement. Those chosen to serve are typically friends of the grand marshal, in keeping with Southern Decadence's origins as a celebration of friendship. With the festival's growth, however, it is easy for friendship to get lost amid the fund-raisers, event planning, dealing with the city bureaucracy, and hundreds of thousands of revelers. The entourages help keep friendship at Decadence's core.

Palmquist's Quistadors included lieutenants Coca Mesa and Frank Perez and entourage members Will Antill, Lulu Blackwell, Samuel Colby Danna, Tim Kinzel, Rip and Marsha Naquin-Delain (2015 grand marshalls), Kevin Petefish, Errol Rizzuto (1999 grand marshal), Jake Stout, and Cam Zimmerman. The press party, like every other event associated with Southern Decadence, was a charity fund-raiser, and it raised $1,237.

Dinner and Drag Show Fund-Raiser, Friday, June 10, Golden Lantern

After feasting on a wonderful buffet laid out by bar baron James Garner, patrons enjoyed a drag show hosted by longtime Golden Lantern fixture Monica Synclaire-Kennedy. In attendance were Mesa, Nikki Monroe, Jessica Champagne, and other members of the entourages. The total raised was $574.

Cocktails and Queer History Fund-Raiser, Wednesday, June 15

Palmquist and Mesa opened their courtyard for a cocktail soiree followed by an LGBTQ history walking tour led by Perez, a local historian and tour guide. At one point during the tour, Phillips was so drunk that she staggered away from the group to pick up a gutter punk lying on the sidewalk whom she found too cute to resist. Several blocks later, she somehow rejoined the tour group. After the tour, the group returned to Palmquist's for a fabulous dinner. The total raised was $2,257.

French Quarter History and Architecture Walking Tour Fund-Raiser, Thursday, June 23

About a dozen people gathered at Café Lafitte in Exile for a walking tour of the French Quarter led by Perez. Highlights included French and Spanish colonial history as well as various common architectural features and the contributions of free people of color, Germans, Italians, Chinese, and Vietnamese. Because most group members were LGBT, a fair amount of gay history was also covered. The total raised was $500.

Pool Party Fund-Raiser, Sunday, July 3

The grand marshals, their entourages, and several others made the short trip to Chalmette for a pool party at Elizabeth Bouvier's home. Approximately fifty people filled the backyard, dining from a local food truck and enjoying poolside cocktails. Skyy Vodka, the official vodka of Southern Decadence, sent the beefy "Skyy Boys" (Liam and Justin) to most of the year's fund-raisers. At this event, they created a flurry of excitement by stripping down to their briefs and jumping in the pool. The total raised was $2,153.

Potato Salad Contest and Fund-Raiser, Monday, July 4, GrandPre's Bar

The third annual potato salad contest hosted by Ken GrandPre was a huge success. Paw Paw Rippy's Kettle Potato Salad with Shrimp and Smoked Sausage, submitted by Rip and Marsha Naquin-Delain, won. The total raised was $260.

Johnny Passion's Smatch Game Fund-Raiser, Saturday, July 9, Allway's Lounge

This annual event, hosted by 2015 grand marshal Misti Ates and her partner, Catherine Gaither, was a satirical twist to the classic 1970s game show, *Match Game.* Phillips appeared as Miss Love, Leggio played Edina from *Absolutely Fabulous,* Penton-Robicheaux appeared as Elton John, and Palmquist was a contestant. Several other former grand marshals also participated, but Phillips's portrayal of Miss Love stole the show. The total raised was $1,830.

More Fund-Raisers

Southern Decadence Carnival, Sunday, July 10, Tulane Avenue Bar

This carnival-themed event featured games, food, and live entertainment. The total raised was $318.

Southern Charm Meets Southern Decadence, Thursday, July 14, Jeffrey Palmquist's Home

This cocktail and pool party at Palmquist and Mesa's home featured food prepared by Wilhemina Bennett, live music, and naked men swimming in the courtyard pool. The total raised was $2,700.

The Sister Sunday Social: Brunch and Jukebox Drag Show, Sunday, July 17, The Friendly Bar

This show was under the direction of Steve Tregre and Marty Curtin. The total raised was $705.

Grill-Off, Wednesday, July 20, the Page

This event pitted Page owner Willie Mackie against Palmquist. Organized by Mackie, Bobby Waggstaff, and Paul Melancon, this event offered participants a delicious buffet. The organizers were also members of the Krewe of Mwindo. Mackie won the grilling contest. The total raised was $475.

Gay Appreciation Awards, Saturday, July 23, Oz

The twenty-ninth annual Gay Appreciation Awards offered a new twist this year—attendees walked a red carpet and were briefly greeted and grilled by the four grand marshals. The total raised was $2,739.

Coming Home: Decadence Takes Biloxi, Sunday, July 24, Just Us Lounge

This all-day event was organized by Penton-Robicheaux, who hails from Biloxi. Grand marshals and entourage members loaded onto a shuttle bus in the morning and drank their way to Biloxi, where they spent the day enjoying live music and great food. The total raised was $1,270.

Southern Decadence S'ingo, Tuesday, July 26, Cheezy Cajun
Organized by Zimmerman, this fun-filled evening featured not only exquisite food but also a series of bingo games. The total raised was $1,653.

An Evening with Vinsantos, Friday, July 29, Allway's Lounge
With Vinsantos at the piano and serving as host, this unusually compelling show featured drag superstars Nicole Lynn Foxx, Angie Z, and Phillips. The total raised was $700.

Mystique and Mystery, Saturday, July 30, Good Friends
Organized by Blackwell and Dana, this event featured a dizzying array of food and two psychics who offered palm and tarot readings. The total raised was $1,889.

Sippin' with the Sisters, Second Annual Deviled Egg Contest, Sunday, July 31, Cutter's
Mac McAll and Kevin Limberg hosted this jam-packed event at Cutter's. The total raised was $358.

Grand Reveler's Cookout, Wednesday, August 3, Double Play
Grand Reveler II Will Antill and Lord of Misrule Frank Perez, both of the Mystic Krewe du Rue Royale Revelers and both Quistadors, served up an amazing buffet to an overflow crowd. The total raised was $1,218.

Turnabout Show and Buy-a-Boy Auction, Thursday, August 4, Oz
In addition to amazing performances by the Oz staff, the auction featured twelve fetching boys. The highest-grossing single fund-raiser in the history of Southern Decadence, the event raised $6,602.

Hooray for Hollywood, Friday, August 5, GrandPre's
Hosted by Phillips and produced by lieutenant Lee "Bunny" Brasseaux, this drag show featured performers dressed as Hollywood royalty. The total raised was $806.

Rummage Sale, Sunday, August 7, Rawhide

Conducted on the sidewalk outside the legendary bar, a wide variety of items ranging from a used stove to erotic art to vintage books attracted a steady stream of passers-by, including some midwestern tourists who had no idea there was always a happy ending at the Rawhide. The total raised was $500.

The French Quarter: A History of Decadence Walking Tour, Wednesday, August 10

Led by Perez, this leisurely stroll around the lower French Quarter focused on the neighborhood's long history of decadence, debauchery, and indulgence. The total raised was $130.

Decadence Gets Dirty, Friday, August 12, the Phoenix

Under the direction of Phillips and entourage member Adikus Sulpizi, this event paired leather men and drag queens switching roles that embodied the seven deadly sins. The total raised was $1,053.

Buddy Jones's Dog Wash, Sunday, August 14, NOLA Bark Market

Professional dog handler Buddy Jones washed pooches. The total raised was $300.

FourPlay Reunion Show, Friday, August 19, Mag's 940

Dozens packed the bar for this light-hearted drag show. The total raised was $1,467.

Quistador Brunch and Portrait Session, Sunday, August 21, Ruby Slipper

The Quistadors gathered for brunch in the Faubourg Marigny, followed by an official portrait session with photographer Larry Graham.

Southern Decadence Charity Fund-Raiser Disco Party and Show, Monday, August 22, Corner Pocket

This Boys-on-the-Bar event attracted a good crowd and, much to the relief of the grand marshals and their entourages, was the last official Southern Decadence fund-raiser of 2016. The total raised was $755.

Quistador Meeting with Jeffrey Palmquist, Wednesday, August 24, Jeffrey Palmquist's House

At their French Quarter home, Palmquist and Mesa served the Quistadors a sumptuous meal. Palmquist then offered logistical details and other information regarding the big day and distributed thank-you gifts to his entourage.

Annual Grand Marshals Luncheon, Sunday, August 28, Marché Restaurant

Eighteen former grand marshals, including Kathleen Conlon, Miss Love, Errol Rizzuto, Lisa Beauman, Regina Adams, Electra City, Paloma, Julian Artressia, Tiffany Alexander, Venus Santiago, Chad Boutte, Steven Mora, Aubrey Synclaire, Misti Ates, Rip and Marsha Naquin-Delain, and Frankie Fierce, along with the four current grand marshals, gathered in the beautiful Marché Restaurant overlooking the Mississippi River. This assembly of Decadence royalty, always held the weekend before Southern Decadence, began in 1995 when Ed Norton, grand marshal at the time, honored previous grand marshals with the first luncheon. After a few short speeches by the reigning grand marshals, each former grand marshal received a gift bag. Palmquist announced the beginning of a new Southern Decadence tradition, the Grand Marshals' Book of Secrets. Palmquist invited all of the grand marshals to write entries in the journal, which would then be passed on to future grand marshals. After the luncheon, some of the grand marshals enjoyed an afternoon bar crawl that started at Café Lafitte.

Southern Decadence Week Begins

Decadence revelers from around the country began arriving in New Orleans on Wednesday, August 31, and Thursday, September 1, with most of the more than 200,000 visitors in town by Friday. Many of these folks were not aware of Decadence's history or of how much work goes into producing the week's events. Many were not even aware of the official parade, assuming incorrectly that 2010 grand marshal Toby Lefort's Friday Night Knights of Decadence parade was the official Southern Decadence Parade.

Visitors who had previously attended Decadence usually arrived with a plan for their stay. Every gay bar in town, even those that had not participated in the earlier fund-raising efforts, scheduled programming for the weekend, and straight bars and businesses benefited as well. Dollars are dollars, so many straight-owned businesses fly rainbow flags. For gay bars and gay-owned businesses, in particular, the weekend is a financial bonanza, helping to offset leaner times of the year.

A sampling of the weekend's events at gay bars included:

- Three-night beer-bust block party at the Phoenix that featured a Nasty Pig Underwear Party, a Renegade Bear Breakfast, a NOLA Pups and Handlers Party, a Decadent Behavior Party with the Lords of Leather, and a performance by porn star Rocco Steele.
- Dick Dancers and celebrity DJs at Oz and the Bourbon Pub.
- Dick of Decadence contest at Café Lafitte in Exile.
- USDA Prime Aged Beef contest at Good Friends.
- Blackout Party at Rawhide.
- Drag shows at the Golden Lantern, the Four Seasons, the Double Play, and GrandPre's.
- Local talent as well as dancers from around the world at the Corner Pocket.
- Renegade Bears Pool Party at GrandPre's.
- Radical Faeries' Prince of Perversion Ball at Mag's 940, featuring the Heavy Petting Zoo, Pups Lube Wrestling, a Boots and Boxers Party, and Underwear Karaoke.
- Guest DJs and dancers, a Labor Day Bar-B-Que, and the Krewe of Mwindo Rainbow Party.
- Imported talent at the Corner Pocket, with expanded show times.

In addition, the Decadent Ducks, a national travel and social club, celebrated its nineteenth visit to Southern Decadence by commandeering a straight bar, One-Eyed Jacks, for two shows.

Thursday, September 1—Reception for the New York Media at the Ambush Mansion

The Naquin-Delains opened their home to a few journalists visiting from New York City, serving them spirits and food as well as quotes. This has become an annual event and helped to promote Southern Decadence as a national festival.

Friday, September 2—Kick-Off Drag Show at the Golden Lantern

The official home of Southern Decadence was jam-packed as revelers began a weekend of decadence and debauchery. The tradition of hosting a drag show extravaganza at the symbolic "eye of the storm" began during the Lucille era, when Lou Bernard, aka Lucille, owned the bar and hosted the first shows as a way to bring former grand marshals back into the fray.

Saturday, September 3

The Saturday night before the day of the parade was more or less reserved for hitting the bars. Special events were held at Oz on Bourbon Street, with special hostesses Chic Chi LaRue from Los Angeles. DJ Ben Baker sparked the air with his beats. The krewe of the Lords of Leather hosted a "decadent behavior party" at their home bar, the Phoenix, in the Faubourg Marigny. Rocco Steele, porn legend, was live on stage. Saturday night also continued the block party at the Phoenix, a much-anticipated Decadence tradition. Persona Shoulders, a well-known New Orleans drag diva, hosted the Krewe of Amon-Ra's "Girls Gone Broadway!" show at the Joy Theatre.

The Official Southern Decadence Parade 2016, Sunday, September 4

As the Quistadors were having brunch at Palmquist's home, Leggio was also hosting a brunch and an open champagne–and–Bloody Mary bar for his entourage, the Plundering Purple Pirates. In addition to lieutenants Elizabeth Bouvier, Barrett and Beaux Delong-Church, Princess Stephaney, Laura Tennyson, and Gary Vandeventer, Leggio's entourage included David Aranda, Chris Arthur, Tim Chandler, Rich Daigle, Daryl Dunaway, Michelle Dunnick, David Forth, Justin Graci, Clint Grow, Pat Johnson, Cheryl Lemoine, Edward Leon, David McCoy, James McDaniel, Jake Morris, Larry Porter, Rhonda Roget, Liam Taylor, Frankie Fierce (2015 grand marshal), and Robert Stainback. Leggio recalled, "I had thirty-five people total walk with me. . . . We had a fourteen-foot pirate ship created as part of the parade that also functioned as a bar."[1]

In addition to having conquistadors and pirates, the parade featured demonic minions from the underworld. Wanting to "put the decadence back in decadence," Felicia Phillips adopted a hellish variation on the overall theme. "It just seemed a given with me to go in a devilishly decadent direction. We decided that I would be Hecate, Goddess of the Underworld, who ascended to this realm, bringing her minions with her to spread decadence and debauchery around the world."[2]

On the morning of the parade, Phillips and her group met at Brasseaux's Esplanade home. In addition to Brasseaux, Phillips's lieutenants were Misti Ates (2015 grand marshal), Monica Synclaire-Kennedy, Adikus Sulpizi, and Eureeka Starfish. Her entourage included Nicholas Andrews, Brandon Brown, Electra City (2007 grand marshal), David Chase, Anita Daniel, Jerek Edora, Shane Feddersen, Catherine Gaither, Ryan Gomez, Hunter Kilpatrick, Bradley Latham, Karli La Corre, Aaron McCoy, Trey Ming, Timothy Robicheaux, and Jeremy Weinberg.

Penton-Robicheaux's lieutenants were Vanessa Carr, Desiree Chevalier, Kathleen Conlon (1986 grand marshal), Bill Hincks, Jon Penton-Robicheaux, and Persana Shoulders, with an entourage of Michael Bingham, Adrian Claveria, Bonita Folse, Gia Givanni, Monique Michaels, and Aaron Yeager. In honor of his Cherokee heritage, Penton-Robicheaux was costumed as a Native American.

By 1:00 p.m., all four grand marshals and their entourages had arrived at the Friendly Bar in the Faubourg Marigny, the traditional staging area for the parade. More than two hundred people thronged the bar and its corner intersection, including some walking groups and other parade participants. Revelers admired each other's costumes, taking pictures and drinking. Around 1:30 p.m., parade captain and Southern Decadence grand marshal 2015 Steven Mora began lining up the parade participants. Palmquist was the lead grand marshal because his Quistadors had raised the most money of the four groups. When everyone was in place, the parade began making its way to the Golden Lantern for the official start. Leading the procession were two scantily clad men, Tyler Rosebush and Joshua Smith, holding a banner announcing Palmquist as Southern Decadence grand marshal 2016. Behind them on each side of the street were Quistadors Will Antill, dressed as a Russian Cossack, and Frank Perez, dressed as an Egyptian pharaoh, bearing the official Quistador flag. Palmquist followed closely in the middle of the street, slightly behind his flag-bearers. Behind Palmquist was an electric car bearing Rip and Marsha Naquin-Delain as well as a couple of ice chests loaded with booze, primarily vodka. Behind the car were the remaining Quistadors and then the other three grand marshals and their attendant entourages, followed by the other groups and individuals participating in the parade.

As the parade made the turn from Decatur Street onto Barracks Street, a massive crowd nearly blocked the view of the Golden Lantern, at the intersection of Royal and Barracks streets. On a stage just outside the bar, Synclaire-Kennedy introduced the grand marshals. Just before the parade started, Palmquist, costumed as a Spanish conquistador, mounted a horse and then blew the traditional silver whistle to start the festivities. The forty-third Southern Decadence Parade had officially begun.

The crowds lining Royal Street were larger than usual and offered cheers, applause, and drunken catcalls. A lot of people appeared in drag, while others wore little or next to nothing on a typically hot and humid day. Rainbow flags were everywhere. Many parade viewers were already drunk, and the mood was festive until the parade reached the intersection of Royal and St. Ann streets. A small group of about a dozen Christian protesters had gathered there with large signs proclaiming not only that "God Hates Fags" and "Homo Sex Is Sin" but also that hell awaits vegans, skateboarders, and people who do yoga, among others. Because the parade route was filed with the city and published in advance, protesters had no difficulty staking out a spot along the route. The protesters were for the most part ignored and were certainly outnumbered. Above them, on the balcony of Perez's corner apartment, several members of the LGBT+ Archives Project of Louisiana waved and offered support.

The parade turned onto St. Louis Street and headed toward the financial district. Palmquist stopped the parade at the Double Play for drinks. The bar was already packed, and some participants ran up to the Corner Pocket, hoping to score more cocktails and a bathroom break. The parade then continued to North Rampart Street and then Toulouse Street for another pit stop at the Page. The parade made its way back to North Rampart for a stop at GrandPre's and then to Dauphine and on to St. Ann Street. As it neared Good Friends Bar, the crowds, which had thinned out along North Rampart, began to increase until they reached the Fruit Loop, a stretch in the Upper Quarter that includes several gay bars. As the parade approached Bourbon Street, rain began and quickly turned into a downpour. No one was deterred—New Orleans knows how to dance in the rain.

The intersection at St. Ann and Bourbon was teeming with shirtless men of all types—muscle studs, beefy bears, slender twinks, and everything in between. Once past Café Lafitte in Exile, the parade dissipated at its usual designated finish line.

Annual Bead Toss

After a brief break to dry off, use the restroom, and replenish their cocktails, the grand marshals and a few members of their entourages gathered at the

Ambush Mansion for the twenty-third Southern Decadence Bead Toss, hosted by Rip and Marsha Naquin-Delain. The grand marshals and their guests rewarded members of the crowd who showed their dicks by tossing beads down from the balcony.

The bead toss began in 1993 during Ms. Fly's reign as grand marshal. Her close friends the Naquin-Delains decided to throw her a party, dubbing it the Yellow Party after her favorite color. Rip, Marsha, and Adolphus "Mumbo" Spires wore wrap-around yellow towels and nothing else, leading guests to think that they had arrived too early, since the hosts appeared to still be getting dressed. Ms. Fly's wig got caught on the iron gate opening onto the carriageway, leading partygoers to joke, "Who will wear it next year?" and to the party the following year. The event evolved into the bead toss.

After the 2016 bead toss, several revelers gathered for a pool party at Palmquist's. Some participants were ready to pass out from drunkenness and exhaustion while others were ready to keep partying deep into the night.

Survivors' Bar Crawl—Monday, September 5

Around 2:00 p.m., the grand marshals and a couple of dozen revelers, some looking like zombies, gathered at the Corner Pocket to begin the Survivors' Bar Crawl. Led by Rikki Redd, the group meandered through the French Quarter, making stops at the Double Play, the 700 Club, the Page, the Voodoo Lounge, and GrandPre's.

Like the bead toss, the Survivors' Bar Crawl also originated with Ms. Fly. During the first bar crawl, in 1997, and for several years thereafter, the idea was for participants to show up in whatever they went to bed in. After Ms. Fly's death in 2000, Ted Mahaffey became the leader; he passed the baton to Redd in 2016. *Ambush Magazine* described the bar crawl in 1999: "The 3rd Annual Southern Decadence Survivors' Underwear Bar Run kicked off at 11:00 a.m. Labor Day at the Corner Pocket. DB Carnes brought in some gourmet Krystals [hamburgers] to help the early risers maintain. Then cruise director Ted of Golden Lantern fame arrived and distributed his garbage bag of goodies: black bras, slips, teddies and other women's black undergarments. Ted's biggest problem was finding some that would fit the large number of jumbo petites in the crowd. Once this chore was accomplished the gang was off and running. First on the agenda was Footloose, then Voodoo, TT's, and the Phoenix, ending up at Lucille's Golden Lantern. This was quite a feat considering all these lovelies had such giant Southern Decadence hangovers."[3]

The Aftermath

In 2016, more than 216,000 people participated in Southern Decadence, with an economic impact conservatively estimated at more than $259 million. The official charities, ARNO and NOAGE, received $27,345.[4]

This success resulted from an enormous amount of work by hundreds of people and support from dozens of businesses. Southern Decadence is now recognized by the New Orleans mayor's office and has become part of the fabric of the French Quarter community. No longer a humble end-of-summer party, it has transformed itself into a weeklong festival that beckons people to come and enjoy themselves in the city that defines the term.

2

The Birth of Southern Decadence 1972–1980

The originators were black, white, straight, gay—
really just rapidly aging hippies.
—Frederick Wright, Southern Decadence Grand Marshal, 1974

Through the Looking Glass

By 1972, political upheavals only underscored the continuing rift in society, especially the roles of men and women, who were exploring alternative modes of sexuality and expression. David Bowie, Elton John, Led Zeppelin, and Roxy Music reflected these trends in popular music, while films such as *Cabaret, A Clockwork Orange, The Godfather,* and *The Last Picture Show* were box-office successes. President Richard Nixon visited China, and U.S. ground troops began withdrawing from Vietnam. On June 17, burglars struck the Democratic National Committee's headquarters at the Watergate Hotel in Washington, D.C., setting in motion a chain of events that would topple the president. The flower children, who had come of age in the late 1960s, began reassessing their lives, a process that included reconsiderations of the meaning of friendship.[1]

clockwise, top left: Frederick Wright (1974 grand marshal) costumed as Bad News, 1975. Robert Laurent (1977 grand marshal), one of the founders of Southern Decadence, 1978. Maureen Block, the Mother of Southern Decadence, 1976. Charlie Block, one of the founders of Southern Decadence, 1976. Michael Evers, whose departure from New Orleans helped to prompt the founding of Southern Decadence, 1974. Photos courtesy of Robert Laurent.

The founders of Southern Decadence were also products of this 1960s counterculture. Opposing their parents' cultural standards, especially racial segregation, war, sexual repression, materialism, and anti–civil and anti–women's rights, invigorated the Decadents and allowed them to establish their own lifestyle, traditions, and mores while absorbing the nuances and atmospheres of New Orleans.[2]

Toward the end of August 1972, Frederick Wright returned from Chicago to New Orleans on a visit to his close friend, Michael Evers, who had recently moved in with his lover, David Randolph, in the Faubourg Tremé neighborhood, a run-down, neglected area. They were soon joined by Maureen Block, who would be working on her doctorate at Tulane University, and her husband, Charlie, who was looking for acting roles, as well as by Robert Laurent and Tom Tippin from Lafayette, and Robert King and Robert Gore from Louisiana State University in Baton Rouge. As Maureen recalled, "This seems very unusual in hindsight, but it was very organic, as if fate had made us all come together—like minds and like spirits."[3] Others who would make the old tenement their temporary home included Bruce Harris, Preston Hemmings, Kathleen Kavanaugh, David Red, Ed Seale, Judy Shapiro, and Jerome Williams. In May, most had attended Wright's graduation party in Chicago, where they had promised to spend the rest of the summer together in New Orleans. Race and sexual orientation had little influence on the members of this tight-knit group, who playfully called themselves the Decadents; rather, their bonds were created simply by their strong sense of camaraderie. This trend spread during the 1970s, but in the Jim Crow South, rigid societal restrictions still applied.[4]

Belle Rêve and Faubourg Tremé

Randolph owned the dilapidated dwelling and adjacent slave quarters at 2110 Barracks Street in the Faubourg Tremé. The Decadents dubbed it Belle Rêve after Laurent declared, "Why, it's like the faded and withered spirit of Blanche Dubois's Belle Rêve from *A Streetcar Named Desire.*" The former slave apartments lacked electricity and water and were subsequently condemned by the

The first Southern Decadence invitation to a simple costume party, 1972, with the ambiguous graphic of an iconic Southern Belle at Belle Rêve.

city. Randolph and Evers lived in the rather large ramshackle main structure along with Randolph's collection of yard-sale finds, figurines, paintings, chipped vases and bowls, tarnished silver, statuettes, and doodads, as well as what could only be called junk. Each week he would circle all the yard sales in the newspaper and plot out his strategies for acquiring yet more "treasures." Randolph did not believe in air-conditioning and even had "summer blankets" at the ready. Lying within the boundaries of the Faubourg Tremé, Belle Rêve sizzled during the dog days of summer.[5]

Recalled Michael Crutcher Jr., "Stepping out of New Orleans's lower French Quarter, one crosses Rampart Street and enters the Faubourg Tremé. The quick crossing into Faubourg Tremé may be thought of as simply leaving one neighborhood for another—tourist for residential, affluent for poor, white for black, safe for dangerous, dangerous for deadly. In fact, one crosses several boundaries and enters many landscapes."[6]

Near the end of the eighteenth century, Claude Tremé had purchased the land of the Morand Plantation, as it was above the river and the Vieux Carré. On one side was Congo Square, where slaves had gathered on Sundays to dance and sell their wares in an open-air market. In the wake of the Civil War, Tremé became home to many of New Orleans's prominent people of color who sought to stake claims to their rights as Tremé residents, including Paul Trévigne, editor of radical Creole newspapers *L'Union* and *La Tribune*.[7] Homer Plessy, the plaintiff in the landmark *Plessy v. Ferguson* case, in which the U.S. Supreme Court ruled that segregation was legal as long as African Americans were provided with "separate but equal" facilities, was a resident of Tremé in 1896.[8] Free persons of color and subsequently Haitian Creoles settled in this area and the adjacent Storyville, which was torn down in the early twentieth century. Urban renewal created Louis Armstrong Park with the Municipal Auditorium on the site of Congo Square, but the rest of Tremé began to suffer from neglect. The Iberville projects were constructed there during the 1950s, and crime soared.[9]

Tremé seems an appropriate birthplace for Southern Decadence, a place where self-described misfit Decadents felt safe enough to celebrate life in their own way. This neighborhood was mostly black and was certainly not gay, but it did have a rich history of acceptance. A few gay men and lesbians were already living there and renovating old homes. The racially and sexually mixed group of friends found Tremé not only welcoming but somewhat of a haven.[10]

Maureen and Charlie stayed initially with some acquaintances in the Faubourg Marigny, because Maureen refused to even consider staying at Belle Rêve. Recalled Laurent, "She complained that it was just too run-down, too godforsaken and bedraggled, too sleazy. But as far as a party location, it was ideal. It was a large house with a large backyard next to an equally dilapidated slave quarter. Very private. It looked like something out of the Old South, practically falling down, in such a ruined state that we all just called it the essence of the decadent South, something from antebellum times."[11]

Aside from Maureen, who attended all the parties despite her reservations, the friends found Belle Rêve welcoming and comfortable despite its decrepitude. Kathleen Kavanaugh, a recent arrival who had come to rejoin Maureen and Charlie and who battled shyness, "felt protected and safe" there, and "my friends became my family."[12] Echoed Laurent, "Our group was so close that some of us ended up living together. Talk about kindred spirits. And we had so much fun. Everyone was just spontaneous, clever, and smart." When someone later asked Laurent how to "become part of our inner group," he answered without batting an eye: "Just be interesting and fun! That was all!"

For Frederick Wright, the feeling of being safe and loved among the Decadents was particularly important. As a black man, he had to be very careful about where he went in the South, even in parts of the French Quarter; as a gay black man, his existence was especially fraught. But as he recalled, although Belle Rêve was a "celestial flophouse of good-for-nothings . . . in desperate need of repair," he and his friends "all desperately loved it just the same."

Life at Belle Rêve

The residents of Belle Rêve set up a croquet game in the backyard, though the August heat made playing impossible, so the old wooden mallets and chipped and faded balls lay in a heap underneath the giant live oak tree. Nevertheless, the game, at once elitist and Carrollian, represented the spirit of the nonconventional Decadents. Confederate jasmine scented the air, while elephant ears, palmettos, and lush banana trees created a dense wall at the far end of the yard, making the space feel isolated, cut off from the outside world.

Life at Belle Rêve was not luxurious, calm, or full of voluptuousness, as Charles Baudelaire described his hot and humid dream getaway in "L'Invitation au Voyage." The sole respite the house offered from the heat and boredom of a New Orleans summer was the bathroom, painted silver from top to bottom and featuring a huge claw-footed bathtub. The privilege of soaking in the tub was not taken lightly. As the bather enjoyed a long, relaxing session, sometimes for hours, the next person in line would frequently lounge on the long, tattered, and scarf-strewn sofa and read aloud from literature or poetry. Beaudelaire's *Les Fleurs du Mal* and Coleridge's "Kubla Khan" battled against Faulkner's *Light in August* and Capote's *Other Voices, Other Rooms.* Many of the friends were especially fond of Tennessee Williams's *A Streetcar Named Desire* and *Sweet Bird of Youth,* which somehow seemed the most appropriate anodyne to the swelter. Daydreams about *Alice in Wonderland* croquet games also figured prominently in the daily baths.

Many of the friends had backgrounds in literature: Evers had been an English major in college, and Laurent had studied English before switching over to graphic design. Evers introduced Laurent to Flannery O'Connor and other southern writers. Maureen Block, too, was an avid reader. They and other members of the group discussed Williams's odd choice of a name for his fictional plantation: "*Belle Rêve* wasn't correct French by any stretch," as Laurent noted, combining a feminine adjective with a masculine noun, but Williams was quite familiar with the language and would have been unlikely to make such an obvious mistake. Camille Paglia has astutely observed that "Williams understood that the Southern claim of aristocracy, enabled by the atrocity of slavery, was built on lies. Hence in *Streetcar* the ancestral DuBois plantation, lost to creditors, is called Belle Rêve—that is, 'beautiful dream.' But the dream was always a patchwork of illogic." As an adolescent, Williams had used *Belle Rêve* as the title of a poem in which he fantasized about living on a Missouri plantation with his parents, evidently taking inspiration from St. Louis's Bellerive Country Club, where his mother sought social acceptance and where the teenaged Williams slipped on a diving board and knocked out his front teeth. Thus, according to Paglia, "Bellerive/Belle Rêve was a beckoning mirage that led to failure, humiliation, and mutilation."[13] Similarly, Matthew Roudané has written, "The logical assumption is that the plantation was originally named Belle Rive (beautiful shore), and that over the generations the name has been corrupted as the family's fortune dwindled. What had been a *solid shore* is now but an evanescent *dream* of lost splendor. Blanche becomes hysterical as she blames the loss of the plantation on the expense of 'all that sickness and dying,' the long series of family deaths she was forced to witness: 'the struggle for breath and bleeding.'"[14] Moreover, in English, the name is frequently mispronounced as *Belle Reeve,* which is the correct French pronunciation of Belle Rive. Finally, Harold Bloom finds an almost metaphorical quality in the disjuncture between adjective and noun: like the character of Blanche Dubois, the name *Belle Rêve* suggests ambiguity and subterfuge.[15]

The denizens of Belle Rêve and their friends who lived nearby focused on honoring the spirit and essence of their group, which meant frequent gatherings to celebrate all aspects of their lives. In addition to gathering at Belle Rêve and playing games, they often went barhopping, and one of their favorite haunts was Johnny Matassa's Bar, located next to the grocery store at the corner of St. Philip and Dumaine streets. According to Laurent, Evers and Wright "discovered this little gem of a place, so we all naturally followed suit. It was easy to just drop by and have a few drinks. It became our meeting place, our starting off point, if you will, where everyone met for a night in the Quarter, especially after a night of bourré." Sunday-night games of bourré, a Cajun card game that features tricks, were a staple of the Decadents' entertainment.[16]

The bar's namesake, John Matassa, had emigrated to America from Sicily and opened Johnny's Grocery and Bar in 1924. His son, Cosimo, operated a recording studio on Rampart Street, where he made some of the first recordings of New Orleans's emerging R&B and jazz music in the 1940s and 1950s. When he retired from the record business, Cosimo took over the grocery store and bar, where, Laurent remembered, "the jukebox had the greatest selections of early R&B known to man." In addition, "You could shop for groceries at the corner while sipping a beer. It was the most sensible of New Orleans things to do." According to Cosimo's son, Louis, who, along with his brother, John, took over the bar in the late 1960s, Matassa's had two entrances, one for whites and one for blacks, though the Decadents apparently did not notice this acquiescence to southern custom. The bar closed by the end of the 1970s.[17]

A Twist of Fate

At the end of August, David Randolph's stepfather died, and he had to leave for Grand Rapids, Michigan, rather quickly to help his mother. Randolph had

Jerome Williams (1975 grand marshal) in front of Johnny Matassa's Bar with David Red costumed as Indira Gandhi, 1975. Courtesy of Robert Laurent.

David Randolph in the doorway of Belle Rêve, 1976. Courtesy of Robert Laurent.

some different priorities from the other group members, according to Laurent: "David was maybe ten or more years older than" the others, who were all in their twenties.

> He wasn't part of our scene. He rolled his eyes at our antics. I remember Michael saying that Randolph was raised by his grandmother in Chicago, while his mother went out partying. She'd return from a night of fun to be berated by her mother, with little David hiding behind the grandmother's skirts and popping out to say, "Bad girl!" A young prude. At one time I had a small photo Michael had given me of David in drag from the 1950s. He was fancily dressed in a cocktail dress with long gloves looking like Ida Lupino. But that was a distant phase. When I met him he was denim and leather. He had a big dog as a pet. He had a tattoo on one of his butt cheeks and would don a pair of jeans at Mardi Gras with a hole in the rear to show off the design. But that was only once a year! Quite honestly, I don't think we would have ever had the party at Belle Rêve if David had not been called away like that. He was just too straitlaced, not a Decadent like the rest of us. He didn't fit in with all our crazy talk, card games. . . . All he ever wanted to do was to go to garage sales all over town.

At around the same time, Maureen Block was becoming increasingly fed up with the heat and increasingly vocal about her discomfort, boredom, and impatience as she counted down the days until the end of the summer, and as she recalled, "I think they started planning the party just to shut me up. It gave us something to look forward to, and nothing pleased us more than getting together with all our friends. We were all just crazy about each other." With Randolph away and unable to object, the rest of the friends decided to have a party on the Sunday of Labor Day Weekend so that they would have plenty of time to recover before they needed to return to work on Tuesday. Given the city's Mardi Gras tradition, there was never any doubt that it would be a costume party. Laurent, as a graphic designer, volunteered to create an invitation to make the party seem "official"—and more fun. Laurent's invitation appropriated the cutout black-paper silhouette, an iconic antebellum image,

Robert King (1978 grand marshal) on the balcony of the slave quarter at Belle Rêve, 1976. Courtesy of Robert Laurent.

Tom Tippin (1980 grand marshal, right) and friend in the backyard of Belle Rêve, 1974. Courtesy of Robert Laurent.

but depicted a prim and proper southern belle with hoopskirts, long ringlets, beribboned hat, and parasol—and a man on his knees with his head subsumed beneath her skirts. The invitation was thus ambiguous—the "belle" might be exactly what she seemed to be, or she might be a drag queen. Such an invitation open to many interpretations set the tone for the event's future. For five dollars, Laurent had fifty invitations printed up at a little shop near Canal Street.

The Birth of Decadence—Sunday, September 3, 1972

Attendees at the first party were required to dress up as a favorite Southern Decadent. Several dozen friends showed up and congregated under the large trees in the backyard, where the air was somewhat cooler and the setting somewhat sequestered. The Decadents drank spiked punch, indulged in

Charlie Block and Judith Shapiro in Baton Rouge, 1976. Courtesy of Robert Laurent.

drugs, and enjoyed the relative calm of the indolent summer. Candles were lit at dusk, and King and Gore brought out the oil lamps they used for light in the slave quarters. Music filtered out into the yard from within Belle Rêve, jazz and blues mingling with zydeco and bluegrass. The party felt like a safe haven, successful and relaxing, and the participants agreed that dressing up in semi-drag and rags and floating around the lush greenery while dancing and tripping on LSD made for an experience they should repeat.

A Farewell to Michael Evers—Saturday, September 16, 1972

Less than two weeks later, Evers left to join Randolph in Michigan. His imminent departure provided another excuse for a party, and Laurent crafted another invitation, this one showing a lovely southern belle staring out at the viewer with an enticing smile on her lips while entreating everyone to "Come

Back to Belle Rêve!" This party proved even more popular than the first, with more than fifty people in attendance. Some of the attendees paraded around the neighborhood as they made their way to Belle Rêve, although those who came in full drag generally did not for fear of police harassment. Appearing in the street in drag in 1972 was both illegal and provocative. Drag was acceptable only on Shrove Tuesday, the last day of Carnival, when the law permitted all costumes; for the rest of the year, costuming and masking were against the law. Laurent remembered that drag queen Anthony Eschmann "stood in the doorway dressed all in white as the parade arrived at the house. Some drags at the house did not want to join in the parade, didn't feel safe outside its sanctity."

"Get Your Things Together"—Sunday, September 2, 1973

In the wake of their two September 1972 parties, the denizens of Belle Rêve resumed their lives, including their regular game nights, which always segued into a trip to various French Quarter bars that was dubbed the Tour of Tours. As Laurent related, during the summer of 1973, "during our Sunday nights of Bourré games, the anniversary of the summer party was fast approaching and we began to think about the possibility of a second party." He hit on a way to combine the Tour of Tours with the end-of-summer party:

> I thought it would be outlandish for all of us to first meet at Matassa's in full costume and then parade back to Belle Rêve for the party. To my surprise, everyone was in complete agreement. They thought it would be a sensation, and that's just what we did. Before the second annual party [in 1973], revelers met at the bar as decadent luminaries: Tallulah Bankhead, famous actress from Alabama, reputed to be a lesbian; Belle Watling, brothel owner in *Gone with the Wind*; Mary Ann Mobley, actress and Miss America in 1959; Lillian Hellman, writer and Jew from New Orleans; and Miss Kitty, bar performer in the popular TV show *Gunsmoke*. We then all marched up the Esplanade [Avenue] median to the old house. Along the way, we stopped at the Rampart Street bars as well as some in the Tremé district.

The invitation again featured women, showing two matrons in conservative late-nineteenth-century dresses: an older woman sitting at an old-fashioned sewing machine, apparently showing a younger woman how to work the machine. The invitation proclaimed, "Get Your Things Together!" which was what Wright said to Maureen Block so that she would come to Belle Rêve despite her misgivings about the place. Below the first image appears the outline of a more contemporary woman contemplating what kind of woman to be for the Decadence party and parade. Would she or others cross-dress? Sailors and prostitutes at the seedy Gallatin Street bars near the river had at times cross-dressed, seemingly as farce, and the Decadents' parties followed in this "established" New Orleans tradition.

"We all felt like outcasts either because of political views or sexual orientation or race. The impulse to head back to Belle Rêve to party was natural. We didn't feel we belonged in the streets," recalled Wright. "The originators were black, white, straight, gay—really just rapidly aging hippies. The party returned to the house at the end of the night partially to avoid Eighth District police, who were suspicious of if not openly hostile toward the parade. We didn't want to get a permit. We modeled ourselves after Zulu, who used to lead the parade wherever he wanted to go."[18]

Belle Rêve came to symbolize shelter from the storm, a place where everyone felt part of a larger group, tucked away from scrutiny. All were welcome. Belle Rêve was indeed a type of hothouse utopia, carefully crafted to enfold its residents in a cocoon of timelessness.

The Belle Rêve Times—Sunday, September 1, 1974

When Wright received Laurent's invitation to the third annual Southern Decadence Party, he read with astonishment that he had been named "Parade Marshal." The invitation was designed to resemble a newspaper, recalling the packaging of Jethro Tull's seminal *Thick as a Brick* (1972), which declared that the album was a musical adaptation of an epic poem by fictional eight-year-old genius Gerald Bostock. Laurent's *Belle Rêve Times* instructed guests to arrive at Matassa's between 2:00 and 3:00 p.m. on September 1: the "pavement parade" would begin when Wright blew his whistle and would follow whatever route the marshal chose before ending in a party at Belle Rêve. The invitation featured a picture of a steamboat that supposedly would bring out-of-towners to the festivities, where they would be greeted by southern belles in front of Belle Rêve. Once again, people were to come dressed as their "favorite Southern Decadent." However, Laurent also used photos of bare-breasted women and other half-clad persons from "last year's fun and hijinks," adding to the allure and sensationalism and promising a repeat.

According to Maureen Block, "Frederick simply had to be the first grand marshal. There was no question about it." Though he did not live in the city, "he would always make time for a stopover in New Orleans for his job travels. . . . Everyone fought to pick him up at the airport. He was the guiding spirit of the group, a natural force. No one knew what he'd do next, the life of the party, but with a huge heart. Just a lovely man."

Grand Marshal Frederick Wright as Uncle Sam in the doorway of Johnny Matassa's Bar, 1974. Courtesy of Robert Laurent.

Despite his surprise, Wright embraced his role as grand marshal. He immediately went out and bought a whistle and a baton and then began planning the first official parade route, which included stops at the Golden Lantern and Jewel's Tavern. He thus firmly established the tradition that the grand marshal was in complete control of the parade. As the parades grew to encompass upward of one hundred people in costume, Pat O'Brian's and some other bars did not welcome the spectacle, and as Laurent recalled, Harry Connick Sr., who served as New Orleans district attorney from 1973 to 2003, "was not pleased with the dozens of rowdies filing into Cosimo's as he departed." Many other places were far happier to host the traveling party—Marti's Restaurant, the Old Absinthe House, the Acropolis, the Safari House, Café Lafitte in Exile, the Bourbon Pub, Pete Fountain's, Jewel's Tavern, Funky Butts, Wanda's, the Midship, and the Golden Lantern, which became the official last stop. On one occasion, according to Laurent, he and Wright tried to have a drink at Wanda's, "but Frederick didn't have an ID on him, and so we couldn't. It was just another example of discrimination against our black friends. I have a photo of him and Ruthie the Duck Lady, sitting outside on the curb."

At 3:00 p.m. on September 1, Wright arrived at Matassa's Bar, where he found a group of costumed revelers—including some decked out as legendary locals Ruthie the Duck Lady, the Bus Lady, and the Bead Lady—ready to begin the parade. For his costume, Wright had chosen to invoke the iconic Uncle Sam, wearing a tight-fitting white tank top with a red and blue stripe across the chest, tight white leggings, an American flag scarf tied around his waist, and a red, white, and blue top hat. Whether Wright did so deliberately or subconsciously, the sight of a black man costumed to resemble the quintessential manifestation of American patriotic emotion and pride—and leading a parade, no less—constituted a provocative and powerful statement against the prevailing racial order. Though the Supreme Court had struck down "separate but equal" laws over the preceding two decades and Congress had passed the Civil Rights Act of 1964 and the Voting Rights Act of 1965, segregation and Jim Crow continued to have a strong influence in the South, and it was still rare to see mixed groups on the street together.[19] The significance of Frederick Douglas Wright's appearance at the head of the parade was further enhanced by his having been named after Frederick Douglass, a noted former slave turned abolitionist, and by Wright being homosexual. Although the French Quarter had a reputation as a safe haven for gay men and lesbians, African Americans were relegated to the fringes, while black neighborhoods such as the nearby Iberville Projects and the St. Claude and Ninth Ward areas further downriver were particularly dangerous for gays. Wright's presence at the head of the Decadence parade thus signaled that it represented a departure not only from the racism present in southern society but also from its homophobia. After the grand marshal had his cocktail in hand, he blew his whistle, and off they went, setting the pattern for all future Southern Decadence parades.

Preston Hemmings, who was living at Belle Rêve at the time, recalled that "everyone along the route was utterly astonished. Several of the lads were in drag, and there were at least seventy-five, maybe one hundred people."[20] As the procession made its way along Rampart Street, Laurent recalled, Wright halted everyone when he smelled fried chicken coming from a car stopped at a red light. After smiling at the black women in the car, Wright reached in and grabbed several pieces. Despite their initial surprise, the occupants of the car recovered quickly—after all, parades and second lines are common in New Orleans—but the participants in the parade were unaware of exactly what was going on and merely heard someone screaming from the car, "Don't touch my breasts! Please, child, don't touch my breasts!"

After stops at numerous bars as well as Marti's Restaurant, a posh spot where a chic clientele dined on gumbo and *boeuf bouilli,* and Big Marshall's Shalimar Club on the fringes of Faubourg Tremé, the parade reached Belle Rêve and began a party that lasted all night and into the early hours of the morning. For the first time, the crowds included people who were not part of the group of friends, and someone stole a large bag of marijuana from Robert King's bedroom in the slave quarters, spoiling the party atmosphere. In addition, David Randolph was planning to sell the property, meaning that everyone would have to find someplace else to live. Henceforth, as Laurent put it, "the bar crawl, with all the costumes and zaniness, became the party."

The Third Annual Belle Rêve Southern Decadent Parade—Sunday, August 31, 1975

For the invitation to the 1975 Southern Decadent parade, Laurent depicted Bourbon Street cabaret performer Chris Owens as a megalithic Godzilla goddess perched high atop the newly opened Louisiana Superdome. At one of their Sunday card games, the Decadents selected Jerome Williams to serve as the next grand marshal. Recalled Laurent, "It was a no-brainer that Jerome would be next. Jerome was gay and had a wicked sense of humor, especially as his alter ego, Miss Pickle. . . . It was only natural for him to be the second marshal." When Williams saw the invitation, he screamed, and decided on the spot to lead the parade in drag as Chris Owens, wearing a black feather boa and a slinky black gown.

By 1975, Southern Decadence had become much anticipated not only among the Belle Rêvers, as Laurent now called the core group, but among other locals, both gay and straight, although it remained very much an underground affair restricted to those in the know. Although, as Laurent noted, "the parade of costumes and bar crawl now became the main focus of the Southern Decadence event. . . . the creative life force of Belle Rêve served as our guide and continued without pause. . . . The parade had become the party, and that would ignite even more audacious behavior, more outrageous costumes, and even more potent drugs. You just can't underestimate the importance of drugs back then, like Quaaludes and Black Mollies [amphetamines]."

Agent Provocateur—Sunday, September 5, 1976

Preston Hemmings was selected as the grand marshal for 1976. As Laurent remembered, Hemmings "lived upstairs from the Blocks in the early 1970s on Napoleon Avenue." During the 1975 parade, Hemmings stood "in front of a truck with a large smiley face painted on the side" and did "a little dance movement." When film of Hemmings's performance was shown at one of the Sunday night bourré games, "the crowd howled in delight. It was a natural assumption he would be the next marshal." Since 1976 was the U.S. Bicentennial, Hemmings recalled, "I came as the Delegate from Louisiana, wearing my granduncle's old tuxedo, my straw hat with four little flags protruding. I cut up several feet of red, white, and blue crêpe and had myself delivered to a cheering crowd in a White Fleet cab. I told everyone that I only had one request for a bar stop. Funky Butts. I started up to the bar on Rampart Street, blowing my whistle and rolled a pair of dice up the street. At Funky Butts, I mounted the stage and sat at the piano. In keeping with the political theme I played and sang 'Every

Man a King,'" the theme song of Louisiana political kingpin Huey P. Long, who served as the state's governor and U.S. senator during the early twentieth century.[21] Unlike the first two grand marshals, Hemmings was straight.

By this time, the group had expanded further, adding not only Hemmings but also others such as Martha and Becky Theriot, sisters from the small South Louisiana town of Golden Meadow, whose father was the wealthiest self-made millionaire in the state. The Theriots occasionally had use of their father's company jet, and according to Laurent, "We enjoyed their dad's airplane, and we traveled quite a bit, flying together." Another member of the "core entourage" who often joined in on these field trips was Douglas Bourgeois, a young artist who was working as a waiter at Restaurant Jonathan on Rampart Street. Bourgeois went on to establish an art studio in St. Amant and to become a noted painter, and many of the Decadents have subsequently collected his work.

Laurent's film of the 1976 Southern Decadence bar crawl shows costumed characters surging in and out of Matassa's—hula girls and gypsies; a frog man, complete with headpiece; and Indira Gandhi. Also on hand was the Lady Russell (Russell Simpson), another twilight creature from the dark corners of the French Quarter. The Lady Russell idolized Maria Montez and other almost-forgotten starlets but especially New Orleans native Dorothy Lamour, frequently performing her sultry song, "The Moon of Manakoora," from 1937's *The Hurricane.* Jack Smith similarly venerated Lamour and Gloria Swanson, but his favorite was Montez, the Cobra Woman. Many other gay men felt drawn to these early screen sirens, who subsequently became camp references for the men. According to Laurent, Russell and those like him "did not live in the real world but floated high above it." When Laurent would "arrive at Matassa's on Decadence Sunday, I'd go in search of Russell. He was always willing to accompany us on our travels and he seemed to have such a good time. He was a gentle, yet crazed spirit, with such energy, you never knew what to expect from him." According to Laurent, Simpson "didn't do typical drag . . . just crazy thrift store cast-offs—always witty, campy costume outfits. One of his lines was 'Do tell me about yourself, but nothing, of course, I'd be forced to reveal under heavy torture.'" When some kind of problem arose, Simpson would announce, "You're jammin' my aura!" Nick Pinkerton described Simpson as "the transvestite who makes a travesty out of being a transvestite, tweaking her tortured bleach job and absolutely nailing dive-bar glamour—that'll cost you $2.50 extra—remove yourself from my presence!"[22]

Dixie's Land—Sunday, September 4, 1977

By 1977, the Southern Decadence celebration had gained even more momentum, attracting increasingly diverse groups to the Matassa's Bar starting point. On the night of September 3, Dennis del Buno and Kevin Flot began looking through the closets in their small French Quarter apartment, pulling out remnants of Carnival costumes and other props that they transformed into some of the devastatingly tackiest drag ever devised. "It was about having fun with a group of people who were not judgmental," said Flot, a black man who had found his place among New Orleans's gay community. "I wanted to be included in all the fun, and I wanted to create the fun along with my friends."[23] This attitude encapsulated the mind-set that made Decadence so appealing in these early years.

For 1977, Laurent himself was designated as the grand marshal, and he set about creating an invitation that invoked all the failings and falterings of the Old South as well as a big jolt of comic relief. The invitation featured a cartoon alligator with his head in his hands and the words "Dixie's Land," along with the lyrics to Daniel Decatur Emmett's song by that name. The lyrics were rendered not in standard English but in the dialect that so often accompanies stereotypical black performances, especially minstrel shows. Emmett and his Virginia Minstrels had first appeared in New York in 1843, and his song (also known as "Dixie") not only became a standard, portraying the Old South and its cotton plantations, but ultimately became a rallying cry for the Confederate South, with its nostalgia for the antebellum era. Laurent's inclusion of the distorted lyrics and alligator (the symbol of Louisiana) revealed a sophisticated critique of and answer to the complex conundrum of the South in general. The Southern Decadence initiates would not allow themselves to be divided by

left: The Lady Russell (Russell Simpson), 1977. Courtesy of Robert Laurent.

above: Frederick Wright (1974 grand marshal) as Sheik Yerbouti in a costume he brought back from Egypt, 1979.

these outdated notions of race, sexuality, possessions, or money. The alligator himself appeared fed up with the song, with the Old South, and especially with these antiquated notions.

Laurent's costume as grand marshal paid homage to a dead bird—a parakeet, Dennis Devine, who had been named after the former roommate of a Belle Rêve resident. In addition, Laurent recalled that he had "fashioned a large red piece of poster board into a sign lettered 'The Original Belle Rêve Southern Decadents Have Arrived.' It was affixed to a lightweight wooden art easel that could be easily carried. For a few parades it accompanied us and would be stationed outside the bars while we imbibed inside. It was sort of a proclamation and warning!"

One of those who joined the Decadence crew around this time was Ron

Smith. He and a friend made a pilgrimage to a church mission outlet near Baton Rouge and bought several white wedding gowns, which they began wearing to the Decadence parades. The wedding dresses were a hit, especially when the parade invaded the newly refurbished Jax Brewery, which had been turned into tourist boutiques and shops. As Smith related, "There seemed like hundreds of drunk drag queens riding up and down the escalators, which only served to entertain and shock the tourists. It was just a moment. What a thrill that was!"

But 1977 was also the year that religious conservatives began appearing at Southern Decadence in earnest. According to Hemmings, "a scuffle broke out between paradegoers and a pair of protesters. Somewhere on Bourbon Street during the 1977 parade, two guys appeared waving signs. One said, Homosexuality is a Sin against God."[24]

The Daring Duo—Sunday, September 3, 1978

In 1978, two grand marshals were chosen, "apparently because people were worried that one of them would get too drunk to lead the parade," according to Preston Hemmings. The two were Robert King, a gay schoolteacher, and Kathleen Kavanaugh, a diplomat's daughter who had lived in Europe. King refused to conduct the parade in drag, preferring to wear shorts and his tuxedo tails. Kavanaugh came dressed as President Jimmy Carter's redneck brother, Billy, wearing a silly hat and fun false teeth. The grand marshals led the crowd, which again exceeded expectations, from bar to bar, dancing in the streets and at times pulling pranks on passers-by. Members of the police stared menacingly at the crowds, but relative calm prevailed. This precedent, however, of more than one grand marshal per parade would reappear many years later.

Roller Skates and Dixie Beer—Sunday, September 2, 1979

For 1979, the grand marshal was Bruce Harris, whom Preston Hemmings described as a "French Quarter barfly." Harris, who was straight, was a carpenter and wood craftsman known, according to Laurent, "for loving beer, which is why his invitation was of a can of Dixie on skates. He wore roller skates as the grand marshal."[25]

About four hundred people were on hand as the parade set off from Matassa's Bar. At each bar along the way, Laurent placed his large red sign and easel outside to warn people in the vicinity that the Belle Rêve Southern Decadents had arrived. The crowd swelled at each stop until nearly eight hundred people were participating, many of them also on roller skates.

Hard Times—Sunday, September 7, 1980

The 1980 Southern Decadence represented a turning point in the event's history. The grand marshal was Tom Tippin, Maureen Block's brother, who had been chosen some weeks back at one of the bourré games. Tippin had always been a willing part of the core group, which held numerous parties throughout the year—for holidays or birthdays or for any reason, no matter how flimsy. Maureen and Tim's parents had even joined in. Though often risqué, the parties were never so overtly sexual that someone would be uncomfortable.

Tippin had carefully planned his costume, fashioning orange yarn into a wig and adding a crown to play the King from the *Wizard of Id* comic strip. When he arrived at Johnny Matassa's, he was greeted by a huge crowd of at least a thousand, including many Decadents—the Blocks, Kavanaugh, King, Wright, Laurent, Hemmings, and David Red—as well as members of the Pair-O-Dice Tumblers, a rock group that often played the dives on Frenchmen Street in the Faubourg Marigny.

When Tippin blew his whistle, he started the parade down St. Phillip Street. Eventually the massive crowd reached Jackson Square. When Tippin motioned for the group to head toward the Greek bars, the leader of the Tumblers objected, and Hemmings "watched in disbelief as the band took off in one direction and the parade marshal in the other. Since the band was going where they wanted to go, naturally the whole parade, with few exceptions, went that way. Decadence, on that very spot, as we had known it, died. The entire parade,

The traditional arrival of the grand marshal at Matassa's Bar to begin Southern Decadence, 1980: *left to right*, Mike from the Pair-O-Dice Tumblers (with trombone), unidentified band member, Bruce Harris (1979 grand marshal), Kathleen Kavanaugh (1978 grand marshal), and Grand Marshal Tom Tippin costumed as the King of Id.

thinking the band knew where they were going, simply went on into history with an infuriated marshal sitting in a dark corner somewhere. We were all just in shock."[26]

According to Laurent, "the crowds were so large that when the parade hit a bar, you couldn't get a drink easily. So Frederick and I thought we'd be clever and at the Moonwalk asked Tom what his next stop would be. We went ahead and felt so smug sitting on barstools with a cocktail and waited and waited and waited." But the parade had been hijacked and never arrived. Wright and

Grand Marshal Tom Tippin as the King of Id, 1980.

Robert Laurent (1977 grand marshal), Ruthie the Duck Lady, and Fred Wright (1974 grand marshal) outside Wanda's bar, waiting for the Decadence Parade to arrive, 1980. It never arrived.

Laurent finally "got to a pay phone and called the Blocks' house in the Quarter to see if we could maybe see what had happened. Tom answered and was still livid. As grand marshal, he wanted the parade to go down Decatur Street toward the Greek bars and Canal Street, and the Tumblers wanted to head back to the Lower Quarter and the Marigny."

Nearly fifty years later, Tippin was still irritated by what happened: "I was already discombobulated at Matassa's, having arrived fifteen minutes or so after the announced time—which was as early as any of the rest of the parades—only to be dressed down by the uninvited band. . . . We made maybe two bars, heading to Jackson Square, from where I was headed toward the Greek sailors' bars on Decatur and Canal. The band's spokesperson told me they didn't want to go that way. That's when I reminded them all that this was our parade, our traditions, and they had no say about it. Following a stout but useless verbal confrontation, I headed down Decatur toward Canal along with my family and friends, who were aware of what was going on. The band headed downriver, with the crowd following behind."[27] With the crowds disappearing in the distance, Southern Decadence as it had been for almost a decade would never be the same.

A Farewell to Decadence

Looking back on the early years of Southern Decadence, Hemmings (grand marshal 1976) recalled fondly: "There has never been a group of friends I've loved more in my life. . . . It was the most wonderful feeling to sit with friends who accepted you for who you were, no matter what—even if the guy next to you was a forty-year-old man with a beard in a dress. I never laughed more or had better times with friends. That whole crowd, gay and straight, was filled with smart, witty people, any of whom might drop you to the floor with laughter at any moment. And they were warm and cared about each other and did things for each other on a constant basis. Sometimes they sacrificed for each other. They gave me much solace and support."[28]

Soon after serving as the 1978 grand marshal, Robert King and a friend were moving a large mirror into his second-floor apartment when he fell over the railing, suffering a spinal-cord injury that confined him to a wheelchair. Nevertheless, he continued to join in the Southern Decadence festivities every year until his health prevented him from participating. After King's death in 2007, Andrew Block, son of Maureen and Charlie Block, and King's godson, described him as "an example of warm spirit, good times, and true friendship."[29] That description applies just as well to Southern Decadence itself.

3

The French Quarter Gay Community

One of the worst aspects of living in a satellite culture, in a colonial outpost like New Orleans (which is having its originality and uniqueness siphoned off daily like the work of some Anne Rice vampire looming over the city with big, dusty bat-wings flared), is that there are always carpetbaggers waiting to pounce, sink their fangs into what passes for local culture, drain it and disembowel it and leave it to jerk spasmodically and systolically as its pitiful life leaches away.

—Jon Newlin, New Orleans writer

Although Southern Decadence did not begin as a uniquely gay event, it was born during a transitional period for both the gay community specifically and the French Quarter in general. By the early 1970s, the French Quarter was in the final stages of its evolution from a primarily residential neighborhood to a tourist destination. The seeds of the tourist economy were planted around 1916, when Elizabeth Werlein published *Wrought Iron Railings of Le Vieux Carré*.[1] In the 1920s, Flo Fields, considered the Quarter's first tour guide, began shepherding visitors around the ancient hub of the city using Werlein's book as the basis of her tour. The metamorphosis of Bourbon Street into the infamous neon strip of today can be dated to around 1926, when Arnaud Cazenave opened Maxime's Supper Club on what is now the site of the Royal Sonesta Hotel. Richard Campanella pinpoints this nightclub as "the birthplace of modern Bourbon Street."[2] By the late 1950s, the humming tourist economy catered primarily to white, middle-class conventioneers, largely ignoring married couples and the gay market. As the tourist industry rose, the French Quarter declined as a residential neighborhood.

Literary and Artistic Renaissance

In the 1920s, the French Quarter was the site of a literary and artistic renaissance fueled in large part by gay men. In 1919, Lyle Saxon convinced the Drawing Room Players to move their little theater, which had been located in the Lower Garden District since 1916, to the Lower Pontalba Building.[3] The Drawing Room Players grew into Le Petit Théâtre du Vieux Carré, which purchased a lot at the corner of St. Peter and Chartres streets in 1922. Architect Richard Koch designed the theater, and Sam Gilmore staged three plays there. Gilmore also was a poet whose work won accolades from the *New York Times,* and he served as patron, associate editor, and contributor to the *Double Dealer,* a prominent journal of literary modernism that published writers such as Ernest Hemmingway, William Faulkner, Hart Crane, Allen Tate, Robert Penn Warren, and Djuna Barnes.[4]

Also contributing to the *Double Dealer* was William Spratling, an artist who had come to New Orleans in 1922 to teach architecture at Tulane University. He lived in the French Quarter and for a while shared an apartment with William Faulkner in Pirate's Alley. Spratling and Saxon served as hosts and organizers of many literary and artistic salons, dinner parties, and cocktail soirees. Writing for the *New Orleans States* in 1922, Natalie Scott described Spratling's apartment as one of the "chosen nuclei of the Quarter."[5]

Spratling was also involved in the very influential Arts and Crafts Club, which was founded in 1919, probably at Saxon's urging. The club originally met in Alberta Kinsey's Toulouse Street apartment until William Ratcliffe Irby donated the use of the slave quarters at his historic home on Royal Street, the

Seignouret-Brulatour mansion. The Arts and Crafts Club, in turn, operated the New Orleans Art Club, which brought modern art to New Orleans. The club offered lectures, hosted exhibitions, and provided art classes, with Spratling teaching sculpting, clay modeling, and sketching.[6]

One member of the Arts and Crafts Club's board of directors, William Weeks Hall, was one of the most interesting gay men involved in the French Quarter renaissance. A painter trained at the Pennsylvania Academy of the Fine Arts in Philadelphia as well as in Paris and London, Hall also owned Shadows-on-the-Teche, an 1834 plantation in New Iberia, Louisiana. Hall had inherited the plantation in 1919 and hired his friend Richard Koch to restore it.[7] Hall often invited French Quarter writers and artists for weekend visits to the Shadows. Hall had no patience for nosy tourists and, according to historian John Shelton Reed, would sometimes deal with them "by impersonating a (nonexistent) idiot twin brother. Other times, he just rushed at them in his underwear, shaking his cane and shouting, 'Get out of here, you goddamn silly women!'"[8]

The French Quarter renaissance also included photographers, at least two of whom were gay. Joseph Woodson "Pops" Whitesell lived and maintained a studio in the slave quarters behind what would eventually become Preservation Hall. William "Cicero" Odiorne had a photography studio in the Upper Pontalba Building before moving to Paris in 1924. Odiorne's Paris apartment became a must-see for New Orleanians in Paris, and he maintained a close friendship with William Faulkner.[9]

In addition to Faulkner and Werlein, many other straight folk contributed to the French Quarter renaissance of the 1920s, including Sherwood Anderson, Grace King, Natalie Scott, Hamilton Basso, Louise Nixon, Jack McClure, Flo Field, Caroline Durieux, Louise Nixon, Alberta Kinsey, Roark Bradford, and many others. But the presence of gay men such as Saxon, Koch, Gilmore, Spratling, Hall, Odiorne, W. R. Irby, and Pops Whitesell demonstrates that the French Quarter renaissance was also not an exclusively straight phenomenon. All of these people knew each other to varying degrees, and all were part of a special moment in New Orleans history, contributing to the bohemian milieu

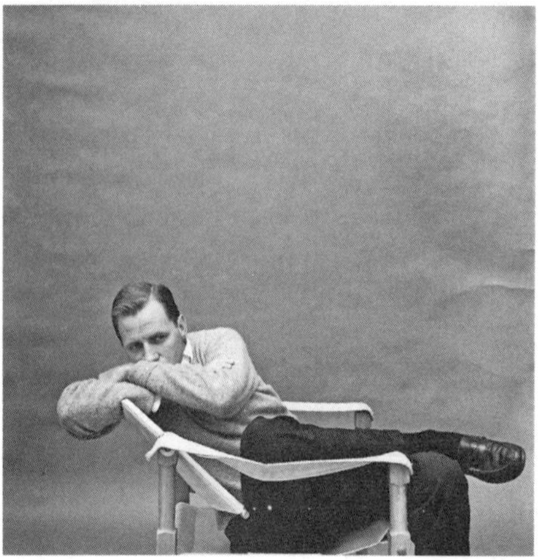

clockwise, top left: Artist George Dunbar in his French Quarter apartment, early 1950s. Artist Tilden Landry in his French Quarter studio, early 1950s. Artist Jean Seidenberg in his French Quarter studio, early 1950s. Portrait of Leonard Parrish, early 1950s. Photographs by Jack Robinson. Courtesy of the Jack Robinson Archive, Memphis.

that still can be sensed today. Fifty years after leaving New Orleans, Spratling recalled that, during the 1920s, the French Quarter "was not known as a chic place to live. . . . [M]any writers, painters, musicians, European and American, who came and went, formed a stimulating background. It was a world full of new ideas."[10]

The 1950s

The French Quarter experienced another artistic renaissance just over two decades later, in the early 1950s. Innovative artists such as George Dunbar, Jean Seidenberg, and Dusti Bongé became nationally known but stayed close to New Orleans. Foremost among the gay artists was a young photographer, Jack Robinson, who took a series of street photographs that recorded the exciting atmosphere during Carnival and the openness of the French Quarter. A friend of Robinson's, Lee Bailey, moved to New York and later penned several popular cookbooks. Other gay artists and socialites of the time with ties to the Quarter included Bruce Butterworth, Leonard Parrish, Tilden Landry, and Russell Bishop.[11] By the late 1950s and early 1960s, New Orleans's mayor and district attorney had scoured the Old Quarter in an effort to clean it up for the tourist trade, and police harassment forced many gay groups to seek venues elsewhere for parties and get-togethers. Other writers who came to New Orleans—most notably Tennessee Williams and Truman Capote—drew inspiration from and wrote about the city in their work.

The 1970s

In 1970, the French Quarter had only 5,257 residents, a decline of more than 50 percent since 1940. At the same time, the number of hotel rooms was increasing from 740 (most of them in the venerable Hotel Monteleone) in 1959 to 2,655 in 1970. The four largest hotels in the Quarter were constructed between 1960 and 1966—the Royal Orleans (now the Omni Orleans) in 1960, the

Bourbon Orleans in 1963, the Downtowner (now Four Points by Sheraton) in 1964, and the Royal Sonesta in 1966.[12] However, the Old Quarter still held on to its allure as a bohemian sanctuary despite the rise of tourist hotels and tacky souvenir shops. For example, Dumaine Nostalgia was a popular shop selling vintage deco items and antiques, including flamingo mirrors, cobalt-blue kidney-shaped end tables, and Maxfield Parrish prints. This deco craze carried on with other shops in the area. Deviation in Design also catered to a more local clientele with off-beat décor and interior design oddities.

Decatur Street Transformed

Another significant change in the character of the French Quarter was the transformation of Decatur Street, which runs along the Mississippi River. Until the 1970s, Decatur Street was a seedy strip of sailor bars and brothels. The French Market underwent a significant renovation from 1973 to 1975, with food vendors generally replaced by sellers of souvenirs. Rents skyrocketed, and many longtime local businesses closed or moved. Morning Call, for example, decamped to Metairie, while on the other side of Jackson Square, the Jax Brewery shut its doors in 1974 and did not reopen until ten years later, when it became a shopping mall. Many locals decried this surrender to the tourist trade. Nevertheless, some local institutions survived the changes, chief among them Tujague's restaurant, Central Grocery, and Café Sbisa, and some locals refused to capitulate to the tourists. In 1974, Jim Monaghan opened Molly's on the Market, a neighborhood watering hole that became something of a literary salon for the Quarter's intelligentsia.

Gay Liberation Movement

Gay rights activism began to have an effect in other U.S. cities during the 1970s but did not penetrate deeply into the French Quarter. A few attempts at organizing occurred, but most were short-lived. A local chapter of the national Gay Liberation Front was founded in 1970 and marched on City Hall in 1971 to protest police harassment. The group then hosted a "Gay-In" at City Park but folded shortly thereafter. Also in 1971, Barbara Scott, who owned the Fatted Calf, a French Quarter eatery popular among gays and lesbians, became the first openly gay candidate in Louisiana to run for the state House of Representatives. Scott lost. The New Orleans chapter of the Metropolitan Community Church was founded in 1971, the Tulane University Gay Student Union was founded in 1972, and the Gertrude Stein Society was founded in 1975. Lesbians in New Orleans were politically active, but with the exception of Charlene Schneider, their activism was oriented toward the women's movement. In 1977, Schneider opened a lesbian bar, Charlene's, which became something of a community center. Schneider encouraged political activism through such actions as hosting voter registration drives at her bar. Gayfest, forerunner to New Orleans Pride, was founded in 1979.[13]

On June 24, 1973, an arsonist struck the Up Stairs Lounge, a gay bar on Iberville Street in the French Quarter where members of the Metropolitan Community Church were having drinks. The fire broke out in the building's stairwell. When the buzzer that usually indicated that a cab had arrived sounded, Luther Boggs, another regular, opened the door to the stairwell and was greeted by roaring flames. As the fire spread, panic ensued. Bartender Buddy Rasmussen led about twenty people through a rear fire exit, although it was not clearly marked. Many patrons dashed for the windows, but they had bars that prevented all but the skinniest from squeezing through.

Passing by at around 7:45 p.m., Katherine Kirsch smelled smoke, opened the door leading to the stairwell, saw the flames, and immediately ran to the Midship Bar next-door to call the police. Fire trucks arrived about two minutes later. They were met by a grisly, horrific scene. The lifeless body of Bill Larson, pastor of the Metropolitan Community Church, was wedged in the window, his face and right arm protruding stiffly over the street. Buddy Rasmussen saw his boyfriend, Adam Fontenot, first on fire and subsequently knocked off his feet by a blast from a fire hose. George Mitchell initially escaped but ran back in to rescue his boyfriend, Louis Broussard; their bodies were found intertwined. A total of thirty men and two women were killed; scores of others were injured. Many of the dead were identified only through the records of local dentist Perry Waters, who also perished in the fire. According to the *New Orleans States-Item,* in the wake of the fire, "workers stood knee deep in bodies. . . . [T]he heat had been so intense, many were cooked together."[14]

The fire was most likely started not by someone with an antigay bias but by Rodger Dale Nunez, a hustler with a history of mental illness who had been thrown out of the bar about half an hour before the fire. While being escorted out after getting into a bathroom fight with a regular customer, Mike Scarborough, Nunez threatened to "burn you all out." No charges were ever filed, however, and Nunez committed suicide the following year.[15]

The media, police, and religious establishment initially responded to the fire with something less than sympathy. Radio commentators joked that the remains should be buried in fruit jars. Erroneously asserting that gay men at the time frequently carried false identification to conceal their identities in case of a police raid, Major Henry Morris, a detective with the New Orleans Police Department, was quoted in the *Times-Picayune* as saying, "We don't even know whether these papers belonged to the people we found them on. Some thieves hung out there, and you know this was a queer bar." Some people refused to claim family members' remains. Church after church refused to hold memorial services. When Father Bill Richardson of St. George's Episcopal Church overrode the objections of many of his parishioners and allowed his sanctuary to host a prayer service, he was chastised by his bishop and received hate mail. A Unitarian church also held a small memorial service, and on July 1, St. Mark's United Methodist Church on the edge of the French Quarter held a larger gathering officiated by the Reverend Troy Perry from Los Angeles, founder of the Metropolitan Community Church, along with Methodist bishop Finis Crutchfield. After the service, Reverend Perry pointed out a side exit that could be used by anyone who wished to avoid the television cameras waiting outside the main entrance. None of the estimated 250 people in attendance took him up on his offer. Perry later criticized New Orleans's gay community for its apathy toward gay liberation. In response, owners of local gay bars who sought to avoid drawing attention to their establishments, as well as other prominent gay men, called Perry and other gay activists who had come to New Orleans "carpetbaggers" and "outside agitators."[16]

Among the survivors was drag star Adrian St. Claire, who wore her fire-scarred back as an emblem of honor. She lost her lover in the fire and nearly lost her own life, but continued to perform at Travis's drag bar on Rampart Street. Her gowns always had their back cut-away to reveal her very real scars so her audience would remember, if only briefly.

In the wake of the fire, however, a handful of activists formed the Gay People's Coalition (GPC), which established a Gay Crisis Phone Line and began publishing *Causeway,* which was edited anonymously by Bill Rushton, a student at Tulane University who also edited the *Vieux Carré Courier.* In a January 1974 editorial, *Causeway* declared, "There are enough gay men and women in New Orleans, who are able to do anything they wish—be it swinging an election or electing a gay city councilman." But as the fire receded into the past, so did the ire of the gay community. The GPC and *Causeway* eventually faded away, as did a similar organization, the Gay Services Center, founded in 1974 by former Baptist minister Mike Stark and located on Burgundy Street in the Faubourg Marigny, and its newsletter, the *Closet Door.*[17]

But the Up Stairs Lounge fire nevertheless constituted a seminal moment in the history of gay New Orleans. A month and a half after the fire, the conservative *New Orleans Times-Picayune* published Joan Treadway's series of six articles concerning homosexuality. The first article, "Gay Community Surfaces in Tragedy of N.O. Fire," was surprisingly objective, with quotes from local gay activists succinctly summarizing the multitude of dilemmas facing gay New Orleanians: police harassment, job and housing discrimination, and general societal alienation. In addition to forcing straight New Orleans to acknowledge its gay community, the fire also forced gay New Orleans to confront itself.

Some people have compared the tragedy of the Up Stairs fire to the Stonewall riots, but such a comparison is not entirely accurate. Whereas Stonewall sparked a movement and resulted in long-term, sustained tangible activism, such was not the case with the Up Stairs fire. If anything, the fire caused the gay community to retreat deeper into the closet, where it remained for several more years.

Anita Bryant

In the spring of 1977, the singer and spokesperson for the Florida Citrus Commission, Anita Bryant, led a campaign to "Save Our Children" by repealing an antidiscrimination ordinance that protected gays and lesbians in Miami. According to Bryant, "What these people really want, hidden behind obscure legal phrases, is the legal right to propose to our children that theirs is an acceptable alternate way of life. I will lead such a crusade to stop it as this country has not seen before." She alleged that because "homosexuals cannot biologically reproduce children . . . they must recruit our children," and she warned that "if gays are granted rights, next we'll have to give rights to prostitutes and to people who sleep with St. Bernards and to nail biters." Either despite or because of her overblown rhetoric, Bryant's campaign succeeded in overturning the law in a June 7 referendum.[18]

Less than two weeks later, Bryant was scheduled to perform in New Orleans. Local activists Alan Robinson and Bill Rushton decided to organize a protest rally. Robinson had been a gay activist while studying at the University of Illinois and had met Rushton while volunteering at the Gay Services Center. The two men began dating, and one night over dinner, they and Ann Gallmeyer founded the Gertrude Stein Democratic Club, which eventually became the Gertrude Stein Society.[19]

The Gertrude Stein Society and more than a dozen other local gay organizations and progressive groups formed Human Equal Rights for Everyone (HERE) to protest Bryant. HERE contacted Rod Wagner, a board member of the New Orleans chapter of the American Federation of Television and Radio Artists, regarding Bryant's bigotry, and the board unanimously passed a resolution asking its members not to air the Bryant concerts. According to Wagner, board members feared "that her appearance could set up even more of a climate for violence here than we're already experiencing. And we are having our troubles. For instance, several older gay men have been stabbed to death in the French Quarter in the past few weeks, and I understand the suspect has said, 'Jesus doesn't like gay people.' What also concerns us are the reports of violence in the Miami area."[20]

HERE also planned a rally at Jackson Square, followed by a march through the French Quarter to the Municipal Auditorium, where Bryant was scheduled to perform. Robinson and Rushton flooded the French Quarter with flyers announcing the rally, and many of the area's gay bars stopped serving Florida orange juice.[21]

The June 18, 1977, rally exceeded organizers' expectations, attracting between twenty-five hundred and three thousand people. After the speechmaking, the crowd sang "We Shall Overcome" and began marching from Jackson Square along St. Ann Street before turning right onto Bourbon and left onto Dumaine. Leading the marchers was eighteen-year-old Ron Smith, a recent arrival from Pensacola, Florida, who was pounding on a snare drum and screaming, "Out of the closet and into the streets." As James T. Sears has written, "Supporters on wrought iron balconies wrapped with banners cheered. The march extended four blocks from sidewalk to sidewalk . . . picking up marchers along the way. Marking one of the largest civil rights demonstrations in the city's history, thousands of protesters arrived at the North Rampart Street Municipal Auditorium Entrance."[22]

The rally energized New Orleans's LGBT community and served as a harbinger of the shift in public attitudes toward homosexuality. Similar protests took place in other cities where Bryant performed, and the Florida Citrus Commission dropped her as its spokesperson.

Over the next decade, the gay liberation movement finally reached the Pelican State. The year 1980 saw not only the founding of the Louisiana Lesbian and Gay Political Action Caucus (LAGPAC) but also New Orleans's first Gay Pride Parade. The following year, the first Louisiana State LAGPAC Conference was held at the Country Club, a bar and swimming-pool club in the Bywater neighborhood. *Ambush Magazine* was founded in 1982, the same year that activists started the New Orleans chapter of Parents and Friends of Lesbians and Gays (PFLAG) and the New Orleans Gay Men's Chorus. Other LGBT organizations created over the next few years included the Krewe of Ishtar (1981), the NO/AIDS Task Force (1983), the Lords of Leather and the Krewe of Polyphemus (1983), Celebration (1983), the Krewes of Perseus and David (1984), Project Lazarus (1985), the Krewe of Queenateenas and Eros (1987), and the Forum for Equality (1989). And in 1991, largely as a result of LAGPAC's work, the New Orleans City Council passed a nondiscrimination ordinance.

The Southern Decadence Community

The Southern Decadence summer festival continued to be held every year without pause as the city changed around it. But, in the wake of the 1980 parade fiasco, Decadence, too, began to undergo some fundamental changes. Many of the event's founders drifted away from New Orleans and from the festival, and their places were filled by members of the city's gay community, making their way out of the closet and claiming the festival as their own. The New Orleans gay community has embraced Decadence as well, for good or bad, as a force of visibility and as a touchstone of LGBT cultural expression.

4

The Gaying of Decadence, 1981–1996

Well, here we go again. Decadence is upon us once more. My God, have any of us sobered up from last year yet?

—Southern Decadence Grand Marshal Donald "Donnie Jay" James, 2004

The events of the 1980 parade indicated that the founders of Southern Decadence no longer controlled it, and the original inhabitants of Belle Rêve subsequently withdrew their physical and spiritual energies from the festival, though not solely because of the schism. "We had other things going on in our lives, and we had grown older and more circumspect. The outlandish and outrageous, quite honestly, didn't really interest us anymore," explained Robert Laurent. "I had to have major surgery during the year, and I had gone back to my family in Lafayette to recuperate. I wasn't even in town for the next Decadence." Maureen and Charlie Block had moved out of the French Quarter to Uptown; she had begun teaching at Tulane University; and as their son, Andrew, got older, their priorities shifted to family life. Robert King was now confined to a wheelchair. Judy Shapiro, one of the Muses of Belle Rêve, had moved back to Manhattan. David Red had relocated to Nepal. Frederick Wright was now working at Notre Dame.[1]

As the Belle Rêvers stepped back, they were replaced by members of New Orleans's nascent gay and lesbian community, most of whom lived in and around the French Quarter and who had already developed a strong, almost cultlike affinity for Southern Decadence. However, the only substantive change that occurred around this time involved the starting point: Johnny Matassa's Bar closed, and the Golden Lantern on Royal Street, previously the site of the end-of-the-parade buffet, now became the starting point, in part because of Robert King's ties to the bar. But just as Southern Decadence became a mostly gay-centric affair, AIDS appeared, and over the next decade, the crisis caused by the disease decimated the gay community in New Orleans, as elsewhere, and profoundly shifted its members' worldview.

A leadership vacuum caused Southern Decadence to lose momentum for a

above: Ed "Blanche" Norton (1995 grand marshal) at the Golden Lantern, 1985. Courtesy of Robert Laurent.

right: Tommy Stephan (1981 grand marshal), 1980. Courtesy of Robert Laurent.

couple of years: in the absence of official invitations and people who were familiar with planning the event, attendance fell. But a reinvigoration occurred with the involvement of Miss Blanche's Demented Women, a troupe of terror-drag queens. The Demented Women were the creation of Edward "Blanche" Norton, who had moved from Tuscaloosa, Alabama, to New Orleans in 1978 with his close friend, Donnie Ezell, and had become caught up in the open and vibrant gay community. Norton began working as a bartender at the Golden Lantern, affectionately known as the Golden Latrine and owned by lovers Danny Wilson and Gary Clay. The low-key neighborhood haunt was located next-door to a laundromat, and neighbors would frequently come in to enjoy a beer while their clothes were on the spin cycle. The Lantern hosted not only drag shows by the Demented Women but also motorcycle christenings for the Knights d'Orléans club and after-parties for Carnival krewes. David Jolly and Jack White also worked as bartenders at the Lantern until they converted Jewel's Tavern, a raunchy sailor bar located a few blocks away, into an even raunchier gay bar. These outlying bars were not as well known as the bars on Bourbon Street, but they enjoyed a loyal clientele. Norton was inspired to create Miss Blanche's Demented Women by a high-fashion photo spread he noticed in *Vogue,* which used the term to describe the set-up. The Demented Women became the de facto inspiration for the reconstituted version of Southern Decadence.

1981—Tommy Stephan (Miss Cakie-Tee)

According to Laurent, after he and the other founders lost interest in Decadence, Robert King told his close friend Tommy Stephan to take it over and start at the Golden Lantern. Like King, Stephan was from Lafayette, Louisiana, but was a bit younger. Stephan's drag name was Miss Cakie-Tee, and Laurent remembered him "outside the Lantern posing like the World War II pinup of Betty Grable, but in overalls. He was as crazy as you'd expect for Decadence, just the perfect person to carry on the torch." In the past, only Jerome Williams in 1975 had led Southern Decadence in drag. But with the festival now headquartered at the Golden Lantern, with its bevy of ultra-serious drag queens, drag became more central to the parade's identity. Most participants wanted to emphasize camp and exaggeration, and in the hot and humid weather, clothing could become an enemy. Though many drag queens continued to honor the Belle Rêve tradition of hoopskirts and petticoats, the focus of the parade shifted to the artistry of drag—high camp or low gutter, glittered or tattered, even terror and gender-fuck, but unequivocally drag.

1982—Donnie Ezell

The 1982 Southern Decadence Parade was a near disaster. According to Norton, there was a near calamity that only New Orleans could have proffered:

> Grand Marshal Donnie Ezell had been out all night partying the night before. He was very good at that, but he came stumbling into our apartment about 1:30 p.m. on Decadence Sunday, drunk as a skunk and as high as the sky. I panicked at first, because he was out like a light as soon as he walked through the door. I quickly set about sobering him up with some strong chicory coffee. He could barely keep down food, and it looked like a losing proposition. But I grabbed him and put him in a really cold shower, and he sobered up enough to put on his Preacher Woman costume, something not very complicated. It was a tight shift dress, all in black, with a nun's habit and a succession of large silver crucifixes. If you didn't know better, you'd think you were in church. I called for a taxi. We lived in the Marigny, way downriver. As the car started to drive off, I remembered the whistle. We backtracked, and soon we were at the Golden Lantern, a bit late, but that only served to stoke the flames of anticipation and excitement.
>
> It was one of those gloriously memorable Decadences, impossible to describe, where everyone was in skanky drag and terrible makeup. I think I only wore a shift and a hat. Had to have a hat in those days, or it just wasn't Decadence. It was a long haul till dusk found us back at ground zero. Donnie took a nap, and I left him in bed. I changed and headed out to the sleazy bars. That usually meant Jewel's, and I think the Phoenix was open by then. At Jewel's, the

place was packed, just like at a beer bust. That's a typical Sunday for you, wall-to-wall tricks everywhere. And then, we were all in the bathroom—or tearoom, as we called it—when the Preacher Woman comes in like a hurricane carrying her Bible and testifying to high heaven. "Don't think the Lord don't see what's happening here. Get thee to church right now, you heathens," she'd shout. Of course, nobody paid her no mind. We had others things to worry about. It was officially still Decadence, after all.[2]

1983—Danny Wilson

Danny Wilson was a kindhearted, oversized teddy bear and part owner of the Golden Lantern. Wilson was chosen to serve as grand marshal because he exemplified the concept of decadence and had proven that fact during the year, which became the most important criterion. Wilson's selection stoked excitement about the celebration: he then became known as the undisputed kingpin of Decadence and was believed to be the source of serious drugs. Norton recalled that he rarely bought drugs but frequently received them as gifts from Wilson: "There was an abundance of drugs in the early 1980s, just everywhere. Crystal meth was the drug of choice, as I recall, but you could still get Quaaludes and Valium—just about anything. I liked speed, so there was plenty of that as well. Acid, too. A lot of people did acid back then, but it was usually cut with speed, so there really wasn't much to it besides the incessant jitters."

For the Decadence to end all Decadences, as some called the 1983 procession, Wilson dressed up as Wonder Woman, and the crowds gathered in front of the Golden Lantern went wild. Wilson's reign also saw a large number of southern-belle costumes, with hoopskirts and large beribboned hats. Norton recalled "lots of high heels that year, lots of Cinderellas and Little Miss Muffets, Southern debutantes, and the like. There were some gorgeous drags that year, more so than usual. Lots of seasoned drags like Alotta Mulatta and Miss Rowena. Girls really got their act together for a real return to Belle Rêve. I just loved this year. I was simply drop-dead in my all-white ensemble with yellow ribbons everywhere, hoopskirt and all, and my golden tresses were dangling all

above left: Danny Wilson (1983 grand marshal) in drag as Wonder Woman, 1985. Courtesy of Lou Bernard.

above right: Adolphus "Mumbo" Spires (1984 grand marshal), 1990. Courtesy of Lou Bernard.

right: The legendary force behind the Krewe of Olympus and several important French Quarter bars, Lou "Lucille" Bernard, 1985. Courtesy of Tulane Special Collections.

the way to the Old Absinthe House, where the tourists went bonkers when we appeared on the balcony and showed off our butt cheeks!"[3]

1984–1985—Mumbo and Fish

Wilson chose as his successor Adolphus "Mumbo" Spires, a popular drag queen from Alabama who worked as a bartender at Lucille's and Friend on St. Phillip Street. Upon learning of his selection, Spires immediately asked the bar's proprietor, Lou "Lucille" Bernard, for a "cordination" party, thereby establishing the tradition of holding coronations for all subsequent Southern Decadence grand marshals. Spires's selection drew Bernard into the festival's orbit: "I got very involved with Southern Decadence the year Mumbo was grand marshal. By then, the person knew in advance and could make plans. We had a big party for him at Lucille's, and for the first time, I presented him with a whistle for the parade. From then on, I presented the grand marshal with a new whistle every year, as was already the established tradition. Couldn't have Decadence without a whistle to start everything!"[4]

Spires had also worked with Michael "Fish" Hickerson at the Phoenix bar in the Marigny and chose his friend and confidant to serve as the 1985 grand marshal. Hickerson was well known in the gay community, in large part because of his involvement with gay krewes such as Polyphemus and Amon-Ra and his fund-raising work for AIDS support groups.[5] Hickerson was especially drawn to the true philosophy behind Southern Decadence, its unique expression of brash outrageousness and in-your-face attitude. Miss Fish would be remembered as one of the most outrageous grand marshals with his drop-dead drag, leading the parade to Canal Street and beyond.

1986—Kathleen Conlon

By 1986, the history of Southern Decadence was already being rewritten from a gay perspective. Patrick Shannon's mid-September article published in *Impact* magazine represented the first detailed written account of the event and focused squarely on the Golden Lantern and its proprietors and patrons, highlighting the role played by Wilson and Clay.

> Southern Decadence, as described by Gary Clay (aka Ms. White Lightning), began about seventeen years ago at a semi-straight bar, Johnny Matassa's on St. Philip Street. Matassa's had a large following of a cross-sectional variety of potential cross-dressers, a nicely balanced crowd of boozers and dopers, and for years this bar offered mixed drinks for four bits and beer for two. One day, a group of the regulars decided that the time was right for a *plein air* expression of their lifestyles and since this was not the Newport Beach or Nantucket Sleigh Ride crowd but your run-of-the-mill Quarter boozers and boozettes, the expression naturally involved costumes and hooch. And of course everyone knows that everything from a hormone injection to a beatific vision in the grits at the Coffee Pot is an excuse for a costume party in New Orleans.
>
> The procession became more and more the province of what in those days were, and perhaps still are, known in polite society as fairies, queers, dykes, fruits and are now referred to as gays, a word I detest. In a hitherto relatively inconspicuous *boite de nuit,* or *vase de nuit* or whatever, at the corner of Barracks and Royal (approximately), the Golden Lantern, under the guidance of La Clay and Danny (Wonder Woman) Wilson, deluges of drags, semi-drags and demi-drags and just some plain old queens began showing up in droves and proclaiming it the starting point of a parade and promenade in and about the French Quarter each Labor Day Sunday. Following a route known only to the Grand Marshal, who usually did everything with an extravagantly improvisatory sense of extemporaneity, the march went from one bar to another, and on occasion to the Moonwalk, the lobby of the Fairmont Hotel, and even to Canal Street for a perusal of the windows at Lerner's and Miller Wohl. Wearing heels as tall as railroad spikes and lashes as long as the stinging tentacles of a Portuguese man o' war, these marchers were known to stun many an unprepared tourist en route, transporting them from the land of Ozzie and Harriet to plain old Oz.[6]

Hickerson had selected Kathleen Conlon to serve as grand marshal of Southern Decadence. Three decades later, she recalled, "Lou Bernard hosted a coronation party at Lucille's bar that pulled out all the stops. George Marney Cossitt and Jamie Temple fêted me at the Phoenix." They and others, including Bobby Laezar and Roy Letson, "made this one of the most poignant and wonderful times of my life."[7] The choice of a straight woman might seem odd to outsiders, but the grand marshals have complete authority to choose their successor. As Hickerson has summed up this gesture time and time again, "Kathleen and I were having cocktails at Lafitte's, and Decadence was the very next day. I turned to her in a panic and said you're it. And that is the history of it all. Thank you very much!" Conlon became even more infamous as the grand marshal who led the whole troupe to the Riverwalk Mall along the river to cavort in the large fountain there, much to the surprise and horror of the tourists.

1987–1988—Olive and Jerome Legume

Jeffrey "Olive" Melton reigned as grand marshal in 1987 before handing off the crown to his close friend Jerome Legume. For the first time, the venerable and conservative *New Orleans Times-Picayune* covered Southern Decadence, breaking from its general (though not blanket) practice of not reporting on specifically gay events. Particularly noteworthy, the piece's overall tone was positive and upbeat, though author Christopher Rose threw in some details designed to shock readers as well:

> [On Sunday,] the French Quarter was home to its own autumn ritual—the largest drag queen parade in the South.
>
> "Southern Decadence is one of those gender affairs," said the gowned and bearded Norman Core. "It's a chance to celebrate the end of a summer and a chance to wear a dress." Held annually on the Sunday before Labor Day, Southern Decadence looks a little like a Mardi Gras street party with the button-down celebrants pared away, leaving only the hardcore cross-dressing bohe-

Grand Marshal Jerome Legume on the cover of *Impact*, September 9–22, 1988.
Courtesy of Tulane Special Collections.

mia. Several hundred men took to the Quarter streets after waiting out the rain, all the more primed after spending most of the morning and early afternoon primping and drinking in dark bars.

> Southern Decadence began about 20 years ago in a subtler fashion, as an end of summer party among Quarter neighbors and friends, both straight and gay. Over the years, the party outgrew the indoors and fell out of favor with straight people. It then moved into the streets, evolving into a wandering shock parade. "Year after year it seems the city forgets that this exists," said Jerome Legume, this year's grand marshal. He was selected by last year's grand marshal for a record of exemplary decadence during the past year. Legume said his selection was due, not to any supreme act, but to "a compilation of events." He dressed as a pineapple in drag and led the parade through the French Market in honor of this year's Southern Decadence theme: "Plagues, Pests and Parasites."

> Two stunned visitors from Chicago watched on Esplanade Avenue as the parade sauntered by. "I guess they're all men?" asked Laura, who refused to give her last name because she said she works for the government and it would not look good for her to be here. Asked if this sort of thing happens much at home she said, "No, not generally." She admitted she hadn't anticipated something like this during her visit. "It's what we hope for," she said. "But it's certainly not what we expected."

> Legume blew his grand marshal whistle and led the blocks-long line of high-heeled revelers on an uncharted tour of the Quarter's more free-thinking bars. He confessed that he was concerned that someone from his job might see him and not understand, but he said, "That's not the point." The point, then? To laugh at yourself. And maybe a little at others when they're not looking."[8]

The 1988 parade attracted an estimated eight hundred to a thousand people, showing a significant rebound from Decadence's nadir but not yet returning to the heights of the celebrations that preceded the 1980 disaster. The event's growing popularity was somewhat offset by the AIDS epidemic, which had taken a severe toll on the city's gay population.

1989—George Goode

By 1989, Southern Decadence again grabbed the cover of *Impact* magazine, which featured Grand Marshal George Goode, a longtime bartender at Lucille's, costumed in a stunning one-piece bathing suit with an entourage of equally tacky drag queens. For his cover story, Patrick Shannon asked parade-goers to identify themselves and explain what Southern Decadence meant to them:

"I'm Loretta Mims, a journalist for *Just for the Record*. It's hot, it's great, it's gorgeous, and hopefully, it's going to be decadent."

"I'm Blanche Fury. It's the end of a dead, hot summer and it's the beginning of a lot of fun and enjoyment and tourism and good things for the Quarter. I'm from New Orleans. Seven generations."

"You know me, girl. Hi, all you girls out there. My name is Tuna Melt. Y'all know me as Tuna. It means I can get out of these dresses for the summer, girl, and get ready for the furs for the winter."

"This is another day to go mad. I don't know who I am. I have to look at my label. It means the end of a very hot summer and hopefully, a short cold winter. You know, like some of the tricks we've shared."

"I'm Olive. I was a former Grand Marshal and this is the one day out of the year that I wear a hoop-skirt."

"I'm Miss Petit. It means just get as decadent as ever, honey, and start out at the Phoenix and get a fabulous breakfast. It's free food. Paul Booth wasn't there! I was so surprised. I didn't eat anything. I just hootched, and that's what it means to me, hootched!"

"I'm Jaquette. I'm having fun. The rest of the year I work hard and I slave."

"Formerly known as Miss Drag Joan Rivers of 1987. I am absolutely astounded and it's, it's flawless, what can I say? This day means to me as a Southern gay person that we are the most decadent fabulous lot in the world. Nowhere! Nowhere in my vast travels have I seen such, such [distracted by several hairy-legged ballet dancers doing arabesques down Royal Street]. . . . I'm sorry, I mean, it's those hairy legs that do it for me, I mean it really is!"

"My name is Susan and I think it's wonderful. I'm from New Orleans and I

Grand Marshal George Goode, leading the parade down Royal Street, 1989. Courtesy of Lou Bernard.

think it's probably, if not as nice, probably better than Mardi Gras, because you don't have a lot of other people around. I think it's great for people to be able to go out and do what they want to do. It's definitely demonstrative of real American liberty. Only in New Orleans. I'm just concerned if there's someone here from Omaha, what would they think? But if they're not embarrassed, I surely can't be."

"I'm Julie and I used to live here but temporarily I'm from Washington, D.C. I agree with my friend here that it's nice to have this kind of freedom of expression."

"I'm Molly and now that I know what's going on I'm just appalled that I've missed it all these years. I'm shocked and appalled. I'm delighted to be here. I hope I never miss it again."

"My name is George Goode, this year's Grand Marshal, and I'm scared to death!"[9]

1990—Robbie "Ruby" Haywood

The beginning of the new decade saw Decadence expanding its influence and numbers exponentially. Miss Ruby was named grand marshal, and her theme was "Circus Came to Town." This title came from the lyrics to a popular Melissa Manchester song, "Don't Cry Out Loud," which had resonated with Haywood. This was the first Decadence parade to have an official color as well, and Miss Ruby had to have her Ruby Red. Most of the costumes that year sported this spectacular color theme.

1991—Jamie Temple and the Phoenix

Jamie Temple and his partner, George Cossitt, opened the Phoenix, the first real leather bar in New Orleans at 941 Elysian Fields in the Faubourg Marigny, in 1982. Originally a hardware store, the building had been purchased by lesbian bar owner Charlene Schneider, who turned it into Smoky Mary's restaurant, named after the railroad line that had once run from the riverfront all the way up Elysian Fields to Lake Pontchartrain. The establishment briefly housed a lesbian bar, Clark's Gable, before Cossitt and Temple, a New Jersey native who had come to New Orleans to attend college and subsequently stayed, bought the structure and opened the Phoenix. Several of the bar's other employees, including Hickerson, Spires, Melton, and Legume, had previously served as grand marshal, and the bar became strongly associated with Southern Decadence, hosting street parties as well as indoor festivities.[10]

Temple had become a leader in the New Orleans gay community not only because of his bar's connection to Southern Decadence but also because he had been one of the founders of the NO/AIDS Task Force. His selection signaled a growing shift in Decadence's orientation from a solely social festival and bacchanal to one with a significant charitable fund-raising component. This was the beginning of that trend and would continue to define the real character of Decadence even after its exponential growth in the future. This change in direction would become one of the most powerful tools of the New Orleans gay community in their battle against AIDS.

In October, the *Advocate* published an article on the year's celebration that truly highlighted its provocative nature:

> A motorist and his family lock their doors as a 6-foot-2 drag queen approaches their car and plants one high heel on their front bumper. As the family cowers, the drag queen raises her dress, squats over the hood ornament, and proceeds to simulate an orgasm while a crowd of thousands cheer.
>
> This most *vivant* of tableaux and hundreds like it took place during Southern Decadence 1991, an annual gay and lesbian celebration that all but paralyzes New Orleans's French Quarter. On the Sunday before Labor Day, costumed revelers meet outside a bar to crown a grand marshal, stagger through the streets, terrorize tourists, and generally make *Paris Is Burning* look like *Home Alone.* There's no parade permit, no scheduled route, no political agenda, and seemingly no reason for Southern Decadence.
>
> So what is it? "Mardi Gras for faggots," says a Bourbon Street stripper. "I don't know," says a waiter from the Clover Grill, "but it'll change your life."
>
> Whatever Southern Decadence is, it began in 1972 with a few dozen participants and has grown steadily each year until it now includes hundreds of elaborately dressed carousers trying, in the words of one participant, "to get as drunk as possible and fuck up the tourists."
>
> "These aren't your run-of-the-mill transvestites," says Ken, a bartender and a veteran of Southern Decadence. "These are some really, *really* sick drag queens.
>
> The three-day weekend brought Decadence-related barbecues, drag shows, and parties, including a 9 p.m. to 9 a.m. dance-a-thon, Pee-wee's Adult Playhouse, and the Miss High Hair contest.
>
> Things really began on Sunday at 5 a.m. at the Golden Lantern, where the parade was to begin, with a happy hour. By 2 in the afternoon, several hundred people were braving pouring rain and awaiting the arrival of the grand marshal, Jamie Shirley Temple Black Leather.
>
> Once the rain subsided, the parade swung into bedraggled, bedragged motion, marching a block over to busy Esplanade Avenue, where drivers were confronted with boys in G-strings and hairy-backed men in stained evening gowns.

An enormous Spanish doña threw tortillas like Frisbees, which others seized and began using to wipe car windshields, begging for tips. Drivers' reactions ranged from delight and amusement to sheer terror. A few locked their doors and took their children into their laps until the parade passed.

From Esplanade, the grand marshal led the parade down Decatur Street. Traffic snarled for blocks around as the decadents ran into nearby bars for fortification, vogued for tourists, and dealt with drivers who had attitude. Drivers who weren't in the proper celebratory mood found their cars turned into rolling drink carts, and one car adorned with BORN AGAIN bumper stickers was mercilessly hooted.

When the mugginess got so wretched that it melted makeup, people disappeared into nearby bars. At one club, where partiers drank cold beer faster than it could be shoved across the bar, a real woman announced, "This is Southern Decadence, and I'm going to be decadent!" She then squatted and peed, as even the most decadent headed for the safer, drier corners of the dance floor.

Several New Orleans natives declared Southern Decadence 1991 to be the biggest yet—even though the parade lost its focus before it could invade the tourist-packed lobbies of the Marriott and Sheraton hotels. Oh, well, there's always next year.[11]

1992–1993—Harry "Rhie" Sherman and Lee "Ms. Fly" Featherston

Temple chose Harry Sherman to serve as the 1992 grand marshal. A close friend of Temple, Sherman never actually worked at the Phoenix, though he did spend an inordinate amount of time helping and was considered part of the bar family.[12] Sherman was also a graphic artist who designed various posters and invitations for the Lords of Leather, a gay Carnival krewe.

The following year, Southern Decadence emerged on the national scene as a gay celebration, with singer and drag queen RuPaul, whose 1993 song, "Supermodel," brought him international fame, appearing at the House of Blues in what was billed as "RuPaul Comes to Heaven: A Southern Decadence Celebration." Ms. Fly, the grand marshal, joined the party after leading the parade, continuing to celebrate Decadence with the Parents and Friends of Lesbians and Gays (PFLAG) at their convention.[13]

1994–1995—Miss Alain and Miss Blanche

The 1994 grand marshal, Alain Simard (Miss Alain), was a well-known New Orleans drag queen and bartender. Her admirers included her successor as grand marshal, Edward Norton in his Miss Blanche persona. Norton described his philosophy of drag: "I took drag very seriously. It was something new and exciting and a way to transform myself into something spectacularly alien, foreign, uncertain, different, and tantalizing, or all of the above. It created a sense of self and liberation [that] made anything and everything possible. We were in our own heads and our own universe. And it was something unique and fantastic. I was just so happy to be part of it all. In a way, I made my contribution by elevating the whole thing to an art form."

Norton had plotted and planned for the day when he would be chosen as Southern Decadence grand marshal. He knew that it was inevitable:

> My take on the parade and the costumes, I suppose, started the whole tradition of choosing a theme. Before me, it was just scrap something together. I, however, wanted a return to the origins of Southern Decadence, to the time I first realized that this was all possible, when there was a carefree attitude and spirit that had somehow faded from the scene. I looked to resurrect the Belle Rêve vibe, come hell or high water. I was a very close friend with Robert Laurent and Frederick Wright, and we got together for an informal luncheon with other former grand marshals the weekend before Decadence. Thus began that great tradition. I loved the founders. They inspired me to really get into Decadence and its true meaning. It meant self-expression and joy, friendship and love of our fellow participants, not just drunken abandon. . . . Once I wore a white dress with petticoats, trimmed in yellow satin ribbons, and a similar hat of course—a wide-brimmed number that just exuded the prim and proper. It was all about contrast, don't you know!"[14]

1996—Wayne White

Norton chose Wayne White as the 1996 grand marshal. The two were good friends, and Norton "wanted to redirect the energies of Southern Decadence to bring in some new blood. Miss Wayne was from Lafitte's, and I wanted to see what those gals could do. I had high hopes, and Miss Wayne—well, she deserved the honor of being grand marshal, more than anyone I knew, because she was one sick puppy, very decadent, and knew how to treat her friends. I loved her to death, and she came through as a spectacular grand marshal." White's reign drew the Bourbon Street bars into the whirlwind of Decadence, swelling the crowds to unprecedented levels. The traditions continued, although the Grand Marshal Luncheon held a week before the parade added a sponsor, Bud Light, and reached an unprecedented level of elaborateness with a formal invitation: "Clover Grill Closed by Order of the 1996 Southern Decadence Grand Marshal, Wayne White. Saturday, August 24, 1996. A Breakfast For Royalty, honoring His Highness Mr. Wayne White, 1996 Southern Decadence Grand Marshal, also Former Southern Decadence Royalty and Their Guests. Tom Wood and The Management and Staff of The Clover Welcome You. Proud to be the Official Diner of Mr. Wayne White. The Clover Grill, New Orleans Counter Culture Specialists."

However, Southern Decadence had turned a corner. It had outgrown the streets and had become more than a single grand marshal and his or her bar entourage could handle. As Lou Bernard remembered, "It took sometimes over an hour for the parade just to stop at a bar and everyone get drinks. It was huge, and now the parade made stops at all the gay bars and everything in between. And everyone had to have another cocktail." In 1996, people realized "that the whole French Quarter was affected by Decadence—the hotels, the taxis, the restaurants, the bars, of course, and then the massive cleanup."[15]

In a pointed letter to the editor of the *New Orleans Times-Picayune,* Robert M. Carter, a concerned resident of the French Quarter, called out the city for failing to support what some were calling "Gay Mardi Gras":

> Another Southern Decadence Day has come and gone and the New Orleans media and civic leaders still don't seem to notice. It is odd that the local media don't respond to the increased tourists and their money being spent in the city. While actual attendance numbers are not available, the impact on the city's coffers and local merchants' income could and should be calculated. I would venture to say that the impact is sizable. Why was this overlooked once again? Is it because it is a gay-inspired holiday? Is it because it is not condoned by the city? Where else in this city is there a parade with thousands of participants and onlookers where no portable toilets can be found? Where else is there a noticeable lack of police and police barricades to protect marchers and reroute traffic for a parade? Maybe Decadence Day should be held somewhere else next year and end its 20-year addiction to New Orleans. New Orleans truly doesn't deserve the revenue this event provides.[16]

An End to the Little Bar Crawl

Southern Decadence was on the brink of another major shift in its lifespan. The crowds had become hordes and, in order to accommodate everyone, a change was required. Now that the festival was raising money for AIDS charities, its survival was paramount. Its exuberance and fierce sense of community and celebration also were now an integral part of the city's lifeblood. Carter's poignant letter was a not a cry for help but a warning. City involvement, although unwanted by many celebrated grand marshals, was key to the future of Decadence. Given a chance, the city would support the festival. The city would begin to listen to such calls and would eventually embrace Southern Decadence as yet another facet of the city's rather complicated and essential persona.

5

Southern Decadence and Carnival

New Orleans is a sensual, sybaritic city, and it is for her pleasures that she has long been celebrated.
—Henri Schindler

On the surface, Southern Decadence appeared to be a standalone festival marking the end of summer, with few links to Mardi Gras six months earlier. A closer examination, however, shows not only that some common threads connect the two events but also that they can be seen as complementary, two halves of a whole. Though Southern Decadence is now often called Gay Mardi Gras, it is more accurately seen as an inverted, distorted Mardi Gras, a Mardi Gras as reflected in a funhouse mirror, almost unrecognizable but nonetheless intricately linked to traditional Carnival. Carnival in New Orleans has always been inviolate, a sacrosanct tradition etched into the fabric of the city. Decadence, by contrast, became the profane image, distorting the traditional processions, costumes, and merrymaking with a parallel vengeance. Even some aspects of gay Carnival seemed to find a way to insinuate themselves into Southern Decadence from the very beginning.

Traditional Carnival

The Carnival season stretches from January 6 (Epiphany) until Shrove Tuesday, which might fall sometime in mid-February or even early March. In New Orleans, the season features a series of tableau balls, usually put on by clubs, known as krewes, and held in secret. For the last two weeks or so of the season, however, parades snake their way around the city, with the krewes devising elaborate floats and intricately costumed krewe members throwing trinkets down to excited revelers in the streets. The old-line krewes paraded down Canal Street, often ending up at the French Opera House on Bourbon Street, or some other equally exotic theater. In 1875, the State of Louisiana declared Mardi Gras a legal holiday. Though war and economic, political, and weather conditions have at times led to the cancellation of some or all of the major Mardi Gras parades, the city has always celebrated Carnival. Since 1973, however, New Orleans has prohibited large parades from traversing the narrow streets of the French Quarter as a consequence of safety concerns posed by large floats and uncontrollable crowds.[1]

Although traditional Carnival krewes have remained mysterious and exclusive, the public has always participated in the parades by wearing costumes that make them more than just onlookers, by drinking and dancing in the streets, and by interacting with the masked figures on the floats and in the parades. In essence, New Orleans's version of the Old World Carnival gives the city's population the freedom to let go, particularly on Shrove Tuesday, in ways that were unimaginable during the rest of the year.[2] As early as 1729, a young clerk dressed in full drag, donning "a corset of white dimity, a muslin skirt, a large pannier, right down to the chemise, along with plenty of beauty marks too." He wrote that, "unless you looked at me closely, you could not tell that I was a boy."[3] In Gallatin Street near the river, denizens of these sailor bars wantonly cross-dressed as well, establishing a custom of masking and costuming that not only defined these celebrations, but also heedlessly rejected any attempt at gender roles. New Orleans's Mardi Gras came to define itself by this very love of costuming. By the late nineteenth century, walking clubs had joined in the festivities, with costumed characters walking alongside the floats. These walking clubs and the extravagant Mardi Gras traditions they represented clearly inspired the founders of Southern Decadence. From its inception, the Decadence parade featured a participatory ethos in which everyone was welcome to join in the festivities, with no "official" sanction required.

Carnival Walking Clubs

Costuming as public display has been an integral facet of the city's identity for centuries. Although appearing on the streets in anything but standard attire had been the legal norm, on Shrove Tuesday the citizenry of New Orleans embraced the idea of becoming something different—decked out in fantastical raiment, transposed to another reality by way of colossal parade floats, costumed royalty from the courts of the Carnival krewes, and hiding behind a separate identity—all had become part of the collective consciousness of the city. Beyond the surreal floats that rolled down the streets every Carnival season, there was a long-standing tradition of the "walking club." Traditional walking clubs date back to the late nineteenth century, and even early krewe parades had costumed characters walking alongside the floats.[4]

The Buzzards

The Jefferson City Buzzards are the oldest Mardi Gras marching club in New Orleans, dating back to 1890. The Buzzards have an all-male membership. Early on Mardi Gras morning, they begin marching Uptown at the edge of Audubon Park in traditional costumes. The club walks down a series of side streets, down to Magazine Street, eventually parading down St. Charles Avenue to Canal Street so as to precede the much-anticipated Rex parade around noon. The walking club then continues on to Rampart Street, then down to Magazine and Poydras streets, where the parade ends. The Buzzards, named for the birds that frequented the area slaughterhouses near the river Uptown and across the river in Algiers, walk or dance along with canes, decorated with paper flowers to give to parade goers with a kiss for ladies, along with beads and doubloons.

The Corner Club

Organized in 1918, the Irish Channel Corner Club is the second-oldest marching club. It is an all-male carnival organization that marches in parades during Mardi Gras—donning colorful custom carnival costumes with their signature Corner Club beads—and St. Patrick's Day with their traditional green vests. Their members also walk with colorful canes given away for kisses while they dance and drink in the streets. The club parades on Shrove Tuesday through the Irish Channel and down St. Charles Avenue with the Pauline Bros. Brass Band. They also parade in the Thoth Parade the Sunday before Fat Tuesday.

The Half-Fast Walking Club

The Half-Fast Walking Club is a New Orleans Mardi Gras krewe, founded in 1961 and led by Pete Fountain. Beginning at Commander's Palace Restaurant on Washington Avenue in the Garden District, the club proceeds downtown on St. Charles Avenue to Canal Street, entering the French Quarter at Bourbon Street and ending up at the Monteleone Hotel in the early afternoon. Fountain and other local jazz musicians play through much of the parade. The original name was "The Half-Assed Walking Club" and was an excuse to take a spirited musical stroll down the parade route. Fountain later changed the name with urging from the organizers.

La Société de Sainte Anne

Known for its fabulous costumes and colorful revelry, the Société de Sainte Anne has marched every Mardi Gras since 1969. Fueled by a healthy dose of cynicism, humor, and an obsessive devotion to Carnival, friends Henri Schindler, Jon Newlin, and Paul Poché founded the parade to continue the tradition of walking clubs and eventually to rebel against an ordinance that banned traditional parades from the Vieux Carré. Schindler named the parade after the street most of his friends lived on, but it was deemed an appropriate twist of fate when they learned Sainte Anne was the grandmother of God. Beginning early on Mardi Gras morning, the band of costumed revelers kick off their march in the Faubourg Marigny with a mixed group of gay and straight, black and white, but always in fabulous and incredible costumes, which some would describe as the best of the season. There are no invitations or exemptions as fantastically costumed paraders join in the march along the route, which culminates on Canal Street to view the Rex parade.[5]

Gay Carnival

In 1972, the first year of Southern Decadence and its costume party, gay Carnival krewes had already been well established and were thriving, although still secreted away and in the shadows. The first gay krewe, the Krewe of Yuga, was formed in 1958, probably in jest, to emulate the traditional Carnival krewes from the nineteenth century. Elaborate costume parties were thrown innocently enough to view parades along Carrollton Avenue, and these celebrations suddenly transformed themselves into an organized Carnival krewe. Others quickly followed suit: the Krewes of Petronius, Amon-Ra, Ganymede, Armeinius, Apollo, Olympus, Ishtar, Lords of Leather, Polyphemus, Dirtie Dottie, and Désimé held lavish balls where royal courts reigned over their subjects much like those of Comus, Rex, Proteus, and Bacchus.[6]

After the original core group had left its mark on the Southern Decadence festival, it was only a matter of time until members of the gay krewes were chosen as grand marshals. This was serendipitous, as members of krewes also worked as bartenders and managers of many of the gay bars sprinkled throughout the French Quarter. Michael Hickerson, who worked at the Golden Lantern and at the Phoenix, brought his knowledge of gay Carnival to the Decadence parade, having been a member of the Krewes of Polyphemus and Amon-Ra. Jamie Temple, the owner of the Phoenix Bar, arguably the only real leather bar in the city, was a member of the Lords of Leather and served as its Lord King in 1998. Robin Malta, former manager of Café Lafitte in Exile, was also the Queen of Petronius in 1990, and Lee Featherston likewise was a

Petronius Queen in 2000. Roy Haylock, who would become famous in his drag persona of Bianca del Rio, served as queen for the Mystic Krewe of Satyricon, and Electra City, along with Tittie Toulouse and Tami Tarmac, all served as queens of the Krewe of Amon-Ra. Errol Rizzuto, also a member of Amon-Ra, served as ball lieutenant and captain. Rip and Marsha Naquin-Delain, the publishers of *Ambush Magazine* and for a long time the force behind Southern Decadence's survival, also have celebrated Carnival with their Krewe of Queenateenas. Aubrey Synclaire was also named among the queens of the krewe. More recently, Jeffrey Palmquist was designated as the first Grand Reveler of the Mystik Krewe du Rue Royale Revelers.[7]

Whether by chance or by dynamics, traditional Carnival in the city of New Orleans has had a profound effect on Southern Decadence. This spirit of celebration, of public display and costuming, does not wither away after Ash Wednesday, but hovers about as a disembodied spirit awaiting a glorious transformation. Halfway around the calendar, Decadence took shape within this grand tradition and molded itself into something almost as sacred, and quite unexpected with more than a dash of the profane attached to its revelry. Carnival, although dissipated after Ash Wednesday, reconstitutes itself in another guise, that of the irreverent and chaotic Grand Procession of Southern Decadence.

6

Bar Culture and the Rise of Decadence

The only thing in life that is truly sacred is friendship.
When you mix that with the pagan and profane,
you would probably get something like Decadence.
—Southern Decadence Grand Marshal
Edward "Blanche" Norton, 1995

New Orleans became a nexus for gay culture even before World War II. In the early twentieth century, New Orleans decadents frequented the numerous bars that sprang up along Bourbon Street, and when the city's gay community developed, its members, too, found a haven there, as did out-of-towners who wanted to explore their desires. French Quarter bars offered more than just drinks, allowing locals to congregate, share news, and establish friendships. Many residents lived within walking distance of their favorite watering holes, many of which never closed—bars were permitted to remain open twenty-four hours a day, 365 days a year. Today, locals generally avoid the strip joints, jazz clubs, and bars along the first half of Bourbon Street, although they remain extremely popular among tourists. Those who want a less frenetic atmosphere where friends can linger, escaping the constraints of time and the outside world, prefer bars in the less-frequented areas of the Lower French

Quarter and along Rampart and Decatur streets. Before the 1960s, when gays and lesbians endured harassment and even arrest when they dared to allow themselves to become visible, these bars became places of refuge. Gay bars were allowed to operate as long as they made payoffs to the appropriate entities. Some of these dives and juke joints fostered not only camaraderie but also revelry and excess that easily translated into a culture fostering the outlandish and decadent.

The Nineteenth and Early Twentieth Centuries

One such center was the Old Absinthe House, located on Bourbon Street. In the early twentieth century, when the French Quarter was run-down and abandoned, few tourists found much of interest there, preferring the thrill of Storyville and the lure of its brothels. Nevertheless, since shortly after the turn of the nineteenth century, the Old Absinthe House has steadfastly promoted its eponymous chartreuse concoction, known as both the Green Goddess and the Green Monster and believed to combine intoxication with poison.[1] Among those who visited during the 1800s were Mark Twain, Walt Whitman, and Oscar Wilde. Though the federal government banned the importation and sale of absinthe in 1912 on the grounds that it was "dangerous to health," Aleister Crowley, a Scottish fan of the occult, visited the Old Absinthe House six years later and described it as the "heart and soul of the old quarter of New Orleans": "I am only sipping the second glass of that fascinating, but subtle poison, whose ravages eat men's heart and brain that I have ever tasted in my life; and as I am not an American anxious for quick action, I am not surprised and disappointed that I do not drop dead upon the spot. But I can taste souls without the aid of absinthe; and besides, this is magic of absinthe! The spirit of the house has entered into it; it is an elixir, the masterpiece of an old alchemist, no common wine."[2] During Prohibition, the bar became a speakeasy, and those who partook of banned beverages there included Sherwood Anderson. It also became known as a meeting place for inverts.

The 1930s–1960s

During the 1930s, other gay bars began to spring up along the periphery of the French Quarter. By 1941, during his second trip to New Orleans, Tennessee Williams discovered the city's openly gay community by visiting such places as Mack's Bar on Canal Street and the St. James Bar at the corner of Toulouse and Royal streets. Williams told a friend that he had a room "right opposite *the* gay bar, the St. James, so I can hover like a bright angel over the troubled waters of homosociety."[3] And a character in Williams's *Orpheus Descending* mentions some of the bars that the playwright must have visited: the Starlite Lounge, the Club Rendezvous, and Miss Dixie's Bar of Music.[4]

New Orleans native Yvonne "Miss Dixie" Fasnacht was a jazz musician who traveled around the country during the 1940s in an all-female band, the Southland Rhythm Girls. When the band folded, she returned to the city and began running a bar with her sister, Irma. When the bar moved to Bourbon Street in 1949, it became known as Dixie's Bar of Music. The establishment welcomed everyone but was particularly accepting of gay men, whom Miss Dixie (a lesbian) protected, using her influence to keep vice cops out as well as bailing patrons out of jail when need be.[5]

A few blocks down at 941 Bourbon Street was another gay bar, Café Lafitte, named after the pirate, which opened in 1933. In 1953, the bar moved to its current location at 901 Bourbon Street (former site of the Mayfair Bar) and was renamed Café Lafitte in Exile. It became the French Quarter's most popular gay bar, especially after Miss Dixie's closed its doors in the early 1964.[6]

Shortly after the end of Prohibition, Emile Morlet opened the Wonder Bar on Decatur Street, where he employed male entertainers to "impersonate various people in the theatrical world." The drag shows brought police harassment, and in 1936 Morlet unsuccessfully sought an injunction against the raids. He subsequently relocated the bar to pilings out on Lake Pontchartrain at the Jefferson–Orleans Parish line and renamed it the Wonder Club. In the late 1940s, the venue became the Club My-O-My, and it continued to operate until May 4, 1948, when a suspicious fire destroyed the building. The club rebuilt at the same location and for the next three-plus decades catered primar-

New location of the Café Lafitte, early 1950s, renamed Café Lafitte in Exile.
Courtesy of the Louisiana State Museum.

ily to tourists, who would descend on the club by the busload to watch the live singers, many of whom had recording contracts. Club My-O-My remained in operation until 1972, when another fire resulted in its permanent closure.[7]

In 1963, John Rechy published a largely autobiographical novel, *City of Night,* that took much of its material from the author's visit to New Orleans during Carnival. Now considered a classic, Rechy's work offered lurid details about some of the city's watering holes, among them the Bourbon House Bar and Restaurant, where gay men, including many of the early members of the gay Carnival krewes, came to gossip, review the happenings of the night before, and plan future parties and outings. Rechy also mentioned several other bars: the Rocking Times (a pseudonymous version of Dixie's Bar of Music, which was located across the street from the Bourbon House), Cindy's Bar, and Les Deux Frères, as well as "Les Petits, where nightly Love Face, a fat Negro woman with bleached hair, made panting, sighing song-love to the mike. And, outside, past the courtyard, was Sandy-Vee's bar—and Sande-Vee is one of the most flagrant, most famous drag-queens in America. Vaunting her imposed exile, defiantly she dangles his/her orange earring for the curious tourists."[8]

Nevertheless, despite New Orleans's general laissez-faire attitude, gays in New Orleans have faced a considerable amount of homophobia. In 1951, Richard R. Foster, chair of the New Orleans Crime Commission (and the man for whom New Orleans's signature dessert, Bananas Foster, is named), told commission members that the city should develop a strategy for discouraging "perverts" from coming to New Orleans since most of the city's homosexuals were "out-of-towners."[9] About a month later, Foster addressed the Civic Council of New Orleans and described what the *New Orleans Times-Picayune* labeled the "homosexual problem" as one of the city's most serious. "In several instances, parents have come to police begging them to save their children," he asserted. "High school boys and girls enticed into places habituated by homosexuals often see an obscene show or something of that nature as a starter," he added. The homosexuals are, he said, "continuously recruiting" and there at least four "places" in the Quarter, which cater to almost no one but homosexuals. "It almost seems as if youngsters who develop homosexual tendencies in other Southern cities are put on a train and sent to New Orleans," he said.[10] Four years later, in 1955, police superintendent Provosty A. Dayrides publicly proclaimed that homosexuals were the city's "Number One vice problem," adding "They are the ones we want to get rid of most."[11]

All of these efforts created a sense of fear in the New Orleans gay community. Beginning in the 1950s, police capitalized on that fear to extort money from bar owners: in exchange for these payments, officers would look the other way and leave patrons alone. Those who failed to pay found their establishments raided. But for the most part, despite these efforts, gay bars in the French Quarter during the 1950s were left alone.

However, in 1958, the New Orleans City Council established the Committee on the Problem of Sex Deviates and named as its chair Jacob Morrison, cofounder of the Vieux Carré Property Owners and Associates and half-brother of the city's mayor, Chep Morrison. Morrison had been a thorn in the side of the gay community for years, often launching legal attacks on gay bars. In 1953, he had led a successful effort to revoke the liquor license of the Starlet Lounge, located at the corner of Chartres and St. Philip streets. The committee's initial report proposed creating a "climate of hostility" toward homosexuals, and Morrison turned his attention toward Tony Bacino's Bar, located at 738 Toulouse. A known "queershop," Tony Bacino's was managed by Roy Maggio, who apparently refused to make "protection" payments. In the summer of 1958, Maggio and other members of the bar's staff were arrested six times and were charged with violating a city ordinance that prohibited "immoral" people, including "sexual perverts," from working in bars and restaurants.[12]

But Maggio and his bartenders, Louis Robichaux and Amos McFarlane, who had previously worked at the Starlet Lounge, refused to fold under the harassment. They went to court and obtained a temporary restraining order against the police. The city attorney responded by arguing that they had obtained the restraining order under false pretenses and that they had committed "lewd acts": they had "kissed," "embraced," and "fondled" patrons of the bar; addressed male patrons as "Darling," "Sweetheart," and "Doll"; had proposed "unnatural sexual intercourse" to U.S. Navy sailors; and had encouraged patrons to "conduct themselves in a lewd and preverted [*sic*] manner." The three men eventually lost the case and abandoned the fight on appeal, and the bar closed within a few years.[13]

Well into the 1960s, the vice squad continued to raid bars and to send undercover officers (almost always young and good-looking) into the bars to make arrests. The *New Orleans Times-Picayune* published the names and photographs of people arrested for crimes against nature or committing a lewd act, frequently resulting in family alienation, the loss of a job, and/or the loss of a place to live. Arrests were often accompanied by a beating and pressure to name other "perverts."[14]

Interior of Lucille's and Friend Bar, St. Philip Street, mid-1980s. Courtesy of Lou Bernard.

1970s–1990s

In the 1970s and 1980s, Johnny Matassa's and the Golden Lantern were pillars of the New Orleans alternative community as well as of Southern Decadence. By the 1980s, the owners of Lucille's and Friend on St. Phillip Street, Lou "Lucille" Bernard and Nick Donovan, had become involved in promoting Decadence and by adding a coronation ceremony for the grand marshals, many of whom were or had been employed there. Lucille's and Friend closed in late 1987, and Bernard worked for a time at the Golden Lantern before buying the bar and renaming it Lucille's Golden Lantern. It continues to serve as the starting point for the Decadence parade and bar crawl, and Bernard played a pivotal role in ensuring the festival's survival through this period.[15]

Other bars also sponsored and promoted grand marshals, and Jamie Temple's selection as 1991 grand marshal brought the Phoenix fully into the Decadence orbit. In addition, the Phoenix Bar has served as the home bar for the

Staff of the Phoenix Bar, late 1980s: *left to right*, Jamie Temple (1991 grand marshal), George Marney Cossitt, Brett Tillman, Michael "Fish" Hickerson (1985 grand marshal), Wilhemina Bennet, Adolphus "Mumbo" Spires (1984 grand marshal), and Don Myers. Courtesy of Jamie Temple.

Knights d'Orléans, a gay motorcycle club; the Lords of Leather, a gay Carnival krewe; the Renegade Bears, a social group for gay bears; and the New Orleans Pups and Handlers. Since 2011, the Phoenix has been owned by Clint Taylor, and it maintains its strong connection with Southern Decadence. Its block parties now have become a permanent part of the tradition of Decadence.[16]

The Phoenix also has the distinction of being the last gay bar raided by police. Police harassment had more or less ceased after the 1970s. When Tom Wood took over Café Lafitte in Exile during the second half of the 1970s, he refused to continue the long-standing weekly practice of presenting an officer with an envelope stuffed with cash; police responded by harassing the bar and its patrons to such an extent that Wood successfully obtained a restraining order against the police to put an end to the harassment.[17] And in 1993, New Orleans finally repealed the ordinance under which the staff of Tony Bacino's had been charged thirty-five years earlier.

Nevertheless, on September 2, 1998, the opening night of Southern Decadence, undercover detectives at the bar on "Underwear Night" found about forty people "dressed in underwear or jock straps." Shortly after midnight, police, whom witnesses described as very rude and as making homophobic jokes, arrested the manager and charged him with "allowing explicit sexual acts on the premises of an alcohol beverage outlet. Thirteen other men, who ranged in age from 24 to 49, were arrested on charges of obscenity." The police department subsequently released a public statement describing the raid and listing the names and addresses of those arrested.[18]

A decade and a half of relatively peaceful coexistence between police and gay bars had preceded this raid, leading to the question of what prompted it. Media reports at the time claimed that a concerned citizen had filed a complaint with city officials and the police department, citing unsafe sexual activity at the bar, which was "extremely out of control on weekends after midnight."[19] According to Edward "Blanche" Norton, a fixture of the New Orleans gay community, the real reason was that Temple had decided that he would no longer make "backdoor payoffs to the police": "Money, booze, and who knows what else used to go right out the door—weekly, monthly." A former policeman backed up Norton's assessment: "All the gay bars, all the straight bars have some kind of payoff. That's just part of the game in the French Quarter. So much money is made down there, and I mean every night, that it has to be protected. Can't get that kind of protection without some kind of payment. And if you don't pay in full, you get a raid."[20] Wood's restraining order two decades earlier apparently did not change things as much as he might have hoped.

Across the street from the Phoenix, at 940 Elysian Fields, was Charlene's, which opened in 1977 and operated for the next twenty-two years. Owner Charlene Schneider was a pioneering lesbian bar owner in New Orleans who, according to Saundra Boudreaux, "cared about her girls" and saw them as family: "She always made us feel loved and safe." As Schneider once said, at the time, "women's bars were like boxing rings," but in the words of Toni Pizani, Schneider "worked toward giving women a better space."[21]

The 1970s also saw the return of drag to the French Quarter when lovers

The original Jewel's Tavern sailor dive bar on Decatur Street, later bought by David Jolly and Jack White and turned into a gay bar. Courtesy of Louisiana Research Collection, Howard-Tilton Memorial Library, Tulane University.

Travis Hickman and Clifford Rednour opened Travis's Bar on Rampart Street. Unlike Club My-O-My, which had featured realistic-looking female impersonators, Travis's Bar featured drag queens who dressed to shock rather than impress, exaggerating their makeup and costumes to appear larger than life, strong-willed, and forceful—escaping the constraints of the everyday. Travis's Bar hosted such drag luminaries as Rowena, Donnie Jay, Alotta Mulatta, Mr. Boobie, and Adrian St. Clair.

Numerous other bars catered specifically to a gay clientele during this era, among them Pete's (later, the Bistro and Oz), the Caverns (later, the Bourbon Pub and Parade Disco), Brady's, Miss Kitty's, Jewel's Tavern, the Safari House, the Up Stairs Lounge, and Wanda's. In addition, the Old Reliable, the Parrot, the Seven Seas, the Acropolis, Regent's Row, Gunga Din, the Abbey, and the Grecian Blue Room welcomed all comers regardless of sexual orientation.

The Twenty-First Century

Historically, gay bars have been centers of gay culture and expression. In the past, bars were virtually the only place where gay men and women could meet other gay people and relax and be themselves. Though the need for gay bars has generally declined across the United States as a consequence of the Internet as well as of the growing acceptance of homosexuality, gay (though not lesbian) bars remain an essential part of the fabric of New Orleans.[22] More than mere venues for serving spirits, these establishments host comedy and drag shows, cookouts, barbeques, and other events that serve the community by raising money for and awareness of AIDS and other important issues and charities.

In addition, gay bars have become an intrinsic part of Southern Decadence. The Phoenix, Golden Lantern, Oz, the Bourbon Pub and Parade Disco, and Café Lafitte in Exile continue to play a prominent role, along with such establishments as the Corner Pocket. In fact, Decadence's symbiotic relationship with bar culture has only strengthened over the years, and most of those now selected to serve as grand marshals are bartenders, representing their establishments, the owners and employees, and the patrons.

7

The AIDS Crisis and Community Building

The shift came after AIDS hit. We knew we couldn't just keep going with Decadence. We had to start fundraising to help our community. We never looked back.
—Southern Decadence Grand Marshal Jamie Temple, 1991

The AIDS crisis hit New Orleans hard in the early 1980s, and although the disease took a heavy toll, it also brought together the city's gay community, whose members rallied quickly and effectively to take care of their own by promoting information, education, and prevention. New Orleans differed from many other cities because its gay community was already organized when AIDS hit—both the gay Carnival krewes and Southern Decadence had already been in existence for more than a decade. The krewes quickly added increasing community awareness and raising money for research and treatment efforts to their social activities, as did Southern Decadence.[1]

NO/AIDS and Project Lazarus

As early as 1983, members of New Orleans's gay community founded the New Orleans/AIDS (NO/AIDS) Task Force in response to the devastation that the disease was causing. In October of that year, gay groups organized a march through the Quarter to raise awareness, honor the deceased, highlight discrimination and prejudice, and advocate additional funding for research and support for its victims.[2]

The following June, as researchers began to emphasize the importance of widespread education about AIDS and gay groups continued to press for additional informational and prevention efforts, Mayor Ernest Morial implemented a program to provide educational seminars to the gay community. Also in 1984, a young man known as Robert H. was released from the city's Charity Hospital after receiving treatment for symptoms of AIDS. At the time, no facility in Louisiana would provide long-term care for AIDS patients. Nursing homes and other facilities were permitted to deny admission based on an AIDS diagnosis, while Charity Hospital provided only short-term acute medical care.[3]

Robert H. was homeless and penniless and had nowhere to go, so a nurse called Tau House to see if they could help. Tau House had been founded by Father Bob Pawell in 1976 as a Franciscan outreach to people alienated from the Catholic Church. Located in a double-shotgun house in the 1000 block of Governor Nicholls Street, Tau House was extremely popular within the gay community, earning a reputation as a nonjudgmental place where persons of any faith could seek spiritual services. A few months before receiving that call, Father Bob had noticed a number of black wreaths on doors as he walked through the French Quarter and had learned that they marked homes where one or more of the inhabitants had died of a strange new disease known at the time as gay-related immune deficiency (GRID). Father Bob gave Robert H. a place to stay, and word soon spread that someone was willing to care for people afflicted with what had subsequently been named acquired immunodeficiency syndrome (AIDS). At the time, scientists and the medical profession knew relatively little about AIDS, and most people who contracted the disease found themselves shunned. Others soon approached Tau House for assistance, and

Father Bob and Father Paul Derosiers of Holy Trinity Church in the Faubourg Marigny in turn approached Archbishop Philip Hannan about providing shelter to homeless AIDS patients. The result was the 1985 creation of Lazarus House, a home for indigent AIDS patients located around the corner from Holy Trinity in a nineteenth-century Benedictine convent. Because of the potential for public hostility, however, the location of the house was kept secret, and Tau House served as the ministry's public face.[4]

Both Father Bob and Jonathan Clemmer, a nurse at Tulane Medical Center, subsequently joined the NO/AIDS Task Force, which began collaborating with Project Lazarus to offer AIDS-related services. A support team then came together, including Dr. Ted Wisniewsky; nurses Carol Pindaro, Jeanne Dumestre, Mike Callais, and Paul Holthaus; and Maurice Geisel, who kept books for the facility. By 1986, Paul Ploché was designated as a fund-raiser and Katie Quigley was hired to provide twenty-four-hour assistance to the residents. By the following year, the staff had grown to ten. Other supporters and volunteers in those early years included Jon Lee Poché, Arthur Roger, Robert Gordy, Madeleine Kohl, Al McMahon, Robbie Haywood, Donnie Ezel, and Ginger Snap. Those suffering from AIDS were no longer completely alone. After a decade during which Lazarus House essentially functioned as a hospice, medical researchers developed drug treatments that enabled those infected with HIV to fight the disease, meaning that an AIDS diagnosis was no longer a death sentence. Project Lazarus has subsequently become less a place to die than a transitional living facility, helping to heal and empower people living with HIV/AIDS by focusing on wellness, providing housing, and offering support services.

Applicants accepted for residency can stay as long as two years, although the average length of stay is about half that. Residents receive training in basic life skills such as cooking and budgeting as well as help in obtaining GEDs, substance-abuse counseling, and other support services as needed. Those who are able to work can receive help finding employment. In addition, patients receive medical care and information on living with HIV.

Project Lazarus now has a twenty-three-resident capacity and an annual budget of more than one million dollars, 60 percent of which comes from the U.S. Department of Housing and Urban Development. The remainder comes from private foundations, individual donors, and the Archdiocese of New Orleans, although it is not part of Catholic Charities. Since its founding, more than twelve hundred people have called Project Lazarus home.[5]

1990s—Belle Reve

In late 1992, as the AIDS epidemic was reaching its peak in New Orleans, David Mesler, Jan Vick, and Peter Drago chartered a nonprofit assisted-living facility—the first of its kind in Louisiana—to house people living with the disease. Using federal grants as well as their own money, they purchased a modest home in the Bywater and renovated it to house eight residents. Like the founders of Southern Decadence, Mesler, Vick, and Drago took the name for their facility from Blanche Dubois's plantation home in Tennessee Williams's *A Streetcar Named Desire.* Belle Reve opened its doors in March 1993.

In 1994, Belle Reve expanded into another property next-door, renovating it to house four families and naming it Belle Esprit. After Hurricane Katrina, the facility expanded again, renovating the warehouse behind Belle Esprit into Belle Grace, which has rooms for seven more residents.[6]

Community Building Continues

Southern Decadence continues to focus on fundraising for AIDS charities, but not exclusively. However, other monies have been donated to such community groups as the LGBT+ Archives Project of Louisiana, which has now become the preeminent group working to make sure the legacy of Southern Decadence and all LGBTQ+ related materials are preserved for the future.[7]

Several members of the gay community passed away from AIDS before they could be named grand marshals. Miss Love lamented that fact in a 2017 interview: "Yes, there were those who passed before their time and we will never get to experience their take on Decadence. Miss Rhie, Ms. Fly got to do it, but even Miss Rhie died before naming her successor!"[8]

8

The Juggernaut 1997–2015

All I can do now is bitch. That's what former grand marshals can do. We can bitch. Ain't nothing going to change, but we can still bitch.

—Southern Decadence Grand Marshal Miss Love (Greg Manogue), 1997

Southern Decadence experienced another seismic shift in 1997. Several days of events preceded the Sunday walking parade of Decadents around the French Quarter. The city government, which for years had viewed Decadence with a raised eyebrow, finally became involved. And the brand-new Internet advertised the event to a worldwide audience, making money an inextricable part of the festival, for both good and ill.

In 1996, Rip and Marsha Naquin-Delain, who published *Ambush Magazine*, registered fifty-seven websites, among them southerndecadence.com. They recognized the Internet's potential as a means of communication and "wanted to make sure we had all the pertinent websites for New Orleans so that the city couldn't come in, or the straight people, and take the website and do what they wanted with it instead of it remaining in the gay community." In its first year of existence, southerndecadence.com averaged three million hits a month. That same year, the Bourbon Pub created a website, southerndecadence.net, that also received substantial traffic. Not coincidentally, attendance at the 1996 festival mushroomed to over thirty-five thousand people. Southern Decadence now meant big business for the entire city of New Orleans.[1]

More traditional media also slowly began to cover Southern Decadence. Though New Orleans's mainstream newspapers at the time still devoted minimal attention to the festival, the local gay press was more forthcoming. However, this coverage included at best sketchy historical information, with a great deal of myth and conjecture, at least prior to the turn of the twenty-first century. Gerard Oncle, a habitué of the French Quarter scene, hearing a conversation that someone should copyright the term "Southern Decadence," did just that and secured a copyright for all print materials.

As the new millennium approached, Southern Decadence began to draw more than 100,000 attendees each year. While many people applauded this growth, others were more skeptical or downright hostile. Some former participants, particularly members of the founding group, merely lamented the loss of intimacy. Christian conservatives, however, saw the festival as celebrating immorality and began to stage protests during the event, tapping into a well of religious criticism of the city that dates back to soon after its founding: Sister Marie Hachard, one of the original Ursuline nuns who settled in New Orleans, wrote to her father. "In the end, the devil here has a great empire."[2] Over the ensuing 250 years, many other preachers and moralizers have condemned the city's tolerance of vice. Ultimately, of course, such Bible-thumping has done nothing to curb the city's penchant for letting the good times (gay, straight, or both) roll.

1997—Miss Love and the Parade Permit

According to Robert Laurent and Frederick Wright, during the 1970s New Orleans district attorney Harry Connick Sr. had followed the Southern Decadence Parade down Esplanade Avenue, wondering what was going on, a sentiment echoed by other city authorities. In 1990, police officers had approached parade participants asking who was in charge. And in 1997, parade organizers decided that it was time to seek an official city permit. Obtaining the permit would ensure police monitoring and protection of the marchers, but it also meant that the parade would have to follow a more-or-less fixed plan. The grand marshal would no longer be able to change the route on a whim or surprise participants with an unanticipated stop. Though many people believed that the city of New Orleans had required Southern Decadence to obtain a parade permit, such was not the case.

The member of the New Orleans City Council whose district included the French Quarter, Troy Carter, had personally witnessed public sex acts on Bourbon Street during a previous Decadence weekend. As the 1997 festival approached, Carter called Larry Bagneris, a social and political activist in the African American and gay communities, and suggested that he reach out to the gay community to work on preventing such incidents. Bagneris agreed and contacted that year's grand marshal, Greg Manogue[3] (Miss Love), and arranged a meeting with Carter to discuss the issues. Bagneris also suggested the idea of securing a permit for the parade. Both Bagneris and Miss Love accepted that some public nudity had always accompanied Southern Decadence, but the increased crowds and exposure also increased the consequences of such displays and the likelihood that things could get completely out of hand.

Greg "Miss Love" Manogue (1997 grand marshal), 1995. Courtesy of Robert Laurent.

Some of Miss Love's friends and others connected with Southern Decadence vehemently opposed any changes in general and the meeting with the councilman in particular. The opponents included former grand marshal Michael "Fish" Hickerson, who told Miss Love, "Don't do it. It should stay like it always has been." Opponents believed that city recognition, a parade permit, and the attendant fees and police scrutiny would strip Southern Decadence of the informality and spontaneity that had always characterized the event.

But Southern Decadence had already changed immensely, leaving behind its origins as a small, intimate jaunt through the French Quarter and becoming an uncontrollable mess. Nostalgia for a bygone time was useless on a practical level: some city involvement was inevitable, and Miss Love's pragmatic approach probably saved the festival. She and Ms. Fly, who was eager to spar with any city official because of the police raids of her bars, met with Carter and were pleased that he expressed no opposition on moral grounds. When he bluntly told the Southern Decadence representatives, "I don't want Joe Blow coming down from Iowa sticking his dick out and getting it sucked on the street. We have to get a little control over this," they were astonished.

Miss Love then applied for a parade permit, paying the twenty-five-dollar fee. But the permit did not arrive until three weeks after parade day. Nevertheless, the parade went on as planned: that morning, before it started, Miss Love handed the officer in charge of the police detail a check for two hundred dollars to cover their fees, and said, "Here you go. Hope it doesn't bounce." As *Ambush Magazine* reported, the parade itself was a huge success:

> The 25th Anniversary of Southern Decadence brought in over 50,000 revelers setting an all time record for the annual end of summer blowout. Hosted over Labor Day Weekend, the event had a $25 million impact on the New Orleans community. Bars, delis, restaurants, and retail outlets boasted record sales doing 14% all the way up to 50% over last year's holiday weekend. Many businesses did better than even Mardi Gras this year.
>
> Miss Love as Grand Marshal XXV led the festivities, "A Wedding to Remember." . . . The Parade saw thousands of costumed participants, many reflecting Love's chosen theme. There were brides, bridesmaids and grooms,

in every shape and size, as well as many participants doing their own thing.

Miss Love's parade route included the kick off at the Golden Lantern down Royal Street to St. Philip with a stop at the Mississippi River Bottom, a popular bar at the time, heading down to Decatur Street, then to Dumaine to Café Lafitte in Exile down to the Quarter Scene Restaurant, taking a left at Dauphine to St. Ann heading over to Rawhide 2010, doubling back to Good Friends Bar, to the Bourbon Pub and Parade Disco, Oz, then down Bourbon to *Ambush* Headquarters for the Official Grand Marshal's Bead Toss.

Some 5,000 revelers cheered as Miss Love came out on the world famous *Ambush* balcony, tossing over 2,000 silver beads, 1,000 commemorative cups and several dozen T-shirts. After cooling down a little, Love and entourage were off. Next up was the annual Grand Marshal's BBQ over at Andy Boudreaux's Mississippi River Bottom bar. The feast was packed as always. Then heading back to the Bourbon Pub's balcony, Love tossed his garter, then dashed down to Lafitte's balcony to toss his bouquet.[4]

1998—Robin Malta

Miss Love chose as her successor Robin Malta, a former queen of the Krewe of Petronius and at that time manager of Café Lafitte in Exile. Malta was both "flattered and flabbergasted" when his longtime friend bestowed the honor. Six years earlier, Malta had come up with the idea for the Red Party, and he and a group of friends from Café Lafitte that included Errol Rizzuto, Big Rick, and Ms. Fly put together the event, which became an annual fund-raiser for AIDS charities such as Belle Reve, Food for Friends, In This Together, and the W.E. Have a Heart Fund.[5]

Hordes of Southern Decadence revelers filled the Parade Discothèque for the Coronation Party, where Bud Light was announced as the festival's official beer. Malta chose as the theme "Deliriously Decadent Divas: A Salute to Sitcom Reruns" and declared that he would appear as Barbara Eden from *I Dream of Jeannie*.[6]

Poster showing Grand Marshal Errol Rizzuto as Cher on her Dark Lady Tour, 1999. Portrait and poster design by Larry Graham. Courtesy of Errol Rizzuto.

1999—Errol Rizzuto

The 1999 grand marshal, Errol Rizzuto, a much-loved figure in the gay community in New Orleans, arrived via super-stretch white limo to meet his court at the Rubyfruit Jungle prior to the annual Southern Decadence Parade, where they received the red-carpet treatment from the restaurant's staff. Rizzuto, all decked out as his version of Cher's "Half-Breed," readied his entourage for the grand parade, for which he had chosen the theme "Dark Lady Tour: Dissidents of Decadence." Precisely at 1:30 p.m., they departed down Royal Street to Lucille's Golden Lantern, where the Southern Decadence Parade would officially begin half an hour later.[7]

Thousands of people followed Rizzuto through the French Quarter, stopping at virtually every gay bar. Rizzuto led most of the parade from his limo's sunroof, the first time a grand marshal had ever ridden to any destination. At Footloose, Rizzuto sang a medley of Cher's hits, repeating the performance later in the day at Oz New Orleans.

The last stop was *Ambush* headquarters on Bourbon Street for the annual bead toss. Rizzuto and his entourage sent more than two thousand strands of black and silver beads and more than five hundred commemorative cups raining down on the revelers below. When the day finally ended after the annual Grand Marshal's BBQ at the Mississippi River Bottom, the parade had become the longest in Southern Decadence history.

2000—Tony Langlinais and Thom "Smurf" Murphy

Rizzuto chose two grand marshals for the next year, hearkening back to 1978, when Robert King and Kathleen Kavanaugh had served. Rizzuto had different reasons for choosing two grand marshals, however: he wanted to unite the two hemispheres of the French Quarter's gay world—the bars on as well as off of Bourbon Street. Tony Langlinais came from Café Lafitte in Exile while Thom "Smurf" Murphy came from the Corner Pocket.

The two men blew their official whistles to kick off the parade at 2:00 p.m. at Lucille's Golden Lantern. The crowd headed down Royal Street before turn-

Southern Decadence, 1999. Photograph by Michael Meads. Courtesy of Michael Meads.

Southern Decadence, 2000. Photograph by Michael Meads. Courtesy of Michael Meads.

ing onto St. Philip. After stops at Second Skin Leather and the Mississippi River Bottom, the parade made the long trek down Decatur to St. Louis Street, with a long stop at Lucky Cheng's. After a few more stops, Langlinais and Murphy hit the Corner Pocket, where they jumped onto the bar for a dance frenzy. After visiting various Rampart Street bars, the parade doubled back to St. Ann Street before finally heading toward its final destination, Café Lafitte in Exile. After that, it was on to *Ambush* headquarters for the bead toss, which featured some seven thousand strands of red beads, five thousand doubloons, and five hundred cups.

The 2000 festival had numerous sponsors, among them the 735 Nightclub and Bar, *Ambush Magazine*, AMBUSHonLine, Bourbon Pub/Parade, Oz New Orleans, Wood Enterprises, Café Lafitte in Exile, Clover Grill, Good Friends Bar, Poppy's Grill, and the Rawhide.[8]

2001—Bianca Del Rio, Pat "Estelle" Ritter, and Ricky Thomas

Langlinais and Murphy chose three grand marshals for 2001. Bianca Del Rio (Roy Haylock), the showgirl star of Oz and queen of the Mystic Krewe of Satyricon, who later became internationally known as the winner of *RuPaul's Drag Race*; Pat "Estelle" Ritter was bar baron of the Voodoo Lounge; and Big Rick Thomas owned the Ninth Circle at Congo Square. The Coronation Party at the 735 Nightclub and Bar revealed the official theme, "Ménage à Trois," as well as the official colors (purple, pink, and red) and the official song ("Lady Marmalade").[9]

2002—"Irish" Mike Sheehan

In 2002, New Orleans for the first time bestowed official recognition on Southern Decadence. Larry Bagneris, executive director of the city's Human Relations Commission, proclaimed August 28 through September 2 "Southern Decadence Festival Days in the City of New Orleans." On the Friday night of Decadence weekend, during a drag show hosted by Lucille's Golden Lantern, Bagneris presented Grand Marshal "Irish" Mike Sheehan with an official mayoral certificate; Mayor Ray Nagin also issued a letter welcoming the more than 100,000 people expected to attend.[10]

However, 2002 also marked another milestone for Southern Decadence: the first time it came under direct attack from the Religious Right as an expression of the "sin" of homosexuality. The crusade was led by Grant Storms, the minister of a small fundamentalist church in Marrero, Louisiana, on the west bank of the Mississippi. Storms claimed that the Lord had instructed him to protest Southern Decadence, so he went to the festival and videotaped people engaging in sex acts in the streets and in bars.[11] A handful of incidents of this type occurred every year, generally involving out-of-town visitors: in 2002, twelve people had been arrested on charges of engaging in lewd conduct. The New Orleans gay community by and large discouraged such displays, and posters and advertisements warned Decadence attendees that they would be arrested if they participated in public sex. Moreover, New Orleanians well knew that straight tourists on Bourbon Street during Mardi Gras flouted the laws regarding lewd conduct. But, by highlighting the few incidents that occurred during Southern Decadence, Storms hoped to incite a public outcry that would "utterly and totally" shut down the summer festival.

Storms himself had something of a checkered past. Twice divorced, he had been removed as pastor of the Uptown Assembly of God Church near Coliseum Square in 1994 after "a moral failing." He had also previously been arrested for protesting outside an abortion clinic in Wichita, Kansas, and for inciting a riot while preaching outside a New York bar. While preaching door-to-door in Westwego, Louisiana, he had offended patrons of a beauty salon, who then called the police. The city's police chief, Dwayne Munch, described Storms as "very stubborn, very rude, and very obnoxious."[12]

Storms showed his tapes to the police, New Orleans politicians, state legislators, and various media outlets, declaring, "There's no economic gain that justifies an orgy in the streets. That's all it is, a three-day orgy in the streets," and stressing that public sex was not merely inappropriate but illegal.[13] Storms met with Mayor Ray Nagin and demanded that he shut down Southern Decadence, but the mayor refused, well aware of the event's importance not only to the gay community but also to the city's economy.[14] Storms's campaign did, however, gain some traction with a few Republican members of the state legislature, most notably Daniel Martiny, who blamed New Orleans's "anything-goes mentality" for the crime that plagued the city.[15] Martiny introduced and the legislature passed a measure toughening the penalties for people convicted of having sex in public.[16] But New Orleans residents were much more concerned about violent crimes—murders, rapes, and offenses involving guns or other weapons—and about drugs than about "moral" crimes. In a letter to the editor published in the *New Orleans Times-Picayune,* Susan Mole Shelley flayed Martiny and Storms: "Crime in New Orleans is bred by poverty and drugs. These so-called religious groups should set up their video cameras, not in the middle of Bourbon Street, but in and around public housing projects at night if they want to see some real crime."[17] Others dismissed Storms as a self-righteous rabble-rouser or simply found him annoying.[18] Still others saw the attack on Southern Decadence as homophobia, citing politicians' and religious leaders' double standard regarding lewd behavior by straight visitors to the Quarter:

> I was absolutely furious when I opened the paper Sunday and saw the letter from Representative Daniel Martiny of Metairie. . . . Rep. Martiny's letter makes it clear that we deserve to live in fear of murderers, rapists and drug dealers 365 days a year because during one three-day weekend, a small number of tourists behave inappropriately.
>
> The weekend in question wasn't the past one, when legions of Texas football fans coerced beautiful young co-eds into baring their breasts for beads. For that matter, it wasn't any weekend when similar activities occur between Canal and St. Ann Streets. The three days each year that have the representative so adamantly convinced our streets should be ruled by criminals the rest of the year is Southern Decadence, held between St. Ann and Esplanade. This weekend was made available for politicians by a group of religious conservatives fanatically obsessed with proving to the rest of America how dangerous gay men and women truly are. These groups scoured crowds of tens of thousands to find small pockets of people behaving, well, decadently. When they couldn't find enough street activity, they went behind closed doors into a few of many gay bars, where only adults are admitted, to videotape the videotapes shown on televisions. Carefully edited out of these tapes are the tens of thousands of party-goers abiding by the law. I'm also fairly certain that no video was shot of the straight girls and boys up the street.
>
> Thanks, Rep. Martiny, for proving that with some video shot by well-placed religious fanatics in the middle of a crowd of tens of thousands, a short-sighted politician can stump for votes while holding an entire city hostage at the expense of an unpopular minority community.[19]

And Rip Naquin spoke up for the gay community as well when he said, "This is just all gay-bashing, and we're easy targets. He thinks we're going to run and hide. We're not. Southern Decadence will go on."[20]

2003—Rusty LaRoux, the First Transgender Grand Marshal

Tensions remained high in the run-up to the 2003 festival. The Louisiana legislature had already increased the penalties for lewd behavior, and in mid-August, Roman Catholic archbishop Alfred Hughes denounced Southern Decadence on the grounds that it "promotes and glorifies" gay and lesbian sex. He went on to declare that the "city's image is marred by the celebration" and that "the glamorizing of such behavior diminishes the moral fabric of our community and cheapens our reputation around the country."[21] The archdiocese asked the city to deny permits for the festival, but officials demurred because they refused to give credence to such exaggeration and for the simple fact that they needed the revenue it produced.

Emboldened by the archbishop's condemnation, Storms planned several protests against the festival, including a rally at City Hall and a march from Armstrong Park through the French Quarter to Jackson Square on Friday night and a gathering of "one thousand Christians" on Sunday afternoon to block the parade and ensure that "the French Quarter does not turn into Sodom and Gomorrah."[22]

The gay community fought back, not only working to increase awareness of the new law against public sex and nudity but also, as Rip Naquin recalled, organizing "forty volunteers who had flashlights and wore bright yellow T-shirts for the newly formed Southern Decadence Security Team," which provided information, directions, and general assistance to visitors. In addition, a group of Stormwatchers gathered on the balconies of French Quarter gay bars with bags of glitter, cans of Silly String, confetti, noisemakers, signs, and streamers, vowing to "drown out [protesters'] hate with our own cheers and laughter and music."[23]

On Friday night, Storms and a few hundred followers paraded from North

Rampart Street to St. Louis Cathedral. Though the police prepared for violence, none occurred. Storms and his crew yelled and preached, while the Decadents jeered and poured bucketfuls of confetti on the marchers.[24] Storms's effort to block the parade also failed: although his supporters gathered at various points in the French Quarter with placards that denounced homosexuality and sodomy, police largely kept the protesters away from the celebrants. When members of the two groups did come into contact, festival attendees limited their weapons to sharp tongues and flicks of the wrist, and violence was avoided.

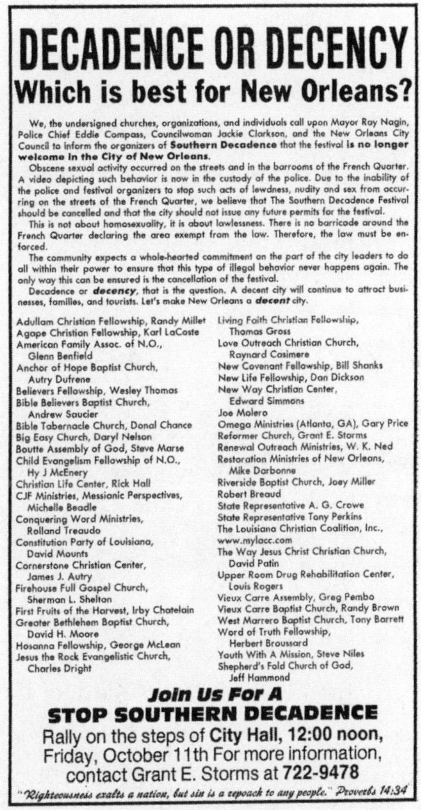

Advertisement for a rally to "Stop Southern Decadence," appearing in the *Times-Picayune*, Friday, October 11, 2003.

The controversy certainly did not harm Southern Decadence, which set a new record with more than 120,000 participants and added almost $100,000,000 to the New Orleans economy. In addition, the gay community capitalized on the protests as a fund-raising tool, as "leaders of three gay support organizations began an email campaign asking backers to pledge money based on the number of hours Storms and his followers protested." The effort raised an estimated $2,000 for the groups.[25]

Much of the credit for the festival's success went to Grand Marshal Rusty LaRoux, who made history as the first transgender person to lead the festival.[26] LaRoux and the gay community worked closely with the city of New Orleans and the New Orleans Police Department to ensure that visitors and locals alike had a safe and fun Southern Decadence.[27]

Writing in *Ambush Magazine*, Phyllis Denmark reflected, "The crowds in the street were something to see. I have not seen this many people at Decadence in years. I think all the drama in the news only served to bring more people to town."[28]

Storms did not stage any further protests against Southern Decadence and faded into obscurity, only to resurface nine years later when he was arrested at Metairie's Lafreniere Park and charged with public masturbation.[29] Convicted on obscenity charges in 2012, Storms was sentenced to three years' probation. His erstwhile targets had no sympathy for him. Bar owner Chuck Robinson told one reporter, "He's done everything through the years to end Southern Decadence and try to make it into something nasty, which it's not. . . . [I]t is ludicrous and heinous that he would have the nerve to complain about any kind of sexuality." Longtime French Quarter business mogul Earl Bernhardt found Storms "just repulsive" and was "not surprised at all that he got caught doing that. Serves him right."[30]

2004—Donald "Donnie Jay" James

The 2004 Southern Decadence Grand Marshal Donald "Donnie Jay" James was already infamous in the French Quarter, where he was also known for his work at Travis's Bar, a drag establishment on Rampart Street. He took seriously his role as grand marshal, and under his watch Southern Decadence not only prospered but increasingly focused on fund-raising for gay krewes and for charitable efforts in the gay community. The weeks leading up to Southern Decadence weekend included Rip and Marsha Naquin-Delain's Magnolia Cotillion, which did double duty as a party in honor of their thirtieth anniversary and as a fund-raiser for the NO/AIDS Walk, as well as "Celebrity Lube Wrestling" at Cowpokes' to benefit Belle Reve. On Saturday night during Southern Decadence itself, the grand marshal hosted a fund-raiser show at Body and Soul to benefit Buzzy's Boys and Girls.[31] Buzzy's is a fundraising organization named in honor of William J. "Buzzy" Fanning and works with HIV/AIDS charities.[32]

2005—Hurricane Katrina

Monday, August 29, 2005, will long be remembered as one of the darkest days in New Orleans history. Hurricane Katrina made landfall just east of the city in the early morning hours, and the storm surge from Lake Pontchartrain caused numerous breaches in the concrete seawalls that line the artificial canals connecting the lake and the Mississippi River. By the end of the day, 80 percent of the city was flooded. With the city in ruins, Southern Decadence, which had been scheduled to start on Wednesday, August 31, was canceled. Grand marshals Lisa Beaumann and Regina Adams would serve again the following year.

Despite the official cancellation, however, a Southern Decadence Parade took place on Sunday, September 4. Javier Sandoval, former owner of Starlight by the Park, and about thirty others "gathered at the Golden Lantern [and then] marched to Johnny White's. . . . Thank God for booze."[33]

Katrina offered religious right-wingers another opportunity to engage in gay-bashing, Perhaps most notoriously, the Reverend Rick Joyner told an audience in Fort Mill, South Carolina, "Katrina hit New Orleans the day before they were supposed to have that Day of Decadence; Katrina, that same storm, hit Key West on the same day they were going to have their gay pride parade. There is a message here: that is something the Lord is not going to put up with."[34]

2006–2009 Picking Up the Pieces

The Decadence celebration in 2006 was in essence a continuation of 2005. Hurricane Katrina had stalled the festival, and it would not only pick up where it had left off, but it gained even more momentum with a renewed purpose and a focus on the festival's survival. Regina Adams and Lisa Beaumann returned as grand marshals and led the charge by declaring "Southern Decadence's Rebirth" as the theme. Although the crowds did not even come close to the pre-hurricane numbers, the event was significant nonetheless as New Orleans continued on the road to recovery with its spirit of celebration intact. With grand marshals Electra City, Marcus Martinez, and Guadalupe in 2007, Decadence raged on and brought in over 100,000 participants.

In 2008, Hurricane Gustav cut short Southern Decadence. After the weekend got off to a promising start on Thursday, August 28, and Friday, August 29, the impending storm caused Mayor Ray Nagin to issue a voluntary call for evacuation at midday on Saturday. Though many hotels closed, leaving guests with nowhere to stay, the festival continued on Saturday night. However, a mandatory evacuation order the next day forced the cancellation of all the Sunday–Monday events.

Once again opponents to the festival came out of the woodwork. Religious homophobic rants continued against the festival as a moral outrage. Comments included "Gustav could do the world a favor if he times his visit just right and washes the filth away that Katrina missed on her visit."[35] However, Grand Marshal Paloma explained how Decadence was actually viewed by its participants. "Every year, it gets bigger and bigger and better and cleaner. It's a great way to get people's minds off the doldrums of summer. The Internet has had a lot to do with its success. It put us on the international map. Decadence used to be a just New Orleans thing, or maybe a Gulf South thing. Now, we get people from Europe, Asia and Australia, which blows my mind."[36] Instead of viewing hurricanes, which have always been a threat for the Gulf Coast, as divine punishment, Decadence has come to symbolize celebration and survival. Paloma summed up this philosophy: "It's for everybody. Lots of people bring their straight friends and relatives to watch the parade. After all, New Orleans is decadence. New Orleans is a decadent chocolate cake, so rich and tasty from the first bite."[37] The next year, Decadence came back strong when returning grand marshals Paloma and Tittie Toulouse led the parade down the streets of the French Quarter. No shrinking violet, Miss Paloma embraced her role as grand marshal with renewed excitement and commitment: "If you aren't the grand marshal in the parade, you are just eye-candy. When you are grand marshal, you have to make a big statement. I'm going to be glowing!"[38]

2009—Dykeadence

Since 2009, Southern Decadence has included Dykeadence,[39] a series of events targeted at lesbians. In 2010, according to Maggie Migliozzi, "Southern Decadence activities aimed at women attracted more than 1,500 people"; the following year, there were "multiple events for queer women every night of Southern Decadence," and NOLA Dykes on Bikes participated in the Sunday parade. Another 2011 addition was Fleurt, a party sponsored by GrrlSpot. Since 2006, GrrlSpot, founded by Christine Johnson, has hosted monthly pop-up queer and lesbian bars at various sites around New Orleans, and attendance has grown from 15 women at the first event to an average of more than 150. By 2016, Fleurt had officially become the biggest indoor party at Southern Decadence.[40] Their mission states that they "inform our community of high quality safe events specifically designed for them and to help the organizers to promote their events. We also aim to provide assistance for people coming from out of town to New Orleans who are seeking resources for women, transpeople, and people of color."

2012—The Scandal

The 2012 Southern Decadence festival suffered two severe blows. The first came from Hurricane Isaac, which made landfall on the night of Tuesday, August 28, just southwest of the mouth of the Mississippi River. Louisiana governor Bobby Jindal had declared a state of emergency on August 26, and the New Orleans airport was closed until Friday, August 31. As many as 100,000 visitors, who had planned to come for Southern Decadence, were unable to make the trip. Although the French Quarter never lost power during the storm, much of the city did, including the Faubourg Marigny and Bywater neighborhoods, where many Southern Decadence events were scheduled. Some venues remained open, powered by generators, and between 25,000 and 30,000 people, many of them locals, participated in the festival.[41]

The second blow to strike Southern Decadence that year came from a financial scandal. Since 2010, the festival had featured an official charity, and the 2012 grand marshals, T. J. Conard and Pat McArdle, chose Belle Reve, the AIDS hospice house inspired by the original home of Decadence. At some point in the summer, Conard made the highly unusual announcement that he was going to keep all the money from his fund-raisers until the end of Southern Decadence.

According to Rip Naquin, Conard "had a couple of alleged cons in his entourage, [and] we think most probably [they] ended up with three thousand dollars or so of Southern Decadence money."[42] And then Conard simply disappeared, leaving McArdle to serve as the sole grand marshal. Blake Miller and others donated money to Belle Reve to cover the shortfall, but Conard never returned to New Orleans to account for the missing money.[43]

Because the hurricane closed New Orleans city offices, McArdle was unable to secure either a parade permit or a police detail. For the first time since 1997, therefore, the Southern Decadence Parade was not restricted to a predetermined route, hearkening back to Decadence's origins as a bar crawl.[44]

This particular year was also not without its religious zealots descending into the French Quarter to confront attendees. Nine so-called preachers were arrested for yelling "anti-gay slurs over bullhorns." A city law specifically targets any aggressive solicitation between the hours of sunset and sunrise. One member of the group was arrested for battery for punching "an officer when he attempted to confiscate his bullhorn."[45]

2013–2014—Repairing the Damage

The disappearance of the Southern Decadence money severely damaged the event's credibility, and its future was called into question. The 2013 grand marshals, Tami Tarmac and Venus Santiago, recognized the problem and approached James Garner, owner of the Golden Lantern, and Rip and Marsha Naquin-Delain, publishers of *Ambush Magazine,* and requested that they, as representatives of the gay community, form a nonprofit organization to manage Southern Decadence's money and provide financial accountability.

Naquin initially refused: "People thought we were trying to take control of Southern Decadence . . . and we didn't want all of the grief that went with that." Ultimately, however, he, Marsha, and Garner agreed to create the nonprofit New Orleans Southern Decadence Inc. despite the strong objections of some members of the gay community. Naquin explained that all of the money raised by Southern Decadence was "turned into us, [and] we put [it] in the bank. Then at the end of Southern Decadence, we paid all the bills, and what was left over minus a thousand dollars to keep the account going was given to charity."[46]

In 2013, nearly one-third of the former sponsors and donors refused to contribute. Support subsequently rebounded, as the creation of the nonprofit restored credibility. Although the fiscal scandal finally prompted the creation of an entity that could provide Southern Decadence with financial and organizational oversight, some former grand marshals had long recognized the need for such a body. City officials, for example, had grown tired of dealing with new grand marshals every year and wanted organizational continuity to ease the process. Larry Bagneris, the de facto gay-community liaison at City Hall, had for years promoted this idea, and consequently he persuaded "Irish" Mike Sheehan to call a series of meetings to discuss the issue before the 2013 Decadence frenzy. Fifteen people attended the first meeting, which was held at the Country Club; the second and third meetings were held at the Healing Center on St. Claude Avenue and attracted even fewer people. Those in attendance for at least one of the meetings included Regina Adams, Tiffany Alexander, Julien Artressia, Larry Bagneris, Michael Hickerson, Toby Lefort, Rusty LaRoux, Robert Laurent, Miss Love, Pat McArdle, Errol Rizzuto, Miseal Rubio, Michael Sheehan, Tami Tarmac, and Frederick Wright.

Miss Love recalled, "It was old school versus new school. It turned into an ugly situation. We were trying to do what we could, what we felt was right as the old-timers, who have a love affair for it and knew what had to be done to save it. We felt that Decadence was on the brink of disappearing. Larry Bagneris was a big pusher of the reorganization. He tried to get us together again. Here we go, third time's a charm and we can't all get along. It was ugly, ugly, ugly at those meetings. A lot of things were said. Rusty LaRoux was there at one of them, but she wisely kept her mouth shut because she just wanted to see what was going to happen."[47] Regina Adams remembered that people in the past had volunteered to perform various tasks but ultimately failed to do so. This created double work for everyone. There was also discussion of assembling a guidebook for the new grand marshals that would include a to-do list for dealing with the city, a list of relevant names and phone numbers, current sponsors, and contact information. Unfortunately, not much was accomplished at these meetings, but a board of directors for the new nonprofit became a reality out of necessity.

2014—The Gayest Show on Earth

This year's Decadence was the testing ground for the new order, and grand marshals Chad Boutte, Reba Douglas, and Aubrey Synclaire chose as their theme "Under the Big Top: Welcome to the Gayest Show on Earth." Over 160,000 participants bombarded the city, and the reborn festival appeared to be back on the right track.

2015—Swimmin' with the Gods and Goddesses

With New Orleans Southern Decadence Inc. up and running, Southern Decadence 2015 could return to celebrating New Orleans's gay life. The event's five grand marshals—Steven Mora, Rip and Marsha Naquin-Delain, Misti Ates, and Frankie Fierce—chose "Swimmin' with the Gods and Goddesses" as the theme, selected three official charities (LGBT+ Archives Project of Louisiana, Louisiana Equality Foundation, and PFLAG New Orleans Scholarship Fund), and lined up eighty-two sponsors. The result was more than thirty thousand dollars for the three charities.[48]

An enormous amount of effort went into raising the money and producing the show. All of the grand marshals devoted the entire summer to Southern Decadence: as Frankie Fierce put it, "Once you are announced as Southern

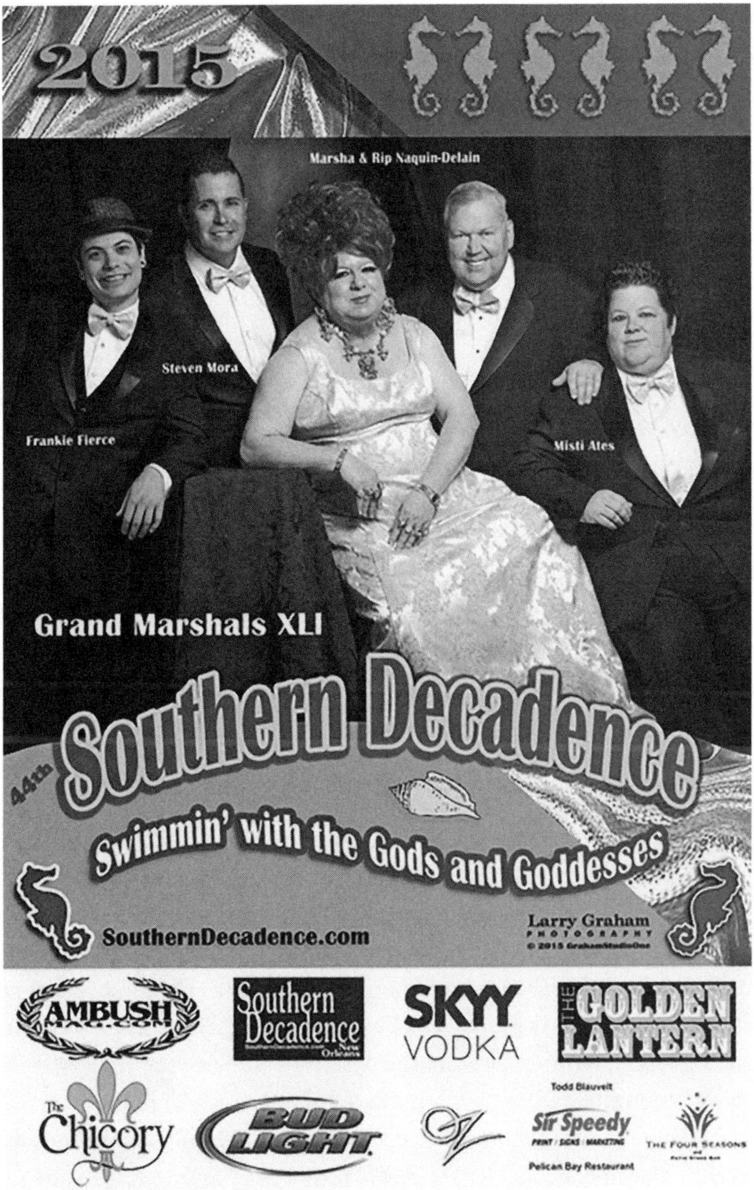

Official poster for Southern Decadence, 2015. Photography by Larry Graham. Courtesy of Rip and Marsha Naquin-Delain.

Decadence grand marshal, your whole life changes in twenty-four hours. You eat, sleep, and breathe Decadence till the day of the parade. I'm on my phone every day from when my eyes open to when they close. All I'm doing is answering emails, text messages, and phone calls regarding Decadence. All you do all summer is find ways to create different events from the year before to be as creative as possible to raise more money than the year before. . . . But in the end, it's worth it because everything you're doing is for a good cause and to help others." And as Mora noted, despite the hard work involved, "the title is quite coveted, as I found out along the way. As a matter of fact, the night I was announced as one of the grand marshals, I literally had people holding onto my arm—before I could even grasp the magnitude of my new role—asking if I could select them next year as a grand marshal. I also had people asking if they could be one of my lieutenants or even the parade captain. It was quite amusing, not to mention social media blowing up with friend requests." For Grand Marshal Misti Ates, the role came with "a lot of pressure to raise money. . . . There are a lot of critics, as with anyone who is in the public eye, but there are more of those who are supporters. Being grand marshal is not just about who can party the most anymore; it's about representing the LGBT community in a positive light."[49]

The Juggernaut Continues

Southern Decadence's transformation into a formalized, permit-holding, money-generating vehicle has involved gains as well as losses, and some of those involved remain nostalgic for what in many ways was a simpler time. However, simpler is not always better. Few if any members of the gay community look back fondly on the days when exposure as a homosexual could result in the loss of one's job or one's family or when AIDS was cutting a swath through one's loved ones. Despite the periodic efforts of the Religious Right, the gay community has unquestionably achieved a level of public acceptance that was almost unthinkable just a generation ago, and Southern Decadence needed to change to reflect all of these changes. The festival now has the support not only of the businesses of the French Quarter but of the city as a whole. And Southern Decadence now has two complementary purposes: celebrating gay life, music, and culture and helping to support the institutions that make that life, music, and culture possible.

Will Antill leading Grand Marshal Jeffrey Palmquist and entourage, Sunday, October 2, 2016. Copyright by Zachary Krevitt, 2016.

9

Decadence Takes the World, 2016

PART 2

It was very epic during the parade. Near the end it started pouring like no other! Thunder and lightning not too far off. Meanwhile Jeffrey [Palmquist] was in a metal helmet on a horse! It was all very amazing and so dramatic.

—Zachary Krevitt, artist and photographer

Southern Decadence, like traditional Carnival in New Orleans, exists only as a series of intangible and ephemeral exhilarations, lingering in the memory but otherwise difficult to document and almost impossible to convey. Words, photographs, and videos capture but a brief glimpse of isolated moments, perhaps a sense of the excitement, the abandon, and the camaraderie, but never the daily exultations. Nonetheless, a few gifted artists, among them Zachary Krevitt, have captured an essence of the festivities. Krevitt, who holds a bachelor's degree in photography from the School of Visual Arts in Brooklyn, New York, was embedded in the grand marshals' entourages during Southern Decadence 2016. His masterful and artistic images of the event stop time, portraying and preserving key moments so that some fragment of them will always remain.

Nicole Lynn Foxx at her best, Friday, September 30, 2016. Copyright by Zachary Krevitt, 2016.

Krevitt summed up his first exposure to Southern Decadence in the following manner: "My time in New Orleans during Southern decadence was punctuated with tradition, revelry, and men. Frank Perez greeted me when I arrived in the city and took me on one of his famous walking tours, where I learned about the history of LGBT folk in the fabric of New Orleans. My nights were filled with gorgeous men from around the world, every group quick to welcome me into their fold. They were uninhibited, operating in a familial environment that felt safe and free of all the predilections of the real word. Life outside of Southern Decadence's beer soaked and glitter-lined streets seemed to stop existing for these few magical days."

Working the audience, Friday, September 30, 2016. Copyright by Zachary Krevitt, 2016.

Aubrey Synclaire (2014 grand marshal) giving it up for a fabulous lip-sync, Friday, September 30, 2016. Copyright by Zachary Krevitt, 2016.

Reba Douglas (2014 grand marshal) giving face, Friday, September 30, 2016. Copyright by Zachary Krevitt, 2016.

Southern Decadence 2016 grand marshals Felicia Phillips, Jeffrey Palmquist, Derek Penton-Robicheaux, and Tony Leggio receiving mayoral proclamations honoring the event from Larry Bagneris (holding microphone), Friday, September 30, 2016. Copyright by Zachary Krevitt, 2016.

top: The "Three Graces" of the Golden Lantern, Friday, September 30, 2016. Copyright by Zachary Krevitt, 2016.

bottom: Big Easy Sisters of Perpetual Indulgence confronted by homophobic religious zealots, Saturday, October 1, 2016. Copyright by Zachary Krevitt, 2016.

top: Revelers on St. Ann and Dauphine streets, Saturday, October 1, 2016. Copyright by Zachary Krevitt, 2016.

bottom: Rainbow flags flying from balconies in front of the Bourbon Pub and Oz, Saturday, October 1, 2016. Copyright by Zachary Krevitt, 2016.

top: Atikus Sulpizi in costume, with Blaze Blanchard and Samuel Colby Danna in the background, Sunday, October 2, 2016. Copyright by Zachary Krevitt, 2016.

bottom: Quistador Coca Mesa, Sunday, October 2, 2016. Copyright by Zachary Krevitt, 2016.

Grand Marshal Felicia Phillips and Bunny Brasseaux, Sunday, October 2, 2016.

Grand marshals Jeffrey Palmquist, Derek Penton-Robicheaux, Tony Leggio, and Felicia Phillips, Sunday, October 2, 2016. Copyright by Zachary Krevitt, 2016.

Grand Marshal Jeffrey Palmquist on his steed, Sunday, October 2, 2016.
Copyright by Zachary Krevitt, 2016.

Grand Marshal Felicia Phillips, Sunday, October 2, 2016. Copyright by Zachary Krevitt, 2016.

Venus Santiago and Tami Tarmac lead the Pussyfooters, Sunday, October 2, 2016.
Copyright by Zachary Krevitt, 2016.

Fancy flagwork seen from Frank Perez's Royal Street balcony, Sunday, October 2, 2016.
Copyright by Zachary Krevitt, 2016.

top: Revelers enjoying the sudden downpour, Sunday, October 2, 2016. Copyright by Zachary Krevitt, 2016.

bottom: Revelers down below during the bead toss from the balcony of the Ambush Mansion, Sunday, October 2, 2016. Copyright by Zachary Krevitt, 2016.

Monica Sinclair-Kennedy at the Ambush Mansion, Sunday, October 2, 2016.
Copyright by Zachary Krevitt, 2016.

Decadent boys strike a pose. Copyright by Barrett DeLong-Church, 2017.

10

The Future of Southern Decadence

Did you ever happen to see a city resembling this one? Kublai asked Marco Polo. No, sire, Marco answered, I should never have imagined a city like this could exist.
—Italo Calvino, *Invisible Cities*

Among the seemingly endless barrage of visitors to New Orleans every year, there are many who will never see the real city, the one invisible from everyday view. This is not a hidden city per se, but another aspect of the physical city, a complement, a parallel doppelgänger that lies in wait like a sleeping beast. This mirror-image city, this unimagined city is only apparent after spending a significant period of time within its confines, breathing the humid atmospheres and contemplating the almost imperceptible signs that contain an almost unquantifiable quality, one that permeates all those who come to live there and slowly reveals itself as the very essence of celebration, exaltation, and even resurrection. It can be seen most prominently during Carnival and reconstitutes itself during Southern Decadence, for it is the intricate construction of the fabled pleasure-dome and its call is the celebration of life itself, lived to the fullest, and often reduced to the momentary and fleeting. Those who dwell within the grasp of New Orleans know this fact only too well, and revel in it.

For those involved in Southern Decadence, the morning after the festival's end usually brings complete exhaustion, along with vivid memories of long days filled with drag shows, parades, costumes, and carousing and drinking with old and new friends. Although not as elaborate or embellished as the Carnival celebrations, Decadence nevertheless has its own all-consuming set of rituals and still leaves participants feeling euphoric and utterly drained. As participants return to real life, the events of the celebration blur and take on an almost dream-like quality. Perhaps only the Eleusinian mysteries might recall some of its hidden allure and esoteric vestiges. Had that "gay celebration of life, gay culture, and the spirit of revelry of New Orleans itself" really happened?[1] Much like Gay Mardi Gras in Sydney and the techno-rave Love Parade in Berlin, Southern Decadence brings together innocence, gaiety, and an unassailable sense of community. These and other festivals and pride parades around the world include not only gays and lesbians but also a wide range of participants. The notion that these celebrations are only for gays and lesbians is as antiquated as the rigid either/or binary misconceptions about sexuality itself.

One of the strengths of Southern Decadence has always been that it offers individuals an opportunity to express themselves through costume and public display, creating a space that imagines something beyond the everyday. Carnival likewise fabricates a constructed fantasy world, but Southern Decadence focuses more on the individual's role in the street rather than on the group, or krewe, which is defined by its exclusivity and in which participants more or less remain anonymous pieces of the larger whole.

Southern Decadence is this stream of individuals expressing themselves as individuals. Michel Foucault defined these *techniques of the self* or *arts of existence* as "those reflective and voluntary practices by which men not only set themselves rules of conduct, but seek to transform themselves, to change themselves in their singular being, and to make of their life into an oeuvre that carries certain aesthetic values and meets certain stylistic criteria."[2] This raw and unadulterated self-expression also constituted a powerful force in how the original group of Decadents viewed themselves. They refused to allow society to categorize them but instead insisted that they could be whatever they wanted. Russell Simpson, for example, eschewed the traditional tropes of female impersonation, constructing instead a different type of personage unique only to him, one which was readily welcomed into the Decadence maëlstrom. David Red pranced about as the embodiment of Indira Gandhi. Robert Laurent chose to bedeck himself as a resurrected canary. Other participants as well ventured out into their own unexplored territory by recognizing no restrictions, and in the process created a cohesive whole that endures even today.

But society has changed a great deal since the early 1970s. In many ways, the pressures to conform to rigid racial, gender, sexual, and other conventions have relaxed. To cite just one obvious example: whereas the sight of a man with long hair was once an oddity, it is now common even among such pillars of mainstream culture as professional athletes.

In the same vein, gay bars once occupied a monumental role in the lives of the gay community, one of the few places where they could openly express themselves and find like-minded people. Today, however, young gays and lesbians see others like themselves everywhere: among fictional television, movie, and even cartoon characters as well as among political and business leaders, teachers, actors, musicians, soldiers, and athletes. Even many people who consider themselves politically conservative have come to accept homosexuality as simply just another facet of who one is, like having brown eyes or being left-handed. In this milieu, gay bars are no longer needed as a hidden refuge; rather, they have become just one more public space for Queer expression. Gay bars are often filled with straight people, and lesbian bars, once ubiquitous, are virtually extinct. New Orleans, formerly home to a thriving lesbian bar scene, no longer has any such establishments. The focus now is spontaneous parties and get-togethers. During the 2016 Decadence celebrations, GrrlSpot, "a monthly pop-up queer and lesbian bar in New Orleans,"[3] was named the "biggest party of Southern Decadence" with its Dykeadence Fleurt annual event.[4]

While the dissolution of the rigid boundary between gay and straight ultimately benefits everyone, it does complicate the issue of "Queer Space." Despite all the progress society has made in its attitudes toward the LGBTQ community, society remains predominantly heteronormative, privileging straightness over queerness. Moreover, homophobia as well as racism, sexism, religious intolerance, and other forms of bias have experienced a resurgence in American society in the wake of the 2016 elections. The need for Queer spaces thus persists and, for those who continue to speak of non-assimilation, such as gay author Edmund White, it remains essential.

Southern Decadence continues to represent the gay community's unbridled spirit as well as its social conscience. As the festival moves toward its fiftieth anniversary, perhaps organizers will expand the pool of those who serve as grand marshals from its traditional mainstays—bartenders, celebrity drag queens, and other Quarterites—to encompass prominent lesbians, more persons of color, and more members of the transgender community. Perhaps the festival will take on a more inclusive spirit, with efforts to bring in straight allies and families. Such an approach would be fully in keeping not only with Southern Decadence's current aesthetic but also with the spirit of the long-ago residents of Belle Rêve, the men and women who created a party to honor their love and respect for one another.

Southern Decadence in 2017 represented a neon spectrum of costumed participants, decked out in vibrant colors that filled the streets of the Old Quarter with ultra-vivid hot doses of Decadence. As reported in the local newspaper, three infamous drag queens were chosen as grand marshals and electrified their subjects with their outrageous costumes:

> Southern Decadence, the gigantic LGBT gathering sometimes called "Gay Mardi Gras," is underway in steamy New Orleans. The highlight of the annual event is the gorgeous, glittering Grand Marshals' Walking Parade that got started at 2 p.m. Sunday (Sept. 3) in the lower French Quarter. The 2017 parade was led by not one but three spectacularly costumed grand marshals: drag stars Persana Shoulders, Coca J Mesa, and Princess Stephaney. Each was surrounded by an entourage of attendants. Plus, there were hundreds of individual costumers, including scores of Marie Antoinettes, inspired by this year's theme "Let Them Eat Cake." Naturally, The Merry Antoinettes, a Mardi Gras marching group that customarily dresses up like the doomed

French queen with the big hair, were there, too. After twenty minutes, more or less, the glittering procession melted away into the distance on Royal Street on a route that would take it past "every gay bar in the French Quarter," as former Grand Marshal Jeffrey Palmquist put it.[5]

However, the Southern Decadence of 2017, although successful in its own right, would present some of the problems continuing to plague the annual event. Many still regret the growth and expansion of Decadence into such a huge juggernaut, having to discard the simple and often preferable small-scale bar crawl that so many former grand marshals recall with regret. The controversy of 2012 still manages to manifest itself and, even in light of the formation of the governing board with its nonprofit corporation to guide the festival, many questions still remain about its future. One such lingering question is the status of the nonprofit's 501(c)(3) tax status. There is no doubt that New Orleans Southern Decadence Inc. was created as a nonprofit entity in Louisiana in 2013. There is no doubt that thousands of dollars are raised and donated by Southern Decadence grand marshals each year to charities. However, donation forms for Decadence include the 501(c)(3) designation, and donors are now requesting receipts for their donations in order to include these documents for tax purposes.[6] The 501(c)(3) status remains a continuing controversy and must be addressed and solved.

James Garner, owner of the Golden Lantern and one of the members of the governing board, has recently shed light on this subject. For many years the tax status was secured and active. However, because of lingering health concerns with Rip Naquin, the 501(c)(3) designation lapsed. Garner is in the process of securing reinstatement.[7]

Rip Naquin passed away in 2017 as Southern Decadence approached. The entire story behind the transformation of Decadence into such a huge and successful, and controversial, gay celebration may never be known, but Naquin's role in saving, shaping, and transforming it into what it is today cannot be denied. However, it would seem that Southern Decadence must confront any and all questions pertaining to its legitimacy and then regroup its energies into perhaps a new phase of its history. With Rip Naquin's passing, the entire operating structure of Southern Decadence should be reviewed and presented to the community with solutions to any and all pertinent problems.

Strengthening the Decadence community's base has become one of the most important issues at this juncture. Religious zealots have revived Hurricane Katrina as a divine punishment for New Orleans on its anniversary. Southern Decadence remains a target of moral outrage and homophobia. Fanatic preachers once again have appeared in the French Quarter to disseminate their hate-filled rhetoric and vulgar slogans. And now with the reinvigoration of the extreme right, extreme hatred and violence continue to be part of their strategy. One preacher of this group was arrested for assaulting a woman celebrating Decadence.[8] This trend can only worsen as the entire country bristles with anti-homosexual bigotry.

Robert Laurent, upon hearing about the loss of former grand marshal Errol Rizzuto, also wondered about leadership in the future:

> I was stunned yesterday to read in the *Times-Picayune* that Errol Rizzuto had died. He was a past grand marshal and I had just seen him at the last Decadence Luncheon. I didn't know him well. I saw him mostly once a year, but no one enjoyed the whole event more. He was an artist/craftsman and did a lot behind the scenes. He made small wire sculptures of the past marshals some years back; I have one of Frederick. When Robin Malta was grand marshal the theme was the TV show *I Dream of Jeannie*. Errol made a small piece of art: a television set with Robin's face in the screen and everyone received one. It hung from a cord around your neck. I still have mine and wore it at the last luncheon in memory of Robin. Errol always had a smile and seemed to exude joy. He'll be missed. With Rip gone and now Errol, someone will have to step forward to be a behind-the-scenes mover and shaker. Things are just too chaotic in my opinion. Perhaps this book will help consolidate Southern Decadence for the future.

And what of the future of Southern Decadence? Dissension in the ranks of all those who care about the future of the festival serves only to weaken the

The diverse crowds lining the sidewalk around the Bourbon Pub on the corner of Bourbon and St. Ann streets during Decadence. In the foreground is the legendary chronicler of gay culture in the French Quarter, Roberts Batson. Copyright by Barrett DeLong-Church, 2017.

ties of Southern Decadence and allows hatred and bigotry to whittle away at one of the best celebrations of the city. Even the Pair-O-Dice Tumblers Band joined in the 2016 parade,[9] cementing the past with the present. The survival and growth of Southern Decadence now depends upon openness and transparency in order to survive the next vital phase of the festival. Perhaps it is time to take yet another leap, one that will solidify the festival as a legitimate and necessary celebration, like so many others, in this most visible of invisible cities, where the sacred and the profane are allowed their equal spaces for the individual and the community of Decadents.

Grand Marshal Persona Shoulders, 2017. Copyright by Barrett DeLong-Church, 2017.

Grand Marshal Cosa J Mesa, 2017. Copyright by Barrett DeLong-Church, 2017.

Grand Marshal Princess Stephaney, 2017. Copyright by Barrett DeLong-Church, 2017.

Entourage of Grand Marshal Princess Stephaney, featuring Beaux and Barrett DeLong-Church in the center, with members of the Krewe of Armeinius. Beaux was Queen Armeinius in 2017, and Barrett was captain in 2018. Copyright by Barrett DeLong-Church, 2017.

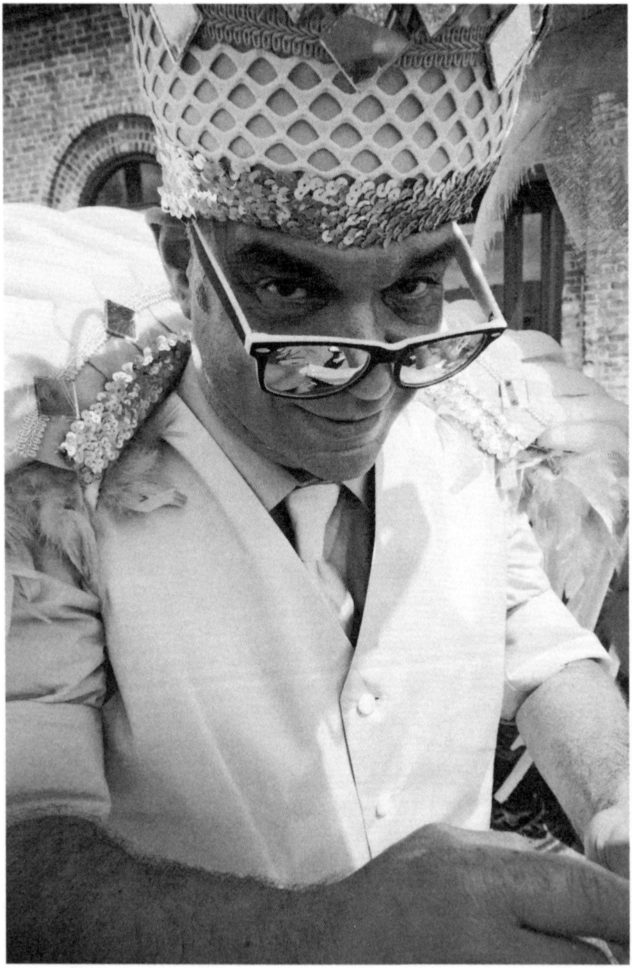

Frank Perez in the entourage of Grand Marshal Coca J Mesa.
Copyright by Barrett DeLong-Church, 2017.

Afterword

Most people think that I was dubbed Mother of Southern Decadence because of my ennui and lament about the sweltering August heat and the fact that we had nothing to do, to which my friends responded with a party the Sunday before Labor Day. In point of fact, I received the title while participating in a panel discussion about the start of Southern Decadence. When I jokingly mentioned my disappointment at never having been named grand marshal, I was given a different—and justly deserved, I think—title. I prefer being known as the Mother of Southern Decadence over being called the Susan Lucci of Grand Marshaldom.

Decadence began almost fifty years ago as a humble party with friends. In retrospect, we were ahead of our time in that we embraced gays, straights, blacks, and whites in a caring, accepting way—people were simply our friends. Despite our hedonistic tendencies, we were not "druggies" or "hippies," as we have sometimes been portrayed. In the early years, children and extended family participated—including my son, Andrew; my parents; and my brother, Tom Tippin, and his children.

I think it's wonderful that Southern Decadence has become a huge celebration for gays; however, for me, it is not a political statement for the community but more of a celebration of life and humanity. I do tend to criticize the commercialization of Southern Decadence over the past four decades, a phenomenon that started when someone decided to copyright the term "Southern

Decadence" in an effort to make money off the phenomenon that my friends and I started.

As it has evolved, Southern Decadence has lost much of the spontaneity and carefree atmosphere that we enjoyed in the past. The celebration has become entirely too official and staged. For example, we chose a single grand marshal each year to lead the parade (except for 1978, when we chose two because we feared—needlessly, it turned out—that their heavy drinking would prevent them from finishing). The person we selected was chosen from among our group of friends to embody the spirit of the occasion, and he or she could dress however s/he saw fit. There were never any official colors or songs.

Currently, however, there are usually at least four grand marshals each year (plus entourages), and it seems as though one is chosen to represent each of the different segments of the gay community: the leather crowd, transgenders, lesbians, and drag queens. I believe there should be only one honorary grand marshal each year.

In the nearly half-century since I helped give birth to Southern Decadence, I have given birth to a wonderful son, completed my doctorate, served as a member of the Tulane University faculty, and had a career in the mental health field. Nevertheless, I am known not for my professional accomplishments but for my contribution to gay culture.

I am proud to be the Mother of Southern Decadence, despite my criticisms of what it has become. It always embraced the spirit of camaraderie and humanity that is so sorely lacking in a still racist and sexist world.

Viva Southern Decadence!

Maureen Block
New Orleans

ACKNOWLEDGMENTS

The authors are eternally grateful to the founders and grand marshals, who have continued to represent and inspire the very notion of Southern Decadence. Heartfelt thanks must go to Robert Laurent, who shared all his photographs, films, invitations, and mementoes; Maureen and Charlie Block, whose encouragement and sense of humor kept this enormous project going; and Tom Tippin, Maureen's brother and one of our dearest grand marshals.

Special acknowledgment goes to the early chroniclers of Southern Decadence: Roberts Batson, Roy Letson, Jon Newlin, and Patrick Shannon for their early work with *Impact* magazine and Phyllis Denmark for her work at *Ambush Magazine*. In addition, Rip and Marsha Naquin-Delain have continued to cover the festival in all its many permutations in *Ambush*. They have played a pivotal role in the growth and survival of Southern Decadence and must be saluted for their commitment to and love of the festival.

In addition, Leon C. Miller, head of the Louisiana Research Collection, and Sean Benjamin, public services librarian, both at Tulane University, have helped in research by allowing access to their collections, especially for issues of *Impact* magazine. Tulane University's Special Collections Department has now become the repository for Southern Decadence materials, initiated by a donation from Robert Laurent of not only his early graphic materials but many newspaper clippings and articles, and all of his early Southern Decadence films. These have been digitized and restored by Dino Everett at the University of Southern California, with the help of Mike Jones at the USC Libraries, realized by way of a generous grant from the LGBT+ Archives Project of Louisiana. Tulane welcomes donations of Southern Decadence materials, such as posters, letters, photographs, and many other related items, for their Southern Decadence Archives.

The LGBT+ Archives Project of Louisiana has been a staunch supporter of all efforts in compiling this history from the beginning. Numerous grants have allowed the authors to travel and conduct research, fund digitization and restoration projects in parallel with the book, and have contributed to the mechanics of such a complex project by way of professional editing and securing publication permissions.

Many people have contributed to this history over the years and have supported the Decadent community of New Orleans. It is indeed an honor to thank two of the best: Lou "Lucille" Bernard and Edward "Blanche" Norton. Lucille has been a vigorous part of the Decadence community in New Orleans for decades, beginning in 1970 as one of the founders of the gay Krewe of Olympus. He and his partner, Nick Donovan, also created one of the most beloved bars of the French Quarter, Lucille's and Friend, which for many years supported the Decadence bar crawl. He refused the grand marshalship three times and preferred to work in the background to make sure it remained the best summer celebration. This continued when he bought the Golden Lantern and worked with the city to insure its success. Blanche was another great Decadent, whom everyone knew and loved at the Golden Lantern. She was a fixture there, and everyone fondly remembers her hurricane parties, where she spun vinyl records of the Talking Heads and Marianne Faithful in the wee hours of the morning. Her troupe of Demented Women fit right in with all the Decadents who came to worship at her altar. Serving as grand marshal in 1995, Blanche began another important tradition by assembling all the previous grand marshals for a pre-Decadence luncheon, honoring their decadent reigns.

Zachary Krevitt, a young and gifted artist, contributed his photographic expertise and love of Decadence to this project without hesitation. His commitment to documenting the festival resulted in the most complete record of the event thus far assembled. Others who have supported, contributed to, and otherwise helped this endeavor are: Michael Joseph Bonnet, Lynn Sipe, Jeffrey Palmquist, Opal Masters, Darwin Reed, Kathleen Kavanaugh, Bruce Harris, Julia Hemmings, Jim Lestelle, John Stevenson, Larry Graham, Michael Meads, Ellen Goldlust, and Rip and Marsha Naquin-Delain.

Finally, the Louisiana State University Press must be lauded for its commitment to this project, especially Rand Dotson, editor-in-chief, who immediately sensed the timeliness, and importance, of this work. Others whom we gratefully acknowledge are Neal Novak at the press and freelance editor Stan Ivester, along with designer extraordinaire Michelle Neustrom.

Appendixes

∽ PUTTING ON THE PARADE ∾

INTERVIEWS WITH SOUTHERN DECADENCE PARTICIPANTS

Edward "Blanche" Norton

Originally from Tuscaloosa, Alabama, Edward Norton and his best friend, Donnie Ezell, landed in New Orleans in 1977. Edward quickly gained employment at one of the most infamous bars in the French Quarter, the Golden Lantern, owned by Danny Wilson and Gary Clay. He bartended with Jack White and David Jolly for a year until they bought Jewel's Tavern on Decatur Street. He remained in New Orleans until the late 1990s and served as Southern Decadence grand marshal in 1995.

Howard Philips Smith: What does Southern Decadence mean to you?

Edward Norton: Decadence is total insanity and fun, guided by traditions, not rules. To my knowledge there are no set regulations as to the parade route. There are also no guidelines as to how the next grand marshal is chosen. It is completely up to the reigning marshal to pick the replacement. Believe me, I asked when it came time for me to pick the next grand marshal, and all I was told was that it was up to me. Of course, you want to choose someone who will carry on the traditions in the proper way, but it is up to the current grand marshal to pass on the whistle.

HPS: What about the parade route?

EN: There is no set-in-stone parade route. This may have changed in the last few years due to the crowds and the need for traffic control, but even in 1995, I went where I wanted. I tried starting my parade at the Golden Lantern and winding through the lower quarter to Rampart as a gesture to earlier years, when the parade started at Matassa's on St. Philip.

HPS: You worked at the Golden Lantern most of the time you lived in New Orleans. What was that like?

EN: I was part of the inner circle at the Lantern. As for Danny Wilson, the owner, I suppose he might have been a dealer, but I can't recall buying anything but black mollies from him. Now the things he turned me on to, that's another matter. Maybe it was just our group or maybe it was everyone, but in the late 1970s and early 1980s, drugs were everywhere. We did acid, MDA, smoked grass, hash, opium, and took Valium, Quaaludes, and those wonderful Tuinals, both green and red. Later on, coke arrived on the scene and then crystal meth. I'm sure I'm leaving something out, but back then when someone turned you on to something, you just said "up or down" and thanked them.

HPS: There are so many legends about Danny Wilson. What can you tell us about him?

EN: Danny liked to party, and he liked others to party. He always had plenty of "chemical enhancements" around. You just had to ask. As all friends do, we had our trials and tribulations, but I was working at the Lantern the day he died, so that says it all about our friendship. But probably his most notorious claim to fame was his being a shower queen extraordinaire. Honey, she was really into her water sports, if you know what I mean.

HPS: What are your memories of Mardi Gras?

EN: Oh, yes, Mardi Gras. It seemed to last longer in the '70s and '80s. There was oil money around so everyone could party, party, party. Seems like it went on for two full weeks in those days. There were more parades and more balls, both gay and straight.

HPS: What about the gay balls? Did you attend any during the time you lived here?

EN: The gay balls were by invitation only, strictly formal, no cross-dressing and no cameras. Being a bartender, I usually got table seats from friends and customers. Actually I enjoyed the balcony seats more. You could see the stage and the floor and you didn't have to make nice-nice all the time. Also you could be totally fucked-up! I was not what they called a "ball queen," but I enjoyed and appreciated how much time and money went into a carnival ball. We had a drag troupe at the Lantern called the Demented Women and we did numbers in many krewe functions and fund-raisers during the year to help raise money. The Carnival balls were serious business, but krewe functions were all fun. I'm not totally sure but I think the Bourbon Street Awards might have come about as a way for krewe members to show off their elaborate costumes to the general public. You might want to check with Miss Woolley (captain of the Mystic Krewe of Celestial Knights) on that.

HPS: What were some of your earliest recollections of Southern Decadence?

EN: My first memory of Southern Decadence was walking out of the gate at 1205 Royal Street by the Verti Mart and seeing a large group of people assembled outside the Golden Lantern in various forms of costume and drag. My roommate, Donnie Ezell [grand marshal, 1982], and I had just moved to New Orleans from Tuscaloosa, Alabama. I think this was in 1977, if memory serves me right. We had done some events and shows while in college, but had moved to New Orleans to be gay young men. We followed this group of people from the Golden Lantern to Johnny Matassa's, a bar up from Matassa's Grocery on St. Philip and Dauphine streets. The group assembled there was gay and straight, and most of the people had on some sort of outfit. Not elaborate like Mardi Gras, but more low-key, some drag, some leather, and what have you. Just the craziest shit imaginable. Being new we asked what was going on and we were told it was Southern Decadence, a Mardi Gras of sorts for locals. At 3:00 someone came out of the bar and blew a whistle and the crowd followed. The bars were all new to me, but they weren't on Bourbon Street. They were on Rampart and over on Decatur. For a walking parade, it moved slow.

Real slow. Not having a thing to wear, we walked behind, a friend of ours, Myron Cole, snapping pictures. By the end of the day, we all swore we would have costumes the next year. It looked to be too much fun!

HPS: What were the times like back then, before AIDS?

EN: Gay liberation was still a baby. While New Orleans was more open than most cities, you still had your unwritten rules. There were male gay bars and female gay bars. Very seldom did the genders mix, even in a social situation. So in the early years it was quite liberating to run the streets in costume and drag and get away with it. It was also well before the AIDS crisis. To me, the early years were the best. There were no events to worry about and it never concerned me who the grand marshal would be or how he/she was chosen. It would be 1981 before I even knew a grand marshal. It was just a great afternoon. After the first year, we always had a costume, and at least we thought they were cute. To be honest, there were always good chemicals in town. That scene was different back then also. They truly were recreational drugs. You didn't do them on a daily basis, and you were responsible when you did them. We never went up unless there was something to bring us down. This has nothing in particular to do with Decadence. New Orleans in general was like that 365 days a year and still is. The rule of thumb was to do what you wanted to do, just don't be late for work the next day. And we weren't! It was a great party afternoon.

HPS: What are your memories of the bar crawl on a typical Southern Decadence Sunday?

EN: You always followed the grand marshal, usually making your way down Decatur Street to the Greek bars and sometimes through the lobby of the Fairmont Hotel. The pace usually picked up by the time we made our way up Bourbon Street. It was picture-city with all the tourists. They loved it. The parade then made its way back to the lower Quarter. The queens would stop at the Golden Lantern and the straights would end up at the Dream Palace on Frenchmen Street.

HPS: What happened when Decadence moved to the Golden Lantern and became a mostly gay event?

EN: The story about the Kazoo Band wanting to go one way and the grand marshal another happened in 1980 with Tom Tippin. As to why the whole thing turned gay, I haven't a clue. Maybe we took over or maybe the straights involved just weren't that interested anymore. I don't remember there being anything done deliberately. I still think the reason it moved to the Golden Lantern when Matassa's Bar closed was that Danny Wilson was the grand marshal. Can't prove it, but that's what I think. After that it began growing into what it is today. I think the first thing added was a coronation for the newly chosen grand marshal and then all the bars wanted to get involved. I know if something doesn't grow, it dies. The old days still hold a lot of memories, but things are different now.

HPS: How did you form your performing drag troupe, the Demented Women?

EN: Now that's a great story. Some friends and I wanted to participate in the drag marathon at the Parade Disco one Christmas. It was just a nonstop show that featured almost everyone in town in the tackiest drag possible. It was just too much. But some of us just wanted to keep changing drag costumes and running out on stage to our favorite songs. I was thumbing through Vogue or something high-fashion like that and saw a photo spread entitled "The Demented Women" and I just knew that was it. High-fashion concept with low-drag presentation. Later we kept on performing at the Lantern and the rest is history, as they say. Danny performed sometimes. I was in drag most of the time. So was Donnie and Tommy, and Mumbo too. All these girls were part of the Dementia. Lord, those were the craziest shows. Good thing nobody taped them. Can you imagine?

HPS: You mentioned that your group of friends continued on partying even though the Decadence parade had ended. What was that like?

EN: Because you always costumed, there came a time in the late afternoon that you went home, showered away the make-up, and put on your sleazy clothes. I had an old pair of jeans that were worn only late Mardi Gras day and late Decadence afternoons. Because it was pre-AIDS, everyone headed back out to be a slut, usually ending up in the backroom at Jewel's. In 1982 my friend Donnie Ezell was grand marshal and he costumed as the Preacher Woman. Complete Southern Baptist Sunday School teacher outfit with the addition of his beard! Donnie was a theater major so he stayed in character all afternoon. So here we were all carrying on in the backroom of Jewel's and in came Donnie, still in costume and character, preaching to us about our evil ways. That was how Decadence was in the early years. Sorry I don't remember more, but as they say, I was too busy having fun to remember what I was doing.

HPS: You became fast friends with some of the original founders of Southern Decadence. How did you meet them and befriend so many?

EN: I was actually real good friends with Jerome Williams (Pickle) and Ed Seale. Over the years, I have gotten to be friends with Robert Laurent. Unfortunately Jerome is no longer with us. Heaven must really be a mess by now! I spoke at length with Frederick Wright, and he gave me a list of people who actually lived at Belle Rêve: Jerome Williams, Robert Laurent, Michael Evers, Ed Seale, David Red, Tom Tippin, Robert King, Kathleen Kavanaugh, Preston Hemmings and Bruce Harris. But not Maureen and Charlie Block. No Sir! Belle Rêve was located at 2110 Barracks. This would put it close to the Tremé area of town. In all my years I never once even drove past it. I vaguely remember seeing a picture in one of the bar rags once, but that's it. The Belle Rêve era was before my time. Even during the Johnny Matassa period, I was still new in town, an outsider looking in, if you will.

HPS: Tell me more about Frederick Douglas Wright. What was your relationship with him?

EN: Fred was as serious as he was frivolous, the life of the party one day and the next off to Yale or Harvard. He was very well educated, as were most of the original Decadents. When he was in town, especially for Decadence, we always got together and had drinks, and I mean lots of drinks. He could really drink. I had trouble keeping up and I consider myself a drinker, as everyone knows. We had this special thing: we'd call each other Orville and Wilbur, you know, like the Wright brothers. He had an incredible sense of history, place, and time. It was almost as if he lived in another century. He considered me special and somehow linked together with him. Isn't that funny? But there you are. I was Wilbur, of course.

Robert Laurent

Robert Laurent met Michael Evers and Frederick Wright while studying graphic design at the University of Southwestern Louisiana (now the University of Louisiana at Lafayette). Laurent graduated and moved to New Orleans in 1970 and became one of the founders of Southern Decadence. He designed the early invitations, using his strong visual sense to help create the celebration's look and feel.

Howard Philips Smith: You met some of the major players in the story of early Southern Decadence in Lafayette. Can you describe your time there at the university?

Robert Laurent: Michael Lloyd Evers and I met through mutual friends at the University of Southern Louisiana [USL] in Lafayette, now the University of Louisiana Lafayette. He was an English major. I'd started out as an English major before switching over to graphic design. We had a similar sense of humor. Michael read more widely than I and gladly introduced me to such great southern writers as Harper Lee and Flannery O'Connor. Michael then moved to New York for a year or so around 1967 or 1968. He went with a friend, and they lived in Queens. Back in Lafayette by 1969, he did a little more college and then went to LSU around 1970, thanks to his Aunt Yvonne. In December of 1971 he and Robert Gore and another friend arrived in New Orleans. Gore I think had graduated, but I doubt Michael ever finished. He never had a career as such. He just got by. When in Lafayette he made ends meet by living at home and running the Lafayette Duplicate Bridge Club. He lived with his aunt when her husband passed away. He also shared an apartment every now and then with friends. As you can tell, he drifted through life, but he was sure fun to be around. By growing up around his mother's bridge games, he emulated them by drinking and smoking at an early age. When I met him I thought he was so sophisticated. He tried to teach me to drink, but it never took that much. I'm just not much of a drinker.

HPS: How did you meet Frederick Wright, the first grand marshal?

RL: I didn't know Frederick Wright that well in Lafayette. I really got to know him after I moved to New Orleans. He was always the life of the party. I can't emphasize that enough. Marie and Steve Dawson, who lived in Uptown, flew him in from Chicago several times on holidays. He stayed with them until they moved to Oklahoma. Frederick then stayed with Maureen and Charlie Block when they lived in the Quarter. When the Blocks and I moved to Magazine Street in 1981, I inherited Dr. Wright on my floor during his visits. Those were the great days of having one long party while he was in town, since Charlie and Maureen were just downstairs. Lots of cards and sitting around laughing.

Frederick Wright was from Lafayette and attended USL. He moved to Chicago to finish college, went to Princeton for his doctorate, and then taught at Notre Dame. He was always passing through New Orleans on his way to or from Lafayette. Michael said Frederick was always the first to skip class before a holiday and the last to return. He was in New Orleans every summer. If he was present, a good time was not far away.

Frederick was not burdened with humility. Maureen's mother once said that he had an exaggerated sense of his worth, which was promptly repeated to him. He thought it a compliment. Friends would argue over who would pick him up at the airport, so they could be the first to enjoy his company. In his company you were assured of a good time. He told me while in college in the 1960s he was already in bed at his mother's when a teacher rapped on his window to hit the streets for a drink. As he dressed and left he heard his mother exclaim, Lord! Lord! The boy's gonna flunk out of school. He eventually received his doctorate in political science from Notre Dame. In the mid-1970s he once stood David Red up at Matassa's. When David expressed his complaint, Frederick simply replied that some of us are arrivers while some of us are waiters. Being the nephew of Chicago bar owners, he loved to hang out with a crowd he knew as familiar company. That was his standard MO. From about 1975 to 1980 Charlie and Maureen lived in the Quarter. While visiting New Orleans, he usually stayed with them. Later when he worked at Notre Dame he stayed with me on my third floor on Magazine Street. He'd go out around 10 p.m. on a work night and I'd go to bed. He'd come in at dawn and when I got in from work I'd hear tales of his escapades. Same thing when he returned from Lafayette while visiting family and friends, returning with boudin sausage, cracklings, stuffed pork chops, all sorts of good Cajun cooking. He was a gourmand. In his younger days he wore off the calories by being so active. In his later years he became very heavy and less active. When in New Orleans in the 1980s, he enjoyed the Wild Side bar, now the Double Play, and Miss Do and all the regulars. His parade movie is a wonderful example of his more youthful spirit.

HPS: When did you move to New Orleans?

RL: I started working in New Orleans in April 1970. Michael Evers and two friends moved to the city in December. They quickly found Matassa's Bar on St. Phillip Street in the Quarter. It was a small neighborhood watering hole that featured seventy-five-cent cocktails and twenty-five-cent shots of Tequila. It soon became our meeting and jumping-off place for further adventures. It was later absorbed into the family grocery store of the same name. Charlie spoke with Louis Matassa this past Decadence and suggested a plaque be affixed to the wall on St. Phillip where the entrance once was. I hope that happens. It's important to remember where it all began.

Michael and Robert Gore soon sublet half a house on Burgundy Street, a few blocks into the Marigny from Elysian Fields. I recall fondly a Halloween party there in 1971 that Frederick Wright flew in for from Chicago. And lots of hearty burgundy. But Michael soon met David Randolph and moved into David's house at 2110 Barracks Street in Tremé.

Michael Evers was my best friend in the late 1960s at USL. Michael was an excellent duplicate bridge player and had his grand-master status at a very early age. With cards in one hand, there was usually a cigarette or drink in the other. Later he introduced the New Orleans gang to the Cajun card game bourré and we began playing every Sunday night at Charlie and Maureen's. Those evenings of fun and laughter lasted ten years. Our tight group of friends had many holiday and birthday parties, most of them costume gatherings. We were in our twenties, carefree for the most part and hung out together in a spirit of revelry.

Michael did stay in Grand Rapids for a while, with David Randolph, but within a year he was back in New Orleans. I lived Uptown near Tulane for most of the 1970s. Michael never owned a car so he didn't visit that often. But I visited my family every month or so and would see him there. Michael died from a stroke in 1994.

HPS: How did the legendary Belle Rêve come about?

RL: Michael Evers moved in with his new lover, David Randolph, in his Tremé house on Barracks. No one else lived there before the first party. David's stepfather died suddenly, and so he had to immediately fly to Grand Rapids, Michigan, to help his mother with their family business. So David wasn't present when we had the party. I don't think we'd have had the soiree there if he had still been in town. Not that he wasn't friendly enough, but I don't think we'd have taken over his place with drinking and partying. David didn't drink or smoke. Two weeks after the first party we gave Michael the going-away party that I with my faulty memory for years remembered as the start of Decadence. With both Michael and David gone, the house needed tenants and rent. Maureen refused to live there. It was too decrepit, so Robert King moved in. At some point David Red, Judy Shapiro, Ed Seale joined him. Jerome Williams, too. With Michael gone to Grand Rapids, I didn't visit Belle Rêve that much.

David Randolph was a northerner who never adapted to the steam and heat of New Orleans. His home was not air-conditioned, and yet he had what he termed "summer blankets." His Saturday mornings started with the *Times-Picayune*'s classified listing of garage sales. He circled ones that looked worthwhile and then plotted them out geographically. He dearly loved objects. Thus his house was filled with items that if you squinted hard enough could possibly be perceived as "antiques." These shabby collectibles might be bent, dusty, tarnished, and in need of repair, but they possessed a worn luster that fit into the rooms. The last room in the place was the kitchen. The back entrance had no screen door and opened onto a yard of greenery that hid surrounding neighbors. The yard had a separate two-story building, an old slave quarter, just steps from the main house, with no electricity or water. It was later condemned by the city while Robert King was residing in it. Sitting at the kitchen table you looked out the door onto a scene, which seemed from another time and place, a century into the past. The view only substantiated the nickname "Belle Rêve."

HPS: One of the most fateful events was the graduation party in Chicago? Why was this so important?

RL: Frederick Wright gave a legendary college-graduation party in Chicago in the spring of 1972. His aunt and uncle ran the Corvette Lounge on the South Side of Chicago and hosted the soiree. I didn't attend. Michael phoned me that he was hitchhiking and wanted me to join him. I demurred. Charlie and Maureen drove from New York. Robert King and Robert Gore attended from New Orleans, met Charlie and Maureen, and were invited to visit them in Manhattan that summer. They accepted, visited Manhattan, and all returned together to New Orleans when the Blocks relocated.

After five years in New York, Charlie and Maureen returned south for her to begin work on her doctorate at Tulane. I met them through Michael Evers and Frederick Wright. At the University of Southwestern Louisiana, I had met Frederick but didn't know him that well. Maureen's brother Tom Tippin attended USL as well, but our paths never crossed. Fate can be strange that way.

Once back in the Crescent City, Maureen began to complain about the heat and everything. It became so irritatingly constant that we would attempt to silence her with, Oh come back to Belle Rêve! It never worked. So the complaints and replies would repeat themselves into the humid evenings as we laughed and partied.

When David left for Grand Rapids to assist his mother in the family baby-clothes business, the house had to be rented out. Michael suggested Charlie and Maureen move in. Maureen refused point-blank. It was just too decrepit. But the nickname "Belle Rêve" stuck. Within days of meeting we decided to have a party. Since none of us had a house, just small apartments, Michael hosted the party while David was away. We chose the day before Labor Day, a Sunday. In a city with Mardi Gras, there was never any doubt that it would be a costume party. I worked as a graphic designer and volunteered to create an invitation. It would make it "official" and more fun. For $4.95 I got fifty 8-1/2 by 11 sheets printed at a little shop near Canal Street. We passed them out, had a wonderful time, and unwittingly began a tradition.

With David Randolph establishing himself in Grand Rapids, Michael was invited to join him. So two weeks after the first Decadent party we gave a going-away party for Michael. With the Blocks declining to rent Belle Rêve, Robert King and others moved in. David Red lived there at some point, as well as these other early Decadents: Judy Shapiro, Ed Seale, Jerome Williams, Bruce Harris, and Preston Hemmings.

HPS: It has always amazed me that there was another party the second year. That really meant the die was cast. How did that come about?

RL: As another year rolled around and Decadence 1973 neared, during our Sunday nights of bourré games we began to discuss a second party. I offered the idea that we meet in costume at Matassa's and then parade back to the house where the party would commence. To my surprise, everyone happily agreed. I took my small Super-8mm movie camera and shot the whole thing on film. Frederick knew Clayton, a high-school friend's mother who ran Big Marshal's Shalimar Club in Tremé. That was a welcome pit stop in the summer heat. Then the crowd marched up the Esplanade median to Belle Rêve.

From the beginning Decadence had an air of provocation. Taking to the streets in costume on an end-of-summer day in 1973 was maybe not scandalous, but it wasn't a common thing to see. Some guys came to Belle Rêve in drag but passed on parading in public. Ed Seale strolled in as Ruthie the Duck Girl in glorious display.

HPS: Who were some of the other denizens of Belle Rêve?

RL: I met David Red through Michael Evers and Robert King. He lived at Belle Rêve and worked for SSI, the agency for doling out food stamps, along with Kathleen and a couple of others at the Sunday night games. David was never a card player, but I was always jealous when state workers would call in sick for the next day. I could never have the opportunity, since I worked for such a small-staffed office. David was in love with the idea of backpacking through India. He did that for a year in the early 1970s and returned to work and saved his money for another trek. He then spent five years in Kathmandu, working at the English Language Institute and living in a small house like the natives with no indoor plumbing or electricity. He'd trek up the mountains to pick his winter supply of marijuana. At that high altitude he could literally see the plucked herb shrivel and dry before his eyes. We corresponded with many letters. David was sophisticated and well read. I once sent him a postcard with a Bourbon Street stripper displayed on it. When the Nepalese postman handed it to David, the postman pleaded to him—I need this. David read my note and relinquished it to the elated worker. For a birthday I wanted to mail him a can of Dixie Beer, a favorite delicacy. I liked the idea of it being sent to the opposite side of the world. When I tried to mail the small package I was informed that I couldn't ship alcohol. So I returned the next day and declared it was a can of root beer. Without a way to chill it, David set it on a shelf as an art object. He returned in the late 1970s to get his doctorate in Austin in languages and now works for the State Department. In one of the parade films, David emulates Indira Gandhi, wearing a sari. In the first parade he dons a black plastic garbage bag and white-streaked face in response to the then recent headlines about Houston murder victims of a gay predator. In the heat David said he almost passed out. David lived at Belle Rêve and would speak about it often.

HPS: What about those two sisters who jetted back and forth from New York?

RL: Martha and Becky Theriot were sisters from the small South Louisiana town of Golden Meadow. We met them when Martha dated a sometime bourré player named Billy Wolfe. Both liked to play cards, so in the old days they were at Charlie and Maureen's a lot. The Theriot girls were the daughters of the largest self-made millionaire in the state. They began as simple country girls, and their father turned a tugboat company into a worldwide oil-service business. The firm had a company jet that sometimes flew Becky to Manhattan, where she lived for several years. Those times coincided with Frederick being at Princeton, and he got rides as well. Martha and Becky's dad made his millions with offshore tugboats servicing oil rigs. Starting here in south Louisiana his business eventually spread to the North Sea. So for years the jet was available at times to his daughter Becky to travel to New York and back while she resided there. This was in the '70s. Frederick sometimes piggybacked on it with her while he was at Princeton. Quite nice. I'm sure it was when there happened to be a reason for the jet to go to the East Coast; I don't think it was available just as a taxi service. But the time of the photos of the party in Baton Rouge, I guess there was no required business use for it; the dad must have let his girls have it for the weekend. It wasn't an often thing, believe me. The dad died of cancer at only forty-nine, and the company slowly faded. Frederick's reply the day Martha told him that the jet had been sold: "Well, Martha, it's been nice knowing you."

HPS: How did you cope with Hurricane Katrina in 2005?

RL: The Saturday before Hurricane Katrina was the grand marshals' luncheon. Lisa Beaumann had access to the Public Belt railcar that was used for private party functions. The head of the Public Belt at that time knew her from the Corner Pocket.

Friday night the forecast was for the hurricane to be east of Louisiana. We woke up Saturday to learn it had turned westerly. I was still staying and got provisions to hunker down. My car was very low on gas, and the lines at the stations were so lengthy I'd have never made it to the luncheon on time if I had filled up the tank. Besides, I thought, I'm staying so why worry.

We met in the Quarter near the Mint, a local bar and cabaret at the end of Decatur Street, to board. The ride could have gone to the top of the Huey P. Long Bridge before returning, but the trip was cut shorter. We still had a fun afternoon. The train ride was wonderful: a bartender, canapés, cushioned swivel seating. I don't remember if we partied back in the Quarter on returning. Maybe other participants can provide more details.

We woke up Sunday with even direr news about the hurricane. Maureen's niece phoned to say that her father-in-law who worked for the local CBS affiliate had told her that this was the Big One and to vacate. I still was not convinced until I heard about possible gusts of 250 miles per hour. Since my car had little gas I packed up my parrot and jumped in the Blocks' car. We drove to Iota, about a half-hour's drive west of Lafayette. Frederick had offered Mumbo a ride. We convened at Bob Mercer's, a longtime friend. He was at an early party and is visible in a parade film, Frederick's I think. Bob has a nice house and lives out in the country. He had a TV, but cable was not available in his rural isolation. We partied without a care, thinking as usual we'd be home in a few days. While many people were suffering from the storm, our only difficulty was locating some Amaretto for cocktails. Mumbo picked some fresh okra from Bob's garden, sliced it, marinated and coated it with seasoning, and prepared the best fried okra I've ever had. We could get limited news but knew the reported flooding a day or so later changed everything. Frederick talked by phone to a couple of bar owners he knew, who had stayed in the city. They said that by Wednesday it began to be scary with gunshots heard around the Quarter. Even they planned to evacuate.

Charlie drove Maureen to Houston to take a flight to New York to begin her treatment for a breast lump that had just been diagnosed. Charlie joined her a week or so later. The Blocks were gone two years. The next weekend Frederick and I were in Lafayette at our respective families. We took Mumbo to the local airport to travel to San Francisco to stay with friends. He's never returned, and I understand from Miss Love his health is poor. One of the local gay bars there held some sort of Decadent soiree on the Sunday before Labor Day, and Frederick of course was feted as the first grand marshal. It wasn't much of a party, just some Sunday afternoon drinks. It was over a month before I could return to New Orleans.

HPS: How has being involved with Southern Decadence changed your life?

RL: Well, nothing so momentous really. If anything, the Blocks and I, Kathleen and Robert King, we were always amused how our little acorn grew to such large proportions. I'm happy to be an asterisk in the scheme of things.

Lou Bernard Jr.

A key mover and shaker within New Orleans's gay community, Lou "Lucille" Bernard not only founded one of the most creative and extravagant gay Carnival krewes, the Krewe of Olympus, but also owned one of the French Quarter's most beloved neighborhood bars, Lucille's and Friend. He also owned the Golden Lantern some time later and renamed it Lucille's Golden Lantern. A native of the Crescent City, Bernard played a pivotal role in ensuring the continuation of Southern Decadence during the years of the AIDS crisis.

Howard Philips Smith: Where did you grow up?

Lou Bernard Jr.: I was born on Canal Street and grew up in Uptown, where we celebrated Carnival every year. If you're from New Orleans, you just take it all for granted. But nothing compares to Carnival for the sheer force of it, year after year. It's in our blood, like river water.

HPS: What were your earliest memories of Southern Decadence?

LB: That had to be in 1984 when Mumbo was grand marshal. Danny Wilson chose him, as was the custom. Even Danny had been chosen the day before Decadence Sunday. That's the way they did it before press parties and announcement parties. Mumbo had moved to the city from San Francisco and came by to ask for a job. I owned Lucille's and Friend at the time. The only thing I had was a cleaning job. But soon he was a bartender, and a good one too. Mumbo was the first black bartender in the Quarter gay bars. Some of my clients told me to get rid of him in very rude terms or they would stop coming to the bar, but I countered with, "Don't let the door hit you in the ass!" Danny chose Mumbo to succeed him as grand marshal a few weeks before Decadence Sunday. He told me he wanted a "cordination" party, and that's just what I gave him. I presented him with his official whistle at the bar, and he was just beside himself with excitement.

HPS: You mentioned that on the Friday before Decadence Sunday there were some drag contests at the Golden Lantern. What was that all about?

LB: On Friday, the Lantern always held a drag contest, as was the tradition. Everyone who was a grand marshal or who wanted to be a grand marshal performed like crazy. It was a mad free-for-all. At least that was the excuse. I don't think anyone was really ever designated as grand marshal from their performance, maybe all except Miss Love.

HPS: During the 1980s, how early did people meet at the Golden Lantern to start Decadence?

LB: The official time was still 3:00 in the afternoon, but some people came early. There were a lot of people still up from the night before. The party just doesn't stop during Decadence. Now the parade starts at 2:00 p.m., so everyone had to prepare for that.

HPS: How did they do that?

LB: Other bars wanted to get involved. The Friendly Bar in the Marigny started hosting a Decadence Breakfast. I guess that was in the late 1980s. This became a big make-up party where everyone could take their time and get ready for the parade. Then everyone would make their way to the Lantern, which was on Royal Street too.

HPS: What was it like at Lucille's during the barrage of drag queens?

LB: The parade stops were the whim of the grand marshal, but they always hit all the gay bars in addition to all the other bars. There were literally hundreds and hundreds of queens screaming for a cocktail when the grand marshal stopped the parade at my bar. I had set up two register stations, one on either side of the bar. I had two bartenders man each register for a total of four bartenders. During the hour or so when the parade was at the bar, they worked their asses off. It was one of my most profitable days of the year, I have to say. Crazy, but worth it. Usually the parade stops followed along the "fruit loop" down from Jewel's, then the Mississippi River Bottom and then up St. Philip to Lucille's.

HPS: Who was the "Friend" in your bar name?

LB: Well, that was Nick Donovan. We both founded the Krewe of Olympus together and we ran the bar together. He was the silent partner, running all the bar events and making sure everything was stocked and the books were right. I ran the day-to-day. We had a big house Uptown with a swimming pool. We had a good life. Nick was the first king of Olympus for the infamous Camelot ball. That was something. One of the highlights of my gay life.

HPS: Tell me more about the bar and bartenders.

LB: George was a bartender at my bar. He named his lover Robbie Haywood or Ruby, as we called him, as the next marshal. Lucille's closed in 1987, so he was grand marshal in 1989. I threw him a party at the Mint, down on Decatur across from the Old Confederate Mint. I managed the place at that time. We had a real shindig. I've seen a lot in my life, but nothing compared to the destruction of Hurricane Katrina.

HPS: What was that like for you? Did you stay in town?

LB: Yes, my partner Jay and I stayed in town. When we woke up on Monday, the house was fine. We had a smallish house above St. Claude, very comfortable. But the next day, when we went to the front door, the water was almost to the top step. The house was raised pretty high on blocks, as many of the old houses are, so we were ok. But then the crime started. Luckily we had a neighbor who had a shotgun and who stood watch over at St. Claude and so we were safe. All around us houses were broken into. It was really frightening. After eight days, the National Guard forced us to leave. We really had to go. The situation was very bad, no electricity, no food. But we had two cats. So we packed them up and they took us to the Convention Center. We had to wait all day with a lot of other refugees and then a helicopter took us to the airport. We had no idea where we were headed, but just seeing the city below us, completely flooded, was heart-wrenching. At the airport we waited for almost twenty-four hours, and then we were off to Raleigh, North Carolina. We stayed there in a refugee center for a week; then, when we were given some money, we rented a car and drove to Houston. We had old friends there and stayed for three months. We had a line to someone at the power company in New Orleans and they would tell us that the electricity was still out. One day we called and it was finally turned on in our neighborhood, so we left. I still have the car we bought in Houston. The rising water destroyed my sports car. I was heart-broken, but many people lost so much more.

HPS: What are your recollections of Mumbo, one of the most decadent grand marshals?

LB: Mumbo's real name is Adolphus Spires, and I think he was from one of the southern states, close to Louisiana. I always walked to the Lantern for the beginning of the parade, but since I was a working bar owner, it was a very busy day for me. No time for fun. The parade was interesting way back then. There was no published route, but the grand marshal brought the parade by all the bars that supported the festival. Yes, I have been active in the gay community in some form for many years—both the Mardi Gras ball organizations and various gay bars that I owned in the French Quarter. I was asked by Larry Graham to pose for an "Icon" photo, but I declined. I felt that an icon should be in his late seventies. I really enjoyed all the roles I played in the gay culture of New Orleans. When I first came on the gay scene, the Vice Squad was still raiding the gay bars. What a horror story. I never got arrested in my whole career—just lucky I guess. Just recently, Mumbo had a severe stroke and is residing in a nursing home outside of San Francisco—very sad.

George Goode was from somewhere in Texas. His family had money, so George was quite spoiled. George was my main bartender for many years. He wore a ladies' one-piece swimsuit or something like that. George died quite some time ago from complications of the AIDS virus. His partner, Robbie, who was also a grand marshal, died not long after him.

Blanche was also an employee of Lucille's and Friend, but not when he was grand marshal. He and I were close friends until his sudden death not long ago. I try to stay in touch with his sister, but she is still grieving.

Jerry Menefee and I were good friends. When I bought my first bar (Lucille's and Friend), I called Jerry for help. He got me connected with his bar manager and made his forms available to me. That helped a lot. I remember several parties at his Uptown home too. Yes, I do remember that great mural in the Parade Disco. Earl Woodard worked on that for some time. Did you ask Earl if he perhaps has any pictures of the mural? I hate to think that it is all lost to history.

I got very involved with Decadence the year that Mumbo was grand marshal. By then, the person knew in advance and could make plans. Mumbo was working for me at the time and he asked if we could do a "cordination party" at Lucille's. That's what he called it. We had a big party at the bar and, for the first time, I presented him a whistle for the parade. That idea caught on, and I presented the grand marshal with a new whistle every year. I also got very involved when George Goode was grand marshal. He also was an employee. Lucille's was very well represented in Decadence. I have been asked to be the grand marshal three times, but I said no every time. I didn't want to be the star; I wanted to be the producer. The real fun has changed with everything announced several months in advance. It has all become very commercial. I still remember the police department talking to me about the parade before the city made the whole event official. I also remember when I backed down that crazy minister who claimed he would prevent the beginning of the parade. I along with two large policemen met him on Royal Street and dared him to interfere. He backed down. Thank goodness! He seemed to not realize the economic impact of Decadence on the city of New Orleans. He got so pissed that he picked a fight with a doorman on Sunday night and got himself arrested. I was interviewed by the local news that year.

I operated Lucille's and Friend from 1979 to 1987. I was working at the Golden Lantern when both partners died. I assumed management until the family could be contacted. They sold the bar to me for a song for all my help. It's a long story. The coronation parties for the grand marshals were at Lucille's and Friend, not the Golden Lantern. I continued the Official Southern Decadence Drag Show at the Lantern. The drag shows were every second Saturday night; they were called the "Golden Age Revue," and Marcy Marcell was my show director. I did the shows approximately four years—2002 to 2005. I bought the Golden Lantern in 1998, not long after I returned from Germany. Someday I will share the long story about me buying the bar.

HPS: I've got plenty of time. Let's hear it.

LB: My landlord wanted to triple my lease in 1987. I just wouldn't do it, so Lucille's was no more. Unfortunately, I borrowed money from the jukebox and penny-arcade fellows to renovate the old site of Buster Holmes. It was a bar but also a restaurant, which didn't work out as I had planned. Two friends from Uptown, who had previously had Flamingos Café came on board, so we called our venture Lucille's Weenie Women Café because they served all kinds of hot dogs, if you can believe it. After about a year I realized there was no salvaging this place. People had grown afraid of Rampart Street, and we were not on the main circuit. That was in 1989 that I had to close it up.

HPS: How did you get involved with the Golden Lantern?

LB: In 1992 I had just returned from a trip to Cancun, when Blanche called me to see if I would be interested in working at the Golden Lantern. I miraculously became the managing partner along with the owner, Randy Russell, who had inherited the bar when Danny Wilson died. As far as I could tell, Russell siphoned all the profits into his own pocket. He liked to party, and the bar was on the verge of collapse. Russell sold the business to Terry Powers for a song in 1995. I came back on board but only as bartender. In 1998 Powers sold the bar to Curtis and Michael, who both passed away within a week of each other. Jay Verona, my partner, and I bought the bar outright, and it became Lucille's Golden Lantern. In 2004 the building was sold to Jules Cahn, who was a real-estate developer. I stayed on till 2005. While we owned the Lantern, I continued the Official Southern Decadence Drag Show on Friday nights before Labor Day. Past grand marshals and grand-marshal wannabes presented their best, and raunchiest, drag so they would get noticed. Sometimes it worked, but I enjoyed the former grand marshals just letting loose with the craziest drag. I miss all that. In addition, during the year we had drag shows every second Saturday night. They were called the "Golden Age Revue," and Marcy Marcell was my show director. I did the shows approximately three years—2002 to 2005. Now early on, in the 1990s, I saw an advertisement in the rags that some other bar had become the "Official Home of Southern Decadence." I don't blame them for trying to get some of the pie, but I went right out and trademarked the phrase. As you can see, I've been very active in Southern Decadence.

Errol Rizzuto

Born and raised in New Orleans, Errol Rizzuto served as grand marshal of Southern Decadence in 1999 and was involved with gay Carnival for many years, including as a member of several gay krewes.

Howard Philips Smith: Tell us about your family. How did Sicilians end up in New Orleans?

Errol Rizzuto: The parents of my great-grandfathers met when they immigrated to the United States in 1910, pledging to one another that they would work together and bring both families to America. They also sealed the promise with a marriage between their families. Here in New Orleans they had a small farm located near the French Quarter, and they sold produce at the French Market, brought up St. Claude Avenue in a horse-drawn wagon. They made enough money to purchase a home in the Marigny, where I grew up.

Frank Perez: What was your childhood like? Where did you attend school?

ER: I grew up in the French Quarter, attending Holy Trinity Catholic School and McDonogh No. 15 on St. Philip Street. I attended mass at St. Louis Cathedral, and I would ride my bicycle up and down Bourbon Street. Frederick Wright, the first grand marshal of Southern Decadence, teased me that I was the only grand marshal who actually played as a child in the French Quarter. I used to say that I went from hot wheels to high heels right here on Bourbon Street.

HPS: You were very much involved with the gay community here in the city. Tell us about your role over the years and how you became active.

ER: I became involved with Gay Pride in 1980. I was elected president in 1984, but we never did have the crowds that other cities have for Gay Pride. Carnival was our Gay Pride, if you ask me. It was the real focus of the gay community. In the years we didn't have an actual Gay Pride Festival, we held an event we called Pride in the Park at Washington Square. Charlene Schneider, owner of Charlene's lesbian bar and member of the gay Krewe of Ishtar, and I performed as the Tangerine Queens. Here I became friends with a slew of former grand marshals, Jamie Temple, Miss Fish, Rhie, and Mumbo, to name only a few. I had also worked on Gayfest, which was a precursor to Gay Pride.

HPS: Carnival was very important to you and the community. To what extent were you involved?

ER: I was in the krewes of Dirtie Dottie and Petronius. I worked with Mickey Gil, who was their captain for many years. Here I learned from the best. Currently I am captain of the Krewe of Amon-Ra as we prepare for the fifty-third tableau ball. I have created costumes for the krewes of Memphis, Apollo Baton Rouge, Armeinius, David, and so many other gay krewes over the years. My costumes have won countless Bourbon Street Awards on Fat Tuesday.

FP: How were you chosen grand marshal of Southern Decadence?

ER: Gay bartenders in the French Quarter have been part of Southern Decadence since the big split in 1980. Miss Blanche at the Golden Lantern, the home of gay Decadence, named Wayne White as grand marshal in 1996. White was a bartender at Café Lafitte in Exile, as was I. Robin Malta was also a bartender there for many years, as was Tony Langlinais. Bars have always been an integral part of Decadence, from Matassa's Bar to all the bars we would stop by during the walking parade throughout the long haul of a Sunday. Wayne initially offered me the grand marshal whistle on the night of his parade. I was part of his entourage, and we ended up at his home on Esplanade Avenue. It was a rag-tag group, including Stan Sanders, Miss Julie Brown, Ricky Taconi (DJ at Café Lafitte), and Miss Marlika (Byson Craig). We were all high on pot, and I asked Wayne who would be his choice. He said that he was still thinking about it and he wasn't sure yet. But then he said, "I was thinking about you, Gurl!" I got so excited that when he offered me the whistle, I said that there are so many others far more deserving and who have worked really hard for you this year. Wayne said, "Like who?" And I named Miss Love, because he had organized Wayne's birthday party and many other things during the lead-up to Labor Day weekend. So he chose Miss Love, which was an insane year to say the least. Miss Love picked Robin Malta, and he picked me.

HPS: How did you get the whistle?

ER: Robin worked at the Hair Asylum salon. There was a second room with two barber chairs. One night we were at Café Lafitte and he invited me over to the salon, which was closed. We plopped into the barber chairs, and Robin looked at me and said, "Sistah, Gurl, Miss Dark Lady, I want to name you grand marshal next year." I responded, "Are you serious?" And he said, "I am very serious! If you want it. It's either you or Miss Lucci Smurf!" Well, I said that of course I would love it! Robin told me to be hush-hush about it, but I did share the news with my friend Paul Overland, or Miss Helga. He mentioned that a couple of his friends were the original grand marshals of Decadence, Fred Wright and Robert Laurent. Paul said he later told them, and Fred said that he didn't even know who the hell I was, but he kept hearing my name everywhere! One day I was making my rounds of all the bars and ended up at the Double Play. Paul was there with Fred and Robert, and we finally got to meet. I loved these guys ever since that day. They were a riot!

HPS: How did you decide on your theme for the parade?

ER: I had already been toying with themes and ideas for some months. I rolled it around for a few more months and finally settled on "The Dark Lady Tour: Dissidents of Decadence." At that time I was performing as Cher and did it rather well, being tall and thin. It all came together perfectly. I used to perform at Travis's drag club on Rampart and at Le Bistro on Bourbon, and even Le Bistro in Hattiesburg and Biloxi. So Cher was inevitable, really.

FP: There were some public events to announce you as grand marshal. What were those?

ER: Things weren't as formal as they are now, but we did have to do it up a bit. My title was officially awarded to me by the reigning Grand Marshal Robin Malta on stage in front of Café Lafitte on July 4, 1999. My press party was at the Corral Bar upstairs, and it was packed, packed, packed with friends and well-wishers.

HPS: And then came the glorious day when you were the grand marshal of it all. What was that like? Were you nervous?

ER: I wasn't nervous. I was Cher! My parade gathered in the Marigny, at Burgundy and Kerlerek. Then we went to Rubyfruit Jungle to organize. That was at Frenchmen and Royal streets. I had a rather large court and a specially appointed court jester. This was Walter Doucet, and I had made a large ornate staff for him to part the masses. He played that part so very well. My court consisted of Robbie Morgan, Chris Cross, Big Rick, James Tompkins, Tony Langlinais, Heath, Maggie Marrero, and Rip and Marsha. Rick got hold of a limousine, which drove behind us. This was taken directly from the lyrics to the song "Dark Lady": "The fortune queen of New Orleans was brushing her cat in her black limousine." Of course, the whole parade officially started at the Golden Lantern, where I performed "Half-Breed." Along the route I did "Dark Lady." These performances were taped, of course, and then played almost every night at Café Lafitte.

HPS: Lou Bernard was a close friend during this time. Why didn't you name him as grand marshal?

ER: Lou has been a part of the gay community for such a long time. He founded the Krewe of Olympus, and he and Nick Donovan ran Lucille's and Friend bar. I used to work for him, and he and I became very close. I created the "Grand Duchess" title especially for him. He never wanted to be in the spotlight. He actually refused the title when I offered it to him. He said, "Hell no! Never!" So I had to create the title of "Grand Duchess" just for him.

FP: What did you do during your reign as the twenty-seventh grand marshal?

ER: I created the first Gay Easter Parade in carriages. We paraded down Bourbon Street on Easter Sunday, and it was fantastic with all the Easter hats. Everyone tried to outdo everyone else. I've never seen such gaudy and humongous hats in my life. Aletha Bryant and Michael Chase, very good friends of mine, were the first Easter queen and king. Of course, this was before we started raising money for various gay charities.

HPS: How did you get along with other former grand marshals?

ER: One tradition I dearly love was the former Grand Marshal Luncheon, held on the Saturday before the weekend of Decadence. I hosted the event at Estelle's Rib Eye and, if you can believe it, there were many grand marshals in attendance: Frederick Wright, Robert Laurent, Michael Hickerson, Miss Love, Robin Malta, Wayne White, Robert King, and Olive. I had Raven (Michael Moyer) as our waitress. When I told the past grand marshals that there would be entertainment and a guest at our banquet, a couple grumbled, saying, It's only supposed to be grand marshals. But they stopped complaining when the dancer came in at the Corner Pocket and Smurf began to perform for us. We got all the grand marshals on the bar with me in spiked heels. Miss Fly kept yelling, "Don't fall off the bar because I ain't got no insurance." Even Frederick Wright got up on the bar and did a jig.

FP: It seems like you and Frederick hit it off?

ER: We sure did. That was Fred's twenty-fifth anniversary year. What a lovely gent he was! He sat right next to me, of course, at the head of the grand marshal table for my banquet. He loved to get high and passed around some joints. Some things just never change.

HPS: There was a precedent of two grand marshals back in 1978. Why did you choose two for your successors?

ER: I picked two for the millennium, one from the younger, Bourbon Street crowd, and the other from the older crowd who frequented bars off Bourbon, like the Lantern or the Corner Pocket. It was my idea that the old and the new should come together to make a bigger and more united Southern Decadence celebration.

HPS: Tell us how you told the designees.

ER: Smurf had a canary when I told him. We were crossing Orleans Street, right in front of the old Buster Holmes restaurant, and she blew a gasket in the middle of the street and refused! But after a while she relented. After all, she had been dubbed the Susan Lucci of Decadence, but I was the one who broke her losing streak. Tony Langlinais, who worked at Lafitte's, and Smurf, from the Corner Pocket, both loathed one another, but after they got to know each other, they were fast and furious friends. Bringing the old and new together was a success in the end. It was a marvelous Decadence to ring in the next thousand years.

HPS: Cher actually toured New Orleans during your reign as grand marshal. I know you attended the concert with friends. Were you excited?

ER: Ms. Fly, who was then owner of the Corner Pocket bar and a mover and shaker in gay NOLA, was the Cher Fan Club president here, and they were friends. I have an original photo of Cher and Ms. Fly signed by Cher, which used to hang in Lee's home then at the Corner Pocket. Ms. Fly was a grand marshal, as you know. I went with my entourage to Cher's concert and her words from the stage were "I hear there is a certain Dark Lady in the house tonight," and Cher proceeded to perform "Dark Lady." Later I learned that Ms. Fly had told her about my Southern Decadence theme. Needless to say I was in da clouds. It doesn't get any better than Cher!

Greg Manogue (Miss Love)

Greg Manogue, known universally as Miss Love, served as Southern Decadence grand marshal in 1997, a key year for the festival because it constituted the first time organizers secured a parade permit, thus bringing the whole series of events under the protection and scrutiny of the city.

Frank Perez: There was a panel discussion on the history of Southern Decadence when you were grand marshal. Tell me about that.

Greg Manogue (Miss Love): Roberts Batson put that together. It was upstairs at the Bourbon Orleans. It was on a Saturday afternoon. I don't think I had time to do anything.

Jeffrey Palmquist: How did you get involved in Southern Decadence?

GM: It was through Bubbles and Candy. They were good friends of mine from the time I started at Mr. B's bar and restaurant. They introduced me to it, but I had seen it before briefly when it was nothing. I do remember going around one of those Sundays. It was maybe 100 or 150 people out at that time. Andy Boudreaux owned Wolfendale's bar then, and that was always a spot that it went to. There was no route at that time. He had a barbeque, and people would gather there. I would say Steven and Warren (Bubbles and Candy) got me involved. We did our first group outfit together because we were flaming flags. That was the controversy—the burning of the flag. This would have been '89 or '90. No, it was '89 because in '90 we were "Queer I Am," the year the aquarium opened up. It was Labor Day weekend and we all went as "Go Go Fish." The balcony across the way from the Golden Lantern, we all got up there in our outfits—our friend Jimmy stayed there—and we did [*sings*], "We're a Grand Old Flag, We're a high flying flag and forever in peace may you wave / the fags I love the home of the homos and the brave." We had blue skirts with stars on them and our hair was all done up in flaming flags and we also had red shirts on. Group things were a big part of it. And Smurf and his group at that time were doing the better group outfit. They would walk around with diapers going "one, two, three, four, five, six, pooh."

JP: Was that the weekend of Southern Decadence?

GM: Decadence didn't have any pre-parties or anything like that, so it was just the one day. And then we went as Go Go Fish in 1990, and in 1991 I got to know a little bit more about who was involved in it. We really didn't know who the grand marshals were. We didn't really pay attention to them. Maybe we got a little more involved and got to know who they were. We got to know Mumbo at that time, and he became a part of our group through the football game. And then we did "A League of Our Own." Estelle then became involved. Mumbo, Jackie Smedley, all those people that were the core group of Decadence at that time.

FP: Tell me about how you were informed or asked to be grand marshal.

GM: You have to understand that Wayne White was grand marshal and before him was Blanche and before Blanche was Miss Alain and before Miss Alain was Ms. Fly, so we all knew each other. It was a hardcore group of people. It was ass-kissing. At the time you were being chosen you were chosen because you were decadent, you were out there. You were also a member of the bar scene. That was very important.

JP: Errol Rizzuto said when he became grand marshal you had to be decadent.

GM: It was a moment when Wayne was chosen, and it was why he was chosen. He didn't do drag. He was Wayne and everyone loved Wayne. I thought he was a great choice because my chance was closer. He got it through Blanche and Blanche worked over at the Lantern and we all worked together. It was that bartender thing. For a while it was all part of that gay-bartending scene. So when Wayne got it I participated a little bit with him. He would have to be the first one I think who got a sponsorship. Budweiser. Blanche I think got a few bucks from Budweiser. But sponsorships really took off with Wayne White.

FP: Tell us about how Decadence has changed, and are those changes good or bad?

GM: I should have ordered a cocktail [*laughs*]. I didn't meet the original founders of Southern Decadence until after I was a grand marshal. I didn't know Frederick [Wright] and Robert [Laurent] and Maureen [Block] when I was grand marshal.

I met them later on. Where it's gone since I was grand marshal? It's had its ups and downs. From the time I had it through the time of Ms. Fly, Mumbo, Blanche, Wayne and then me giving it to Robin and Robin passing it on to Errol was I think at its second growth. It was taking off. Wayne White, I think, really had the largest parade ever. There was no parade permit, no police escort yet. He left from the Lantern and went straight down to St. Louis and followed that route all the way to Rampart Street and then Rampart to St. Ann. The Internet blew up after Wayne White and then it just exploded. I was the first one to go in front of the city and get a parade permit.

FP: Why?

GM: Because at that time, the Internet and videos and the nudity that was happening on the street was beginning to get exposed and the crowds were getting big and the city had safety concerns. And I would have to say Larry Bagneris stepped in there as well and suggested I go meet with Troy Carter and see what we can do. Let's do this properly because we're requiring other groups to do so. So I went with Ms. Fly. At that time she was going through the police raiding her bars and she loved the idea of fighting City Hall. There was a lot of opposition within the group. Some former grand marshals thought it was a bad idea. Some said you can't do that. There's no reason to do that. Michael Hickerson [grand marshal 1985] said, "Don't do it." I looked at it as a way of saying, hey, let's go see what they have to say. So Ms. Fly and I sat in Troy Carter's office and he came right out and said, "I don't want Joe Blow coming down from Iowa sticking his dick out and getting it sucked on the street. We have to get a little control over this."

JP: He really said that?

GM: Yes. Ms. Fly and I were looking at each other like "What?!" Carter was our councilman at that time. I remember the Saturday before Decadence Sunday still not having the permit in my hand. And it was twenty-five dollars. I got it in the mail three weeks later. I remember walking up to Officer Cruz on the corner with a check for two hundred dollars and saying, "Here, I hope it don't bounce." That was for the police escort.

FP: When you met with Carter, did he express any opposition?

GM: I don't recall any opposition. They were just trying to get a grip on what was going on, what was happening.

FP: So where did the idea of a permit originate?

GM: I would have to say Larry, but I don't know the details. In 1990, a police officer would walk up to parade participants and ask, "Are you in charge of this? Who is in charge?" They were wondering what was going on. But really, no one was in charge. It went from bar to bar at that time. Blanche was at the Lantern, Wayne was over here at Lafitte's. I was hanging out there but I didn't really have a home bar. I was going to all the bars—the Pub, here, Wolfendale's, and the Mississippi River Bottom. Andy Boudreaux was another big one because I remember him taking me in the back and saying, "Here's five hundred dollars. Make sure that parade comes by here." That was in the backroom office at MRB. Eddie Folse was there at that time because he also had a barbeque after the parade was over. Then you have to look at Robin's year, 1998. His was fantastic. He followed the rules, but the city relaxed the rules a bit. It was pouring down rain. He was going down Decatur Street with Big Rick and all of them pushing his little cart and they had a National Guard Convention in town and they had all those trucks going down Decatur Street one way and the parade was going the other way. He hopped on one truck and away he went and he caught up with parade somewhere on St. Louis. Those were some fun times with the parade that you just don't see anymore, a little more craziness. I was not crazy. Robin was. Errol was crazy too because his entourage was just a mess, going anywhere and everywhere. Then you got into Tony and Smurf. They were picking it up more. And then after Tony and Smurf, you get into a little bit more of Bianca, Rick, and Estelle. And what changed at that time, and I'll just say it honestly, was the drugs. Drugs were a very heavy part of the scene.

JP: I remember when I started here at Lafitte's in 2000. It was getting lewd again. It had taken a curve back to that, the original decadence.

GM: That's when the Reverend got involved. Reverend Storms. Then Irish Mike got it and his crazy control over the sponsors of the liquor, making sure they did this and that, and then naming Donnie Jay, and then telling Donnie Jay that he had to pick Regina and Lisa. And then when it got to Katrina, we all stepped in as a group to say, hey, what are we going to do. It didn't go over well. We couldn't get along with each other. There were eight, nine, or ten of us and each of us had our own opinion and it ended up with Jägermeister shots and fuck you and do whatever you want and it came down to one thing—you can do it again but you have to keep the same number. That was the conclusion.

FP: I've heard that you have a tradition of writing a letter to the grand marshals with the instruction of not opening it until the morning of the parade.

GM: It's just a little note. I've done it for, I'm going to say, I've done it for the worthy. Is that the right word?

FP: You obviously have a keen appreciation for the history of Southern Decadence. What should people who have never heard of Decadence know about it?

GM: These people will never be able to experience what we have done and what we have achieved. I use Frederick Wright as an example and Robert Laurent. Their history is something that should be passed on. It's not just a party. We are New Orleans, and we created a party for y'all to come down and spend money and be crazy and all that. They need to know why they did it and what they went through at that time to be able to do it. Frederick Wright and Robert Laurent told me there were times when Harry Connick Sr. was following them down Esplanade Avenue when he was the district attorney wondering what are they doing? What are they up to? It was right after the Up Stairs Lounge fire. It was a time when they were arresting people for being in drag or for being who they were over on Rampart Street and going to Night Court. Just to know what it is they started. It might be them saying they started it because Maureen was bored with their bourré games. There is a lot more history of that group of people in the beginning of it. There are stages of Southern Decadence and stages of grand marshals too. And then surviving the AIDS crisis and surviving the time when people didn't have interest in it anymore.

FP: How do you think the AIDS epidemic affected Southern Decadence?

GM: Oh. It affected it big time. You lost a lot of those grand marshals who are no longer here to tell their stories. You look at the list of grand marshals and you can see the names of people that passed. Or look at Rhie. Rhie died before he could name the next grand marshal.

JP: And look how many were lost that would have been grand marshals.

GM: And a lot of the people at the beginning of this were straight. There was a mixture of people. Jaime Temple was in the bar business. So was Ms. Fly.

JP: It was a testament to the bar culture in New Orleans.

GM: Oh, definitely. And then it filtered in a different direction.

JP: Tell about the moment you were asked to be grand marshal.

GM: I kind of knew it was coming. I was downstairs here at Lafitte's. Wayne was working. It was a Monday night. I was a manager at Bacco's at that time. I'd always stop by here for a drink and then I'd go home. And Wayne called me at work and said I want you stop by and I said okay. I kind of knew it was coming because Wayne had given me a few hints and he was being pressured from all areas at that time about who he was going to pick. The pressure was on him from Smurf and others and he leaned over the bar and said I have to ask you a question and I said sure go ahead and he said would you like to be the next grand marshal of Southern Decadence. I said, well, let me think about it for a minute and of course I answered yes and that was the way it went. You tried to keep it a secret as much as you could and you denied it in front of everybody. The announcement party came here. We had already picked the theme of "A Wedding to Remember." I had a cake made and we had a little drag show. Wayne was emceeing it. We had Ms. Fly, Mumbo, Michael Hickerson was there, and Estelle. Wayne was announced at the Mississippi River Bottom. Jaime Temple at the Phoenix—many years it would be announced during their anniversary party. At the Phoenix one time Smurf was halfway on the stage . . . and you just kept on denying it. I remember many nights sitting here at the bar denying it. You told a few people to be a part of your group. And we didn't have a lot of money. I remember going to the boutique shop on North Broad and bought the wedding dress for five hundred dollars and had them put in the rainbow colors and you had the father of the bride, the mother of the bride. We made fun of it as much as we could.

FP: Why did you pick Robin (Malta)?

GM: I picked Robin for one very specific reason. When he was the Queen of Petronius he invited me to sit at his queen's table, which was up on stage at the Municipal Auditorium. You sat up there and you felt like a million dollars. I was contemplating between him, Smurf, and Princess Stephaney. I wish I could find the tape of Smurf calling me three, four times the night before saying, "I guess it's not going to be me." She became the joke of Southern Decadence, but she took the joke in stride because she became the Susan Lucci of it until she finally got it.

FP: So at that time the title of "Southern Decadence Grand Marshal" was something people were vying for?

GM: Oh, yeah. It had become a thing, something that you wanted. My friends Bubbles and Warren were looking at me like why don't you give it to me? Can you imagine where it would be today if I gave it to Bubbles? It could have gone off in so many different directions. I always felt that once you have that you know you have to think it out. Look at some of those choices and how they went down that line.

JP: You have to think about that when you're the grand marshal. Yeah, it's your friend or your lover or whoever but you have to think about what direction is this person going to take it.

GM: Right. And I think that is more important now than it was at that time.

JP: It's interesting you mention Princess Stephaney. Was she decadent?

GM: Oh, very much so. She still rubs it in my face.

FP: When did the unofficial selection criterion change from a person who lived a truly decadent lifestyle to something else?

GM: Who did Regina and Lisa give it to? I think it changed at that point, I really do because Lisa chose her boyfriend, Marcus. And who the hell is Marcus?

FP: Getting back to your reign, why "A Wedding to Remember"?

GM: I always felt it should be something that was going on in the country at the time, what was making news and gay weddings were a part of the news. Same thing for flaming flags. It was always finding something political—a connection to current events.

FP: So you were known as Miss Love at that point.

GM: Yes, I was.

FP: So, that kind of fit?

JP: So who gave you that name?

GM: It was a dishwasher at Mr. B's Bistro. We all had our own drag names—Candy, Bubbles, Big D, Edmond, and then Chris King was a part of our group and his name was Christie Love. I was only twenty-three years old at that time, and the dishwasher, Kim Addison was his name, came up and we were very flamboyant at work, and Kim said "You're such a bitch, they ought to call you Miss Love." So that's how it came about. I didn't really have a drag name associated with me at that time.

FP: Did you perform in drag?

GM: No, we were just going out in costumes.

FP: What else about making Southern Decadence official could you add? Was that good or bad? Would it have survived without city recognition? Would they have shut the whole thing down?

GM: I don't think the city would have shut it down. It was too big of a party, and even the people who lived in the Quarter could tolerate it. You could say however that we almost lost it with Pat McArdle. We tried to come together as a group. It was Michael Hickerson, Irish Mike, Larry Bagneris, Errol Rizzuto, Misael, maybe Regina was there, I'd have to go back and look at my notes—all after the money went missing in 2012 we met at the Country Club and tried to have a meeting and then people said we were trying to create a dictatorship but we were looking at it like, we're about to lose it and then Pat McArdle got up and left. We tried to elect a president and all that, and we got shot down. People said we were trying to take it over and at the same time we were saying no, we're trying to save it because of the so-called missing money and the hurricane. Pat said she was going to do it again and she got up and cried. This was the second meeting we had at the Healing Center over on St. Claude. It was old school versus new school. It turned into an ugly situation.

FP: Tell us about the Southern Decadence Board of Directors.

GM: We were trying to do what we could, what we felt as the old-timers, who have a love affair for it and what we had to do to save it because we felt as if it was going to go away. Larry Bagneris was a big pusher of it. He tried to get us together again. Here we go, third time's a charm and we can't all get along. It was ugly, ugly, ugly at those meetings. A lot of things were said. Rusty LaRoux was there at one of them, but she kept her mouth shut because she just wanted to see what was going to happen. Pat McArdle was very determined that she was going to do it again and we, the old school, were very adamant that no she's not going to do it again. You have probably given a bad name to it or tarnished it with what's his name, who took the money [T. J. Conard]. She finally caved in because it was going to get uglier. Robert Laurent was there; Maureen and Charlie were there and they said . . . Charlie, who was a very wise man said some things that got back to her or that group, hey, you had it once and now move on. We tried to come up with some basic rules such as you can only have it once. Like Rex. Rex is Rex once. If it rains or snows out, he's Rex and then he's Rex no more. Maybe that should have been the one basic rule, but there were absolutely no rules. You can only have it once regardless of an act of God, and she didn't want to go that way. After that they picked Tami Tarmac and Venus Santiago, and I had gotten two packs of paper together with everybody's address and phone numbers and said, "Here, this is what you're going to have to do. You're going to have to meet with the city and such," and I tacked it all up on the back wall of what is now GrandPre's. Tami and Venus really stepped up to the plate. We basically said we're washing our hands of it and that's when I said, "I'm finished."

FP: So at those meetings, who was criticizing you for trying to take it over?

GM: Do I have to name names? It was the old school versus the new school if you could look at it that way.

FP: The new school thought the old school was trying to take it over?

GM: Yeah. There were some bad, bad things said, and that's when Michael Hickerson finally said, "Fuck it. I don't want to have anything more to do with it."

JP: What did she want?

GM: She wanted it to go back to the old way. You were never going to change her mind on that. A lot of that had to do with the way it changed with the fund-raising, the money, and all those events, which her philosophy on that was it could be done in two events and then they can just go on and be grand marshals. She was very hard-line, old school on that. I've been butting heads with her since 1997, and we've never really seen eye to eye. We really lost our friendship over that part of Decadence.

FP: So the effect of the money scandal with T.J. was what?

GM: We were trying to rein it in, to try to make sure this would not happen again. Tami restored some credibility through the nonprofit, and we were already talking about that. A lawyer friend of mine was looking into that, but we could never all agree who would be on that board.

FP: So the idea of a board existed prior to the money scandal?

GM: It was in talks. We were talking about it.

FP: Whose idea was it?

GM: I can't pin down one person, but we were all talking about it.

FP: So the money scandal was the impetus to do it?

GM: Right. Something had to be done. And there was a push from Larry Bagneris. And Toby was fighting for his own parade in that first meeting. I had to go sit up with the sanitation department. It was just Larry and me and they were coming all at me saying the sanitation fee was going to be eighty-five hundred dollars, and this is what you got to have. I sat there and thought what the hell am I doing. That's when I had had it. I told Tami and Venus you gotta do this. So then Rip and Marsha got a little more involved at that time with Tami and Venus and then Toby. The thing was fighting that sanitation fee and Toby with his Knights of Decadence parade on Friday night was not going to have anything to do with it. His feeling was I'm not paying. But you're going to have to pay something because you're part of the mess. That was another ugly little turn. And then attending that first security meeting up there with everybody. And that's when Southern Decadence took a turn. It's getting recognized. And come to find out two years later that sanitation fee had been waived. Well, you're not paying eighty-five hundred dollars. And then Tami Tarmac pursued that a little bit more and pressured them a little bit more and then finally they waived that. I think she used the example of Essence Fest.

JP: So tell us about James, and Rip and Marsha and the board.

GM: That I don't know. With the formation of the Decadence nonprofit, Tami Tarmac asked them to do that. I'm not sure how James [Garner] got in that, maybe because he's the owner of the bar [Golden Lantern]. We've always said they need to have a member of Southern Decadence on that board. I want to touch on the copyright issue.

JP: Did Irish grab that?

GM: Well, he grabbed what he could. Gerard's role in the copyright is an aspect of Decadence. I don't even talk to Gerard anymore. I told him to kiss my ass.

FP: Who is Gerard?

GM: Gerard Oncle. He copyrighted "Southern Decadence" for printed material in 1996. When Robin was grand marshal, and it happened right here in this bar, and we were all saying that we need to copyright this and he went and did it. So he owns copyright on printed materials.

FP: Does he get money from that?

GM: No, but he had an agreement with Tom Wood at one time to be able to use it that year and Tom paid him one dollar for it and it's never been pulled out again until we got a little funky with those shirts a few years ago and Gerard got a little crazy. He's still around and he just renewed it. If he wanted to he could start charging everybody that uses that name. He hasn't. I don't think he's ever going to take it that far. He was very good friends with Big Rick and Robin and Frank and all of them at that time. And if you look at the dates on that one that was originally done, Rip and Marsha then get theirs a month later, a copyright for publications. There are two different copyrights on it—copyright and trademark. They tried to get ugly with each other two years ago and what Gerard has started from Robin in 1996.

FP: In your opinion, who were some of the more colorful grand marshals?

GM: Blanche. She passed out at Wolfendale's. You can find this out through Robert and Charlie and Tom Tippin and Robert King, who I had the pleasure of meeting and getting to know, who was paralyzed. From what I gather, a lot of times you were not picked until two days before, a week before. Mumbo. I remember Olive because she was Olive Oyl. The Saints game also played on that weekend so that worked into what was going on. A lot of people were leaving the Saints game at 2:00 p.m. and getting in drag in the parking lot and then meeting the parade. The NFL later changed the schedule and it's a preseason game, but before it used to sometimes present a conflict.

FP: Anything else, Miss Love?

GM: The board thing is still an ugly part of Decadence.

Rip and Marsha Naquin-Delain
(Robert J. Naquin and Martin Greeson)

Rip and Marsha met in the early 1970s and began publishing *Ambush Magazine* in Baton Rouge in 1982. They moved their whole enterprise to New Orleans in 1985, centered on Bourbon Street. Rip and Marsha were the first to register as same-sex domestic partners in 1993, when it became available in Louisiana, and married in 2014. They were both intricately involved with the Southern Decadence festival, fundraising for the LGBT community in New Orleans, and founded the Krewe of Queenateenas.

Frank Perez: How did Southern Decadence get going online?

Rip Naquin: We registered SoDecadence.com in 1995, among other dot-coms. There was some early confusion with SoDecadence.net, which was the Bourbon Pub. They were selling at that time VIP tickets for all their events. The public erroneously thought, upon first glance, that it was a VIP pass for all the bars and their events. That's the trouble with having two sites, but we soon cleared all that up. The pub, however, did not return any money to customers.

Howard Philips Smith: How were you all involved with the permits?

Rip Naquin: The first big parade, I mean huge, was in 1996. *Ambush* paid for the police detail that kept things in order. Then all the bars paid their cut en route. It was a huge honor back then for a grand marshal to stop at a bar. Very lucrative. Just ask Lucille. Hundreds of people clambering for a cocktail. You know what that means in monetary terms. Now in 1997 Miss Love got the first real permit to parade from the city. We simply had to. It was just out of control, and we needed that support. Thank God it came to that. Without it we would not have Southern Decadence today.

HPS: Who paid for the permits each year?

RN: Well, *Ambush* paid each year until 2011. We did not do it in 2012 because of the potential lawsuits. We had a lawyer look everything over, and we just couldn't risk it anymore. That was the year when Decadence did not have a permit and you know what happened. The money disappeared.

FP: How long have you been attending Decadence?

Marsha Delain: I think we first came down from Baton Rouge in 1977. We just loved it, the bar crawl and all. We kept going until 1980, thereabouts. Then when we moved to town we did it every year.

RN: Every year. That's right. We were in from the start and we saw it change so much over the years.

HPS: What happened with the money in 2012?

RN: Pat McArdle and T. J. Conard were the grand marshals and when it was time to turn in the money after all the fundraisers, T.J. had left town. Now when you put it together you come up with the answer.

HPS: What happened to Decadence in 2013?

RN: Something had to be done. Public sentiment was now firmly against the festival as being corrupt, and I can't blame them. Originally Tami and Venus came to us and we all got together with James Garner from the Golden Lantern and formed the New Orleans Southern Decadence Inc. nonprofit with 501(c)(3) status. We didn't really want to be involved with all that, but we were asked and we had to consider it for the greater good.

FP: Why weren't charges filed against T.J. and Miss Hope [Pat McArdle]?

RN: Yes, the money was gone, but Blake Miller of the French Quarter Suites stepped in and donated the $3,000 to Belle Reve so they wouldn't be out of any money. That was the amount that was stolen. There's your real answer: we did get to donate the money after all, and then T.J. was nowhere to be found. Also, you have to remember, that in 2012 we didn't have a permit and there weren't many people here because of Hurricane Isaac.

HPS: Which brings us to Hurricane Katrina. What was that like for you and Decadence?

MD: We were in the midst of the biggest issue of *Ambush* yet, over 164 pages. Then Katrina hits on Sunday and Monday. Next week was Decadence.

RN: We stayed on till the shooting and looting started and left early Wednesday morning in a caravan. We had to siphon gas from cars just to get enough to make it out of the city. There was no news. We didn't know really what was going on. No electricity anywhere. Lisa Beaumann and Regina went on to a plantation and held a parade on Decadence Sunday with horses and carriages.

MD: We ended up in Lafayette and celebrated at a gay bar there. Yes, we did have our Decadence. I've heard of similar little celebrations from many people. Even Katrina couldn't dampen our festival spirit!

RN: We came back in two weeks but we had to get out again because of another hurricane, so it was really almost a month later that we were back for good. Lafitte's was the first bar to open up. *Ambush* came out on October 11 with money from FEMA. Many homeowners got some money from the government and we used it to get the magazine back out. The French Quarter was the only part to come back right away.

FP: What was it like during those first months?

RN: It was dangerous, especially in the Quarter. Our neighbor Royce had a shotgun and sat on his stoop. This protected our block for sure. Other blocks in the neighborhood were broken into and smashed. Not us, thanks to Royce.

FP: What changes have you seen recently?

RN: I think the gay community has grown here in New Orleans, especially our visibility and money power. Even the straight businesses fly the rainbow flag now. More are getting involved with our events. It's good for all of us.

HPS: What was it like being chosen to be grand marshals?

MD: It was really a dream come true. We always hoped we'd be chosen one day and then it happened. We were so honored. It really is like being crowned royalty.

RN: Decadence in 2015 was bittersweet. Ms. Fly had been murdered and we wanted to honor her in some way. We wore "Sally Fly" pins, that was for Ms. Fly. That year was more of a family feel to our group, especially in our entourage.

FP: How did you come to pick Jeff for 2016?

RN: We had some difficulties among our fellow grand marshals in 2015, so we wanted someone strong enough to withstand all the negativity. I think it's just normal in a group to have disagreements, but you still hang together in the end. We donated our money to our chosen charities: PFLAG scholarships, NOAGE, [New Orleans Advocates for LGBT Elders] and the LGBT+ Archives Project. That's why you keep it all in one, as we say.

HPS: How did the bead toss get started?

MD: That was Ms. Fly. Her favorite color was yellow. So of course we had a Yellow Party. We had yellow towels around us and on our heads, like we just got out of the shower. That was the start in 1993. The bead toss just happened at this party, which was when the grand marshals would come in to recuperate at Ambush Mansion on Bourbon Street for food, cocktails, rest, then the bead toss.

RN: Each grand marshal leaves his/her own stamp on Decadence, and that is as it should be. In 2015 we raised the largest amount of money for charity and we had five grand marshals. That was really a first, and we had that costume by Opal [Masters]. What a masterpiece! We don't allow corporate sponsors now either. It's just too much.

FP: How do you see the future of Decadence?

RN: It just keeps getting bigger and bolder. Now we have three block parties on Friday, Saturday, and Sunday at the Phoenix. So much has changed. And now we have Toby LeFort and his Knights of Decadence Parade on Friday night. Dykeadence. It will continue to grow because our community wants to celebrate and take the world with them. But you know what the queens say. They say I ruined Decadence! But in the end they still come out and celebrate.

EARLY SOUTHERN DECADENCE INVITATIONS

Robert Laurent, who designed the first Southern Decadence invitations, deftly defined the original spirit and image of the festival. Working within preconceived notions of the Old South and especially the camp and often ruinous nature of the term "Southern Decadence," Laurent graphically mined an established store of recognizable and iconic imagery to great effect. These invitations arrived in the mail and excited recipients to celebrate the end of the summer and to "come as your favorite decadent." In addition, Laurent concocted invitations for birthday parties, anniversaries, and all sorts of other events put on by members of the core group. Whether the group ties and their joy in getting together inspired the startling visual graphics associated with the ongoing celebrations or vice-versa, these documents encapsulate the humor and whimsy of Southern Decadence and remain a testament to its artful insanity.

The last Southern Decadence invitation designed by Laurent, in 1980, is perhaps the masterpiece of the series, summing up the entire decade of the 1970s. The invitation itself, entitled "Hard Times," is a comic-strip compilation assembled to create a seamless storyline, with each panel expertly integrated into rows of a grid as if already published in newspapers or comic books. This montage soon reveals itself as a commentary on not only relationships and personalities within the core group of Decadents but masterfully critiques the political and social angst of the time. In hindsight, this invitation as the culmination of nearly a decade of fanciful and irreverent graphic representations would herald an end to the first incarnation of Southern Decadence and its simple pretensions of public display coupled with its grand pretensions of royalty, inspired by traditional Carnival.

The grand marshal for 1980 was Tom Tippin, one of the members of the original troupe, who costumed as the King of Id, transforming his status as marshal and general into one of reigning monarch, in jest perhaps, but this would be short-lived. The *Wizard of Id* comic strip followed the day-to-day adventures of a king and his subjects in the kingdom of Id. However, the story lines sometimes strayed to whatever suited the plot at the moment. A large cast of characters rounded out the king's subjects and were usually caught up in various intrigues and comic situations. The king himself often referred to his subjects as "idiots," and was himself the brunt of many a joke.[1] This comic-strip king ruled over a pseudo-medieval idiocracy, much like the parallel kingdom of Southern Decadence. Robert Laurent expanded on this particular character. "The Wizard of Id also implied the Wizard of Oz and its parallel world. But Tippin took the whole thing one step further with his King of Id. Let's not forget the psychological underpinnings of the term 'id' either. This reference from Freud's psyche represents our desires and impulses, which is quite appropriate for our little excursions into Neverland."[2]

Assuming his kingship with fervor and sincerity, Tippin crafted an elaborate costume which transformed him into this comic-strip royal with a perfection that perhaps startled the decadents who gathered in front of Matassa's Bar for the annual parade of misfits. Tippin wore an elaborate orange wig that he had crafted from thick yarn, and his tunic and scepter mimicked the pint-sized despot with amazing detail. Tippin was an avid collector of comics, and his collection numbered in the tens of thousands, all carefully cataloged, archived, and preserved in glassine envelopes. Laurent recalled the specifics of designing this invitation: "Here's the last parade invitation of the original group. I went out with a bang. . . . 1980 was an election year and we would have just survived two political conventions. I guess the theme stems from the awful picture of the country presented by the Republicans. Anyway, I chose to pick panels of misfortune from a wide array of mostly daily comic strips."[3]

By choosing "Hard Times" as the theme, Laurent channeled an end-of-the-decade zeitgeist, which would eventually outweigh the delirium first generated by the early and carefree Decadence marches, and signaled the demise of the first phase of Southern Decadence. That exuberant and irreverent esprit manifested itself completely in the first invitation, which has become the most iconic. The black-silhouette cutout was a popular representation in the nineteenth century, and this first invitation from 1972 used that image to create an anonymous southern belle, already a cliché, with a man underneath her petticoats, underscoring the subversive nature of Decadence from the beginning, as off-kilter as the odd spelling of "YA'LL." The second invitation—the next party was a mere two weeks after the first—continued on with the facade of the genteel South while anticipating the demise of Belle Rêve. A proper southern belle implores revelers to "Come Back to Belle Rêve," a place depicted on the invitation as a real plantation. For the 1973 invitation, Laurent waged another attack on gender roles in society, women's work, and the drudgery of housework, eviscerated by a dose of Southern Decadence. He placed himself in the lower corner as a tightrope walker balancing himself with stars. However, Laurent's most elaborate reference to the antebellum plantation system was the multilayered invitation for the 1974 parade encapsulated in "The Belle Rêve Times." This complex faux-newspaper announces the Third Annual Southern Decadent Party with news items of relatives coming down to the plantation on a steamboat to celebrate, Canal Street emptied of people who were at the party, and the Decadents themselves anxiously awaiting their guests at Belle Rêve. Included is a grid of photos supposedly from last year's "fun and hijinks," candid and outré pictures of mostly bare-breasted women proud of their open sexuality, and decadence.

The invitation for 1975 revealed a marked shift in the visual message of the event. Instead of irreverent references to antebellum times, Laurent channeled the new and the modern. This was the year the Superdome was at last completed. This iconic landmark illustrated how New Orleans was now one of the premier cities of the nation, and Laurent used this image to convey that Southern Decadence had become larger than life, at least in the minds and hearts of the Decadents. On top of the Superdome stood the legendary Bourbon Street entertainer Chris Owens. Gigantic, like Godzilla or King Kong, Owens replaced these cartoon characters with a real woman as a formidable and gargantuan presence. Here Laurent underscored the changing role of women in society and elevated them to the top of the world. Jerome Williams, aka Pickle, impersonated Owens as grand marshal that year to honor her support of not only the gay community but the French Quarter denizens as well.

For 1976, Laurent used a grid of both cropped square photographs and cartoon characters for his Bicentennial invitation. Recently he recalled how this particular invitation was conceived. "I think of all the ones I put together, this one is my least successful. I evidently wasn't into it; maybe I was too busy at work to devote a lot of time to it. And maybe already it was becoming a duty rather than a fun thing to do. There's no overall theme like the one for Tom's. It's just a motley collection of images. (But, in defense, I could say that's what the parade had become.) The small illustrations aren't from the comics with the exception of Little Lulu, third row, third image. But that's coincidence. I think since they're all the same size that most likely they came from *New York Magazine*'s contents pages at the time. They would be a detail of the different articles inside the publication. I'm rather sure of that."[4]

However, by obfuscating the characters depicted in his invitation, reducing each to a small square with minimal information, Laurent seemed to say that all the kooky and crazy participants of Southern Decadence were all one madcap, amalgamated group that accepted all comers, as long as they were part of the party. These cropped and truncated thumbnails, close-up views, and oddly framed perspectives only served to render all the images of equal weight and importance. They represent the diversity of the devotees of Decadence and at the same time the absurdity of the day as singular stilled moments frozen in time.

Another mini-masterpiece was revealed in 1977, the year Robert Laurent was grand marshal. His brilliant invitation was titled "Dixie's Land," referencing this almost sacred song of the Old South, and a cartoon alligator—as a symbol of Louisiana—who was definitely bored with the whole thing. By including the minstrelized lyrics of the song, Laurent further criticized the lingering vestiges of the Jim Crow South and how blacks were still treated as minstrel-show shadows. The next invitation further explores the transformation of women from the first set of invitations to something startling and bold. Here Laurent attacked the stereotypical representation of women as the antithesis of the demure female figures found in earlier invitations. The southern belle has been transformed into a muscular, almost masculine version, unashamed of her body, probably a weight lifter in her spare time, unflappable in a pair of pumps and a bathing suit. Although there were two grand marshals in 1978, this was the first time a woman was designated as a grand marshal. Kathleen Kavanaugh was an unapologetic participant in Decadence and took on her role as grand marshal with a playful will and confidence, and along with her co-captain Robert King, they ruled the day. The 1979 invitation returned the festival to its roots of celebration by proclaiming "Laissez les Bons Temps Rouler!" We are definitely at the close of the 1970s with roller-skates, possibly for roller disco, and the quintessential libation unique to New Orleans, Dixie Beer, once again referencing the Old South, coming full circle from the first invitations.

But it would be the 1980 invitation, lost until Tom Tippin's sons found a copy in his attic, that brought all of these themes together. This surprisingly innovative and haunting invitation at once announces that "Hard Times" have come again. Using single cells from daily newspaper comic-strip cartoons, Laurent brought together in one piece *Doonesbury, Beetle Bailey, Garfield, Mary Worth, Nancy, Dick Tracy, Crock, Hägar the Horrible,* and *Brenda Starr,* among others. Some of the difficult themes found within this visual display are personal and relational problems, social pariahs (non-persons), women's liberation, regret, body image, frustration, outdated morality, life-threatening situations, critique of the traditional family, elections and politics, family tragedies, career choices, aging and lifestyle issues, the mandatory draft for the Vietnam War, fear and police surveillance, alcoholism, ignorance, and nuclear threat. In addition, Laurent stealthily inserted names and references of various Decadents into the cells. Maureen Block, the Mother of Southern Decadence, was called out in a Mary Worth cell. Robert Laurent used himself and his pet parrot to express his dismay over the 1980 presidential election between Ronald Reagan and incumbent Jimmy Carter. Lee Provost's vanity, Becky Theriot's cooking, Bruce Harris's sarcasm, and Kathleen Kavanaugh's pet were all jokingly integrated into various cells as in-crowd laughs. The Vietnam War was still a sore point for many Americans, and Laurent uses a cell from *Doonesbury* to recall the awful draft. The accident at the Three Mile Island nuclear plant closed out the series on a grand sense of doom and pessimism.

Inadvertently, Laurent realized that the original group had indeed grown up, and this loss of innocence coincided with the hard times lived outside the bubble of Southern Decadence. They became more serious as they grew older. As the decade reached its end, they were moving on with their lives. The original core group would always be close, but some went their separate ways. Robert King's accident only sealed this fate. The Blocks moved Uptown with their son Andrew, and Maureen had begun teaching at Tulane. Kathleen Kavanaugh married and moved away. Laurent had surgery and went home to Lafayette to recover. David Red had relocated to Nepal for teaching. But even with these hard times brewing on the horizon, the invitation also offered a solution, a panacea for all the trials and tribulations. Judy Garland, the ever-bright Dorothy Gale, and a song from the 1950 movie *Summer Stock* closed out the invitation on a positive note: "Forget All Your Troubles! C'mon Get Happy!" This promise of Good Times, however, would soon dissolve as the parade fractured into angry fragments at Jackson Square, and the original Belle Rêvers would subsequently withdraw from the event altogether, paving the way for Southern Decadence to become a gigantic gay super-festival.

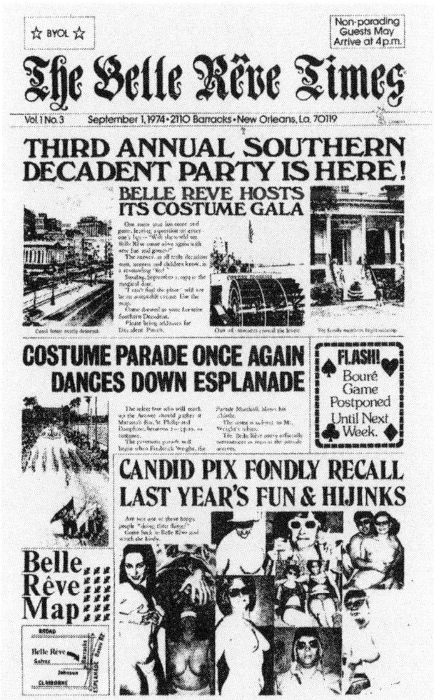

clockwise, top left: 1972, 1972, 1973, 1974

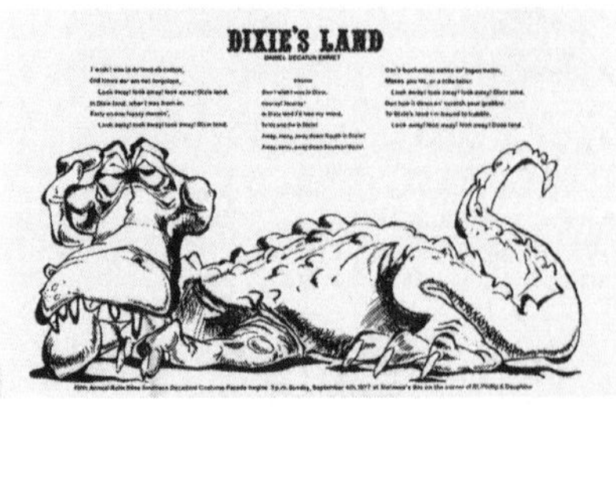

clockwise, top left: 1975, 1976, 1978, 1977, 1979

HARD TIMES
SOMETHING IS BOTHERING YOU, ISN'T IT?
EVERYONE HAS PROBLEMS! ISN'T THAT WHAT LIFE'S ALL ABOUT?
STARTING TODAY I'M MAKING YOU A 'NON-PERSON.'
I'M GOING TO THE BUREAU OF CHILD WELFARE TO MEET MY SOCIAL WORKER—
YOU MADE ME FEEL... CHEAP!
PLEASE TAKE ME HOME!
BUT I'M TALKING ABOUT BRENDA... SHE HASN'T HEARD FROM HER MYSTERY MAN. SO, SHE DECIDED TO FLY BACK TO THE BLACK ORCHID ISLAND!
OH NO!!
MEANWHILE— —FIRST TIME IN THE COMPANY CAFETERIA, MRS. FLOWERS?
YES, MR. GARR— AND I THOUGHT I'D TRY SOME OF THE CHEESE WE MAKE HERE—BUT THERE ISN'T ANY—
I'M PUTTING YOU ON A DIET, THING. YOU MAY HAVE WHATEVER YOU CAN SIP THROUGH A STRAW
MEANWHILE ..
HMMMMMM???!!!
IS HE AFRAID I'M GOING TO THROW SOME KIND OF AN ORGY?
FROM YOUR PAST PERFORMANCE, HIS CONCERN IS JUSTIFIED!
DO YOU SEE ANYTHING?
JUST A DEAD ENGINE!
JE L'AI LAISSÉE DANS MON AUTRE VESTE! NOUS SOMMES DE NOUVEAU À LA PORTE!
OH, NON! NON!
ADIEU, CINÉMA!
A-T-ON IDÉE D'ÊTRE AUSSI...
KLUNK!
—THE RESUSCITATOR WASN'T ANY USE. SIR. I'M SORRY.
WE WEREN'T VERY HOPEFUL. THANK YOU FOR TRYING.
OH, I CAN'T BELIEVE IT!
MARK THRASHES THE WATER IN AN EFFORT TO KEEP THE SHARK FROM ATTACKING AGAIN
I KNEW BETTER THAN TO LET BECKY FIX MY BREAKFAST!
MAUREEN, YOU KNOW EVEN THE BEST OF MARRIAGES REQUIRES HARD WORK AND UNDERSTANDING TO SURVIVE!
ROBERT L., IN MY OPINION, THE COMING ELECTION IS GOING TO BE A FARCE.
IT'S RAINING HARDER.
THE WIND'S COMING IN GUSTS!
WHY IS IT TAKING PAPA SO LONG?
MRS. APONTE GAVE THE JOB TO SOMEONE ELSE.
OH, NO!!!
I'M NOT USED TO LIVING ALONE AND I'M NOT GETTING ANY YOUNGER!
I CAN'T BELIEVE I DIDN'T EVEN KNOW THE DRAFT WAS BEING REINSTATED. I TRY SO TO KEEP UP.
IT'S NOT YOUR FAULT, TONKER. YOU'VE BEEN IN TRAINING.
I FEEL LIKE A FOOL, MRS. WORTH! FEAR OF AGING IS A TERRIBLE THING!
IT IS ALSO A VERY FUTILE EMOTION, LEE!
GET UP, HARRIS. YOU'RE ON K.P.
YOU WOKE ME UP TO TELL ME THAT?
YOU REALLY SHOULDN'T PERMIT A STRANGER TO COME INTO YOUR HOUSE WHEN YOU'RE ALONE, JENNY!
HE HAD AN HONEST FACE!
DARN ZIPPER'S FOREVER GETTING STUCK!
MEANWHILE... BACK HOME...
ISN'T GRANDPA COMING TO DINNER?
NO! I'M AFRAID THE WIDOW BROWN DONE HIM IN!
BONK!
THAT YOUNG MAN IN DARK GLASSES!— I DO BELIEVE HE'S FOLLOWING ME!
I WAS GOING TO QUIT, HUGH! HONEST! JUST AS SOON AS I'D USED UP THAT BOTTLE!
YOU'VE SAID THAT EVERY TIME... FOR THE PAST SIX YEARS, GLENNA!
NOBODY FOOLS ME, LADY!
INTO THE DUNGEON WITH HER, MAKKO! YOU, DOCTOR, GET BUSY ON THAT BOMB!
DAISY'S BEEN MOODY AND UNHAPPY ALL DAY LONG
I'M ABSOLUTELY TERRIBLE, THANK YOU!
WE REALLY SHOULD PREPARE SOME KIND OF RELEASE FOR THE PRESS!
Forget Your Troubles, C'mon Get Happy! Tom Tippin is Parade Marshall for the 1980 Belle Rêve Southern Decadent Costume Parade starting at Matassa's 3pm Sunday August 31

1980

An acerbic comic cell representing Robert Laurent's pet parrot commenting on the upcoming election.

The fear of growing old and being alone, one of the "hard times" depicted in the invitation.

An in-joke about Kathleen Kavanaugh's pet named Thing.

Another joke about one of the core group, making fun of Bruce Harris.

According to Robert Laurent, this cell represents Lee Provost's vanity.

A reality check about personal relationships with a reference to Maureen Block.

Doonesbury comic recalling the draft for the war in Vietnam.

The invitation ends with a reference to the nuclear accident at Three Mile Island.

top: Wedding anniversary party invitation for Charles and Maureen Block.

bottom: Pajama party invitation.

clockwise, top left: Film still from the Super 8mm footage of Southern Decadence celebrants at Johnny Matassa's Bar, 1973. Film still from the Super 8mm footage of Southern Decadence celebrants at Big Marsha's Bar, 1973. The Lady Russell, 1974. Grand Marshal Frederick Wright marching down Rampart Street, 1974.

THE SUPER 8MM FILMS

Robert Laurent procured a Super 8mm camera early in 1972 and filmed various parties and cookouts with his friends. The following year, he began filming Southern Decadence. His recordings feature a strange fluidity, a stream of spontaneous moments and unchoreographed dances, long moments of supreme banality and exaggerated gestures that recall William Eggleston's *Stranded in Canton* (1974). However, Laurent's footage lacks sound, thus recalling masterpieces of the early silver screen, an era when every gesture, facial expression, and movement of the body revealed much more about the subjects and their surroundings. These rare films are part of the Southern Decadence Archive at Tulane University's Special Collections after digitization and restoration at the University of Southern California.

MASTER LIST

OF SOUTHERN DECADENCE PARADES, GRAND MARSHALS, THEMES, COLORS, NUMBER OF ATTENDEES, AND ECONOMIC IMPACT

Year	SDGM No.	Grand Marshals	Color	Theme	Attendees	Economic Impact
1972	First Southern Decadence Party at Belle Rêve, celebrating the end of a long, hot summer. Two weeks later, another party at Belle Rêve, the infamous farewell party for Michael Evers; no parade or grand marshal.					
1973	Informal costumed march from Johnny Matassa's bar back to Belle Rêve for the now annual Southern Decadence Party; no grand marshal.					
1974	1	Frederick Douglas Wright				
1975	2	Jerome Williams (Pickle)				
1976	3	Preston Hemmings				
1977	4	Robert Laurent				
1978	5, 6	Robert King Kathleen Kavanaugh				
1979	7	Bruce Harris				
1980	8	Tom Tippin				
1981	9	Tommy Stephan (Miss Cakie-Tee)				
1982	10	Don Ezell				
1983	11	Danny Wilson				
1984	12	Adolphus Spires (Mumbo)				
1985	13	Michael Hickerson (Fish)				
1986	14	Kathleen Conlon				
1987	15	Jeffrey Melton (Olive)				
1988	16	Jerome Legume		Plagues, Pests, Parasites		
1989	17	George Goode				

1990	18	Robbie (Ruby) Haywood	Red	Circus Came to Town		
1991	19	Jamie Temple	Black	Shirley Temple Black Leather		
1992	20	Harry Sherman (Rhie)	White	Casino Casinot		
1993	21	Lee Featherston (Ms. Fly)	Yellow	Drag-On-Fly		
1994	22	Alain Simard (Miss Alain)	White Gold	Voodoo that You Do		
1995	23	Edward Norton (Blanche)	Virgin White	The Cocktail Tour		
1996	24	Wayne White	Royal Blue Gold	Tour of Da Nile	35,000+	
1997	25	Greg Manogue (Miss Love)	Silver White Teal	The Love Tour: A Wedding to Remember	50,000+	$25 million+
1998	26	Robin Anthony Malta	Color TV Optional	Deliriously Decadent Divas: A Salute to Sitcom Reruns	60,000+	$30 million+
1999	27	Errol Rizzuto	Silver Black	Dark Lady Tour: Dissidents of Decadence	70,000+	$35 million+
2000	28	Tony Langlinais Thom (Smurf) Murphy	Red Silver Black	Taboo X 2: The Forbidden Pleasures Tour	90,000+	$72 million+
2001	29	Roy Haylock (Bianca del Rio) Pat Ritter (Estelle) Rick Thomas (Big Rick)	Purple Pink Red	Ménage À Trois	100,000+	$80 million+
2002	30	"Irish" Mike Sheehan	Any and All	Fairy Tales	110,000+	$88 million+
2003	31	Rusty LaRoux	Vibrant Colors of the Rainbow	Carnival Decadence	120,000+	$96 million+
2004	32	Donald James (Donnie Jay)	Electric Blue Silver Black	Daydreams and Fantasies: Welcome to My Harem	125,000+	$100 million+

(continued)

Year	SDGM No.	Grand Marshals	Color	Theme	Attendees	Economic Impact
2005	33	Regina Adams[a] Reilly O'Wright III (Lisa Beaumann [a])	Red Purple	Jazz and Jezebels Cancelled Due to Hurricane Katrina	—	—
2006	33	Regina Adams[a] Reilly O'Wright III (Lisa Beaumann [a])	Green Pink	Southern Decadence 2006: Rebirth	75,000+	$60 million+
2007	34	Harry (Tip) Varnador (Electra City) Marcus Martinez Mark (Guadalupe) Thomas II	Crimson Teal Gold	Ancient Truths, Lies, and Sacrifice	100,000+	$125 million+
2008	35	Samson Utley (Paloma)[a] Gary Delaune (Tittie Toulouse)[a]	Silver Black White	Decadence Does Disco Cancelled Due to Hurricane Gustav	—	—
2009	35	Samson Utley (Paloma)[a] Gary Delaune (Tittie Toulouse)[a]	Black Silver Red	Hurricane: This Year, They Blow Back	100,000+	$150 million+
2010	36	Julien Artressia Toby Lefort	Powder Blue Black Purple	Leather and Feathers Charity: NO/AIDS Task Force	135,000+	$160 million+
2011	37	Michael Kitchens (Tiffany Alexander) Misael Rubio	Fuchsia Pink Silver Black	Viva New Orleans: What Happens in New Orleans Stays in New Orleans Charity: NO/AIDS Task Force	80,000+	$96 million+
2012	38	Pat McArdle (Miss Hope) T.J. Conard	White Purple Silver	Peace, Love And Hope = Monkey Dance Charity: Belle Reve	30,000+ (Hurricane Isaac)	$30 million+

2013	39	Venus Santiago Richard Hullender (Tami Tarmac)	Fuchsia Pink Tangerine Orange Gold	Live, Laugh And Love Charity: Belle Reve	150,000+	$180 million+
2014	40	Chad Boutte Arthur Severio (Reba Douglas) Aubrey Synclaire	Canary Yellow Turquoise Blue Pearl White	Under The Big Top: Welcome to the Gayest Show on Earth Charity: PFLAG New Orleans	160,000+	$192 million+
2015	41	Misti Ates Frank Joseph Wingerter IV (Frankie Fierce) Steven Mora Rip & Marsha Naquin-Delain	Lavender Lime Green Silver Lamé	Swimmin' with the Gods and Goddesses Charities: LGBT+ Archives Project of Louisiana, Louisiana Equality Foundation, and PFLAG New Orleans Scholarship Fund	180,000+	$216 million+
2016	42	Philip Anthony (Felicia Phillips) Tony Leggio Jeffrey Palmquist Derek Penton-Robicheaux	Ruby Red Pearl White Blue Sapphire Amethyst Purple	Decadence Takes The World Charities: NOAGE[b] and ARNO[c]	216,000+	$259 million+
2017	43	Josh Mesa (Coca J Mesa) Drew Aizpurua (Persana Shoulders) Danny Starnes (Princess Stephaney)	All Neon Colors with Silver Accents	Let Them Eat Cake: Southern Decadence Electrified Charities: NOAGE and Dodwell House	250,000+	$300 million+
2018	44	Frank Perez Adikus Sulpizi	Blue Yellow	House of Bourbon: Unleash Your Beast Charities: LGBT+ Archives Project of Louisiana and Team Friendly	TBD[d]	TBD[d]

[a] Served twice as grand marshals because of hurricanes.

[b] New Orleans Advocates for LGBT Elders.

[c] Animal Rescue New Orleans.

[d] Information not available at time of publication.

∽ IN MEMORIAM ∽

Robert J. "Rip" Naquin and Marion M. "Marsha" Greeson

The current popularity of Southern Decadence is due in no small part to Rip and Marsha Naquin-Delain. Through their publication, *Ambush Magazine,* and its attendant websites, they promoted Southern Decadence tirelessly. Sadly, Rip passed away on Tuesday, August 8, 2017, less than a month from the Labor Day extravaganza he loved so much. His partner Marsha soon followed on Thursday, December 14.

Originally from New Iberia, Louisiana, he and Marsha Delain had been a couple since 1973 and were the first same-sex couple in Louisiana to register as a domestic couple in 1993 when the city of New Orleans made that option available. The two were officially married in New York City in 2014.

Greeson grew up in Baton Rouge and graduated from the Baton Rouge Beauty College. Naquin and Delain met outside a Bourbon Street bar in 1973, moved in together in Baton Rouge, and were soon involved with the International Imperial Court System, becoming the first Grand Emperor and Grand Empress of Louisiana in 1978. They then launched *Ambush Magazine* in 1982 before moving to New Orleans in 1985.

From 1986 until Naquin's death, the *Ambush* offices were located on the first floor of 828 Bourbon St., with the proprietors' residence on the second and third floors. Legendary parties took place at the 1830s Ambush Mansion, especially during Carnival.

In addition to promoting Southern Decadence, Rip and Marsha's contributions to the LGBT+ community were numerous. He and Delain founded the Gay Easter Parade, the Krewe of Queenateenas, and assumed stewardship of the Gay Appreciation Awards from the late Marcy Marcel. Over the course of his illustrious career, Rip served on the governing boards of a number of organizations, including the New Orleans LGBT Community Center; the LGBT+ Archives Project of Louisiana; and New Orleans Southern Decadence, Inc.

As consummate fundraisers, the couple devoted much of their life to raising hundreds of thousands of dollars for local charities, including the NO/AIDS Task Force, Food for Friends, Belle Reve, Buzzy's Boys and Girls, NO-AGE, the LGBT+ Archives Project, NOCCA, PFLAG, the Louisiana Equality Foundation, ARNO, and many others. Their passing marked the end of an era and left a huge gap in the New Orleans LGBT+ community.

Errol Rizzuto

Errol Rizzuto, a longtime beloved fixture in the New Orleans LGBT community, passed away on October 29, 2017. Rizzuto, along with his good friend Robin Malta, was a cofounder of Café Lafitte in Exile's annual Red Party, which raises money for local charities. He also served as the grand marshal of Southern Decadence in 1999 and, in recent years, he became involved in the Krewe of Amon-Ra as captain.

Rizzuto will be remembered for his cheery disposition and his love of life, as well as for being the epitome of selflessness. Word of his death sent shockwaves throughout the community. Those who knew him, both well and casually, flooded social media with fond memories, the universal sentiment being that he was kind and generous. More than a few posts described him as a "prince among men."

NOTES

Introduction

1. *The Collected Works of Samuel Taylor Coleridge, Poetical Works, Poems (Reading Text): Part 1,* ed. J. C. C. Mays (Princeton N.J.: Princeton University Press, 2001), 512–14.

2. William L. Robinson, *The Diary of a Samaritan* (New York: Harper, 1860), 153.

3. Lafcadio Hearn, *Inventing New Orleans: Writings of Lafcadio Hearn,* ed. S. Frederick Starr (Jackson: University Press of Mississippi, 2001).

4. Lafcadio Hearn, *Chita: A Memory of Last Island* (New York: Harper, 1889), 163–64.

5. Justin Hale and Janice Stillman, eds., *Old Farmer's Almanac* (Dublin, N.H.: Yankee Publishing, Inc., 1952).

6. John Brady, *Clavis Calendaria; or, A Compendious Analysis of the Calendar: Illustrated with Ecclesiastical, Historical, and Classical Anecdotes.* (London: Longman, 1812), 84.

7. H. G. Emery and K. G. Brewster, eds., *The New Century Dictionary of the English Language* (New York: P. F. Collier & Son Co., 1927), 382–83.

8. Edward Gibbon, *The History of the Decline and Fall of the Roman Empire* (New York: Modern Library, 1977).

9. Robert V. Remini, *The Life of Andrew Jackson* (New York: Harper and Row, 1988).

10. Clarence John Laughlin, *Ghosts along the Mississippi: An Essay in the Poetic Interpretation of Louisiana's Plantation Architecture* (New York: Scribner, 1948), epilogue.

11. Hearn, *Inventing New Orleans.* The letter was published in the *New Orleans Daily City Item,* January 5, 1878.

12. This paragraph is a condensed version of a longer conversation with Robert Laurent over the course of several years.

13. Jack Kerouac, *The Subterraneans* (New York: Grove, 1958), 1.

14. Charles Maniaci, interview by Howard Philips Smith, 2016.

15. Anaïs Nin, *The Diary of Anaïs Nin, 1947–1955,* ed. Gunther Stuhlmann (New York: Harcourt, Brace, Jovanovich, 1974), 133–34.

16. Alice L. Hutchison, *Kenneth Anger: A Demonic Visionary* (London: Black Dog, 2004).

17. Belle Rêve was the home of Southern Decadence in the first years, the name taken from Tennessee Williams's *A Streetcar Named Desire.* The French spelling has been retained. However, for the AIDS hospice with the same name, they have dropped the circumflex.

18. Edward Leffingwell, ed., *Jack Smith: Flaming Creature—His Amazing Life and Times* (1963; New York: Institute for Contemporary Art/P.S. 1, 1997), 155–67.

19. "Roger Ebert Reviews *Chelsea Girls,*" *Chicago Sun-Times,* June 27, 1967.

20. John G. Ives, *John Waters* (New York: Thunder's Mouth Press, 1992).

21. Pam Tent, *Midnight at the Palace: My Life as a Fabulous Cockette* (Alyson Books, 2004), xiii.

22. Roberta Smith, "Art in Review: William Eggleston," *New York Times,* January 30, 2004.

23. John Kennedy Toole, *A Confederacy of Dunces* (Baton Rouge: Louisiana State University Press, 1980).

24. Tennessee Williams, *Mister Paradise and Other One-Act Plays* (New York: New Directions, 2005), 187–220.

25. William Talsman, *The Gaudy Image* (Paris: Olympia Press, 1958).

26. William B. Tressner Jr., *Queens of the Quarter* (San Diego: French Line 48, 1968).

Chapter One

1. Tony Leggio, interview by Frank Perez via Facebook Messenger, October 2016.

2. Felicia Phillips, interview by Frank Perez via Facebook Messenger, October 2016.

3. "What's Hot," *Ambush Magazine,* September 17–30, 1999.

4. Rip Naquin-Delain and Marsha Naquin-Delain, "45th Southern Decadence Sets New Records: Over 216,000 Participants, over $259 Million Economic Impact, over $27,000 for Charity." *Ambush Magazine,* November 22–December 5, 2016.

Chapter Two

1. The majority of this chapter is based on a series of interviews from 2014 to 2016 with the founding members of Southern Decadence, including Robert Laurent, Maureen and Charlie Block, Tom Tippin, Preston Hemmings, and Judith Shapiro by Howard Philips Smith and Frank Perez.

2. Roger Kimball, *The Long March: How the Cultural Revolution of the 1960s Changed America* (San Francisco: Encounter, 2000).

3. Maureen Block, interview by Howard Philips Smith, 2016.

4. Roberts Batson, "Southern Decadence," *Impact,* August 28, 1998.

5. Robert Laurent, interview by Howard Philips Smith, 2014.

6. Michael E. Crutcher Jr., "Historical Geographies of Race in a New Orleans Afro-Creole Landscape," *Landscape and Race in the United States,* ed. Richard H. Schein (New York: Routledge, 2006), 23.

7. Michael E. Crutcher Jr., *Tremé: Race and Place in a New Orleans Neighborhood* (Athens: University of Georgia Press, 2010).

8. Keith Weldon Medley, *We as Freemen: Plessy v. Ferguson: The Fight against Legal Segregation* (Gretna, La.: Pelican, 2003).

9. Crutcher, *Tremé.*

10. James T. Sears, *Rebels, Rubyfruit, and Rhinestones: Queering Space in the Stonewall South* (New Brunswick, N.J.: Rutgers University Press, 2001).

11. Robert Laurent, interview by Howard Philips Smith and Frank Perez, 2016.

12. Kathleen Kavanaugh, interview by Howard Philips Smith, 2017.

13. Camille Paglia, "Tennessee Williams," in *A New Literary History of America,* ed. Greil Marcus and Werner Sollors (Cambridge, Mass.: Harvard University Press, 2012), 793, www.newliteraryhistory.com/tennesseewilliams.html.

14. Matthew C. Roudané, ed., *Cambridge Companion to Tennessee Williams* (Cambridge, U.K.: Cambridge University Press, 1997), 52.

15. Harold Bloom, ed., *Bloom's Guides: Tennessee Williams's* A Streetcar Named Desire (Philadelphia: Chelsea House Publishers, 2005), 25.

16. Preston Guidry, *Official Rules and Techniques of the Cajun Card Game Bourré,* ed. Benny Graeff and Ivy Lantier (Lafayette, La.: National Cajun Bourré Association, 1988).

17. Keith Spera, "Cosimo Matassa, New Orleans Recording Studio Owner, Engineer and Rock 'n' Roll Pioneer, Has Died," *New Orleans Times-Picayune,* September 11, 2014; Ian McNulty, "Matassa's Market, Back from Brink, Reopens in French Quarter with New Look, Different Menu," *New Orleans Advocate,* February 14, 2017, www.theadvocate.com/new_orleans/entertainment_life/food_restaurants/article_c04984ac-efbf-11e6-826f-9f7c33da97e2.html; Louis Matassa, interview by Frank Perez, 2016.

18. Sears, *Rebels, Rubyfruit, and Rhinestones,* 97–98.

19. Stephanie Cole and Natalie J. Ring, eds., *The Folly of Jim Crow: Rethinking the Segregated South* (College Station: Texas A&M University Press, 2012).

20. Julia Hemmings, "Origins of Southern Decadence Festival," www.nolacitymuseum.org/items/show/980 (accessed October 17, 2016).

21. Ibid.

22. Nick Pinkerton, "William Eggleston in the Real World/*Stranded in Canton,*" Museum of the Moving Image Reverse Shot, August 31, 2005, reverseshot.org/reviews/entry/701/william_eggleston_real_world_stranded_canton (accessed December 2016).

23. Kevin Flot, interview by Howard Philips Smith, December 2016.

24. Hemmings, "Origins of Southern Decadence Festival."

25. Ibid.

26. Ibid.

27. Tom Tippin, interview by Howard Philips Smith, 2016.

28. Hemmings, "Origins of Southern Decadence Festival."

29. "In Memoriam: Robert King," *Ambush Magazine,* August 26–September 8, 2008.

Chapter Three

1. Elizabeth Werlein, *Wrought Iron Railings of Le Vieux Carré* (1916; Williamsburg, Va.: Bookpress, 1946).

2. Richard Campanella, *Bourbon Street: A History* (Baton Rouge: Louisiana State University Press, 2014), 107.

3. Scott Ellis, *Madame Vieux Carré: The French Quarter in the Twentieth Century* (Jackson: University Press of Mississippi, 2010), 25.

4. John Shelton Reed, *Dixie Bohemia: A French Quarter Circle in the 1920s* (Baton Rouge: Louisiana State University Press, 2012), 8.

5. Ibid, 236.

6. Taylor D. Littleton, *The Color of Silver: William Spratling: His Life and Art* (Baton Rouge: Louisiana State University Press).

7. William Weeks Hall, *The Weeks Hall Tapes,* comp. Morris Raphael (New Iberia, La.: Raphael, 1983), 6–7, 26–27.

8. Reed, *Dixie Bohemia,* 221, 234.

9. See Reed, *Dixie Bohemia.*

10. Ibid.

11. Howard Philips Smith, *Unveiling the Muse: The Lost History of Gay Carnival in New Orleans* (Jackson: University Press of Mississippi, 2017).

12. See Ellis, *Madame Vieux Carré,* 78.

13. Sears, *Rebels, Rubyfruit, and Rhinestones,* 274–75; see also www.lgbtarchivesla.org.

14. Johnny Townsend, *Let the Faggots Burn: The UpStairs Lounge Fire* (St. Petersburg, Fla.: BookLocker, 2011),

15. Clayton Delery-Edwards, *The Up Stairs Lounge Arson: Thirty-Two Deaths in a New Orleans Gay Bar, June 24, 1973* (Jefferson, N.C.: McFarland, 2014). Several variations of the name of the lounge have appeared in print. For consistency, the authors use Clayton Delery-Edwards's version as he has confirmed that this is the way it appeared on the original bar signage.

16. Ibid.

17. See Sears, *Rebels, Rubyfruit, and Rhinestones,* 273.

18. Ibid., 243, 275–76.

19. Frank Perez and Jeffrey Palmquist, *In Exile: The History and Lore Surrounding New Orleans Gay Culture and Its Oldest Gay Bar* (Hurlford, Scotland: LL-Publications, 2012), 97–98.

20. See Sears, *Rebels, Rubyfruit, and Rhinestones,* 243, 275–76.

21. Ibid.

22. Ibid., 276.

Chapter Four

1. Robert Laurent, Tom Tippin, and Maureen and Charlie Block, interviews by Howard Philips Smith, 2014–16.

2. Edward Norton, interview by Howard Philips Smith, 2003.

3. Ibid., 2004.

4. Lou Bernard, interview by Howard Philips Smith, 2016.

5. Jamie Temple, interview by Howard Philips Smith and Frank Perez, 2016.

6. Patrick Shannon, "Southern Decadence: Lady Attitude Presides over Decadence," *Impact,* September 15, 1986.

7. Kathleen Conlon, Facebook comment, 2016.

8. Christopher Rose, "Kind of a Drag: Parade Salutes Decadent Spirit," *New Orleans Times-Picayune,* September 5, 1988.

9. Patrick Shannon, "The Wit and Wisdom of Southern Decadence," *Impact,* September 15, 1989.

10. Frank Perez, "The Phoenix Rises from the Ashes of Smoky Mary," *Ambush Magazine,* November 8–21, 2016.

11. Kevin Allman, ". . . And Scandalizes Southern Sensibilities: Scenes From New Orleans's Southern Decadence Celebration," *Advocate,* October 8, 1991.

12. Wayne Phillips, interview by Howard Philips Smith, 2016.

13. Betty Guillaud, "Big Easy Does It," *New Orleans Times-Picayune,* September 12, 1993.

14. Edward Norton, interview by Howard Philips Smith, 2004.

15. Lou Bernard, interview by Howard Philips Smith, 2016.

16. Robert M. Carter, "Decadence Day Overlooked," *New Orleans Times-Picayune,* September 10, 1996.

Chapter Five

1. Henri Schindler, *Mardi Gras New Orleans* (Paris: Flammarion, 1997).

2. Ibid.

3. Caillot, *A Company Man: The Remarkable French-Atlantic Voyage of a Clerk for the Company of the Indies, A Memoir by Marc-Antoine Caillot,* ed. Erin Greenwald (New Orleans: Historic New Orleans Collection, 2016), 135–36.

4. Carolyn Kolb, "Mardi Gras Walking Clubs: Carnival's Feet on the Street," *New Orleans Magazine,* February 2013.

5. Gwendolyn Knapp, "Waiting for Ste. Anne: Herein Lies the True Spirit of Carnival," *New Orleans,* February 2012.

6. Smith, *Unveiling the Muse.*

7. Ibid.

Chapter Six

1. Jad Adams, *Hideous Absinthe: A History of the Devil in a Bottle* (Madison: University of Wisconsin Press, 2004); Mary Ann Wegmann, "Battle of New Orleans: Old Absinthe House," *New Orleans Historical,* neworleanshistorical.org/items/show/619 (accessed August 23, 2017).

2. Aleister Crowley, "Absinthe: The Green Goddess," *The International,* February 1918, 2.

3. Tennessee Williams, *Tennessee Williams Notebooks,* ed. Margaret Bradham Thornton (New Haven: Yale University Press, 2006), 232.

4. Tennessee Williams, *Orpheus Descending* and *Suddenly Last Summer* (New York: New Directions, 2012), 66.

5. Stephen Miller, "New Orleans's 'Miss Dixie' Fasnacht Dies at 101," *Wall Street Journal,* November 25, 2011.

6. Perez and Palmquist, *In Exile,* 37–42.

7. John Kelly, "1972: Fire Destroys Club My-O-My on Lakefront," *NOLA.com,* September 5, 2010.

8. See John Rechy, *City of Night* (New York: Grove, 1963), esp. 322–29; Smith, *Unveiling the Muse.*

9. Meredith Bethune, "The Sweet Success of Bananas Foster Has an Unsavory Past," *The Salt,* September 30, 2016, www.npr.org/sections/thesalt/2016/09/30/493157144/the-sweet-success-of-bananas-foster-has-an-unsavory-past.

10. "Curb Advocated on Homosexuals: Crackdown to Save Young Persons Demanded," *New Orleans Times-Picayune,* April 28, 1951.

11. Various *Times-Picayune* articles from late 1950s.

12. Frank Perez, "Climate of Hostility," *Ambush Magazine,* November 20, 2012.

13. Frank Perez, "The Persecution of Tony Bacino's Bar," *Ambush Magazine,* April 16, 2013.

14. One such example of this type of harassment was the police raid on the Krewe of Yuga ball in 1962, resulting in almost one hundred arrests for "lewd conduct," with all the names of the arrestees published in the newspapers.

15. Lou Bernard, interview by Howard Philips Smith, 2015.

16. Frank Perez, "The Phoenix Rises from the Ashes of Smoky Mary's," *Ambush Magazine,* November 8–21, 2016.

17. Perez and Palmquist, *In Exile,* 46.

18. Petula Dvorak, "Lawyer: Gay Bar Raid an Outrage," *New Orleans Times-Picayune,* September 9, 1998.

19. Frank Perez, "The Phoenix Rises from the Ashes of Smoky Mary's," *Ambush Magazine,* November 8–21, 2016.

20. Edward Norton, interview by Howard Philips Smith, 2003.

21. Frank Perez, "Remembering Charlene Schneider," *Ambush Magazine,* October 13, 2015.

22. Rachel Lee, "Last Call: Stories from New Orleans' Disappearing Dyke Bar Scene," March 24, 2015, www.autostraddle.com/last-call-stories-from-new-orleans-disappearing-dyke-bar-scene-282482/.

Chapter Seven

1. Smith, *Unveiling the Muse.*

2. NO/AIDS Task Force, www.facebook.com/noaidstaskforce.

3. Jessica Wapner, "How New Orleans Became America's Ground Zero for HIV," www.aeon.co (accessed August 2017).

4. Project Lazarus, www.projectlazarus.net.

5. www.projectlazarus.net/history.htm.

6. Belle Reve, bellerevenola.org (accessed June 5, 2017).

7. LGBT+ Archives Project of Louisiana, www.lgbtarchivesla.org.

8. Greg Manogue, interview by Frank Perez and Jeffrey Palmquist, 2017.

Chapter Eight

1. Keith Darcé, "Southern Decadence Means Big Business, Gay Tourists Give Summer a Boost," *New Orleans Times-Picayune,* September 4, 1998.

2. Anne Craven, "The Unsinkable Ursulines," *Country Roads,* May 26, 2015, countryroadsmagazine.com/art-and-culture/history/the-unsinkable-ursulines.

3. Greg Manogue (Miss Love), interview by Frank Perez and Jeff Palmquist, 2016.

4. Rip and Marsha Naquin-Delain, "Decadence Revelers Top 50,000 with a $25 Million Economic Impact," *Ambush Magazine,* September 19–October 2, 1997.

5. Patrick Shannon, "A Dialogue with Robin Malta, Southern Decadence Grand Marshal XXVI," *Ambush Magazine,* July 24–August 6, 1998; Frank Perez, "Remembering Robin Malta," *Ambush Magazine,* November 22–December 5, 2016.

6. Shannon, "Dialogue with Robin Malta."

7. Rip and Marsha Naquin-Delain, "SDGM XXVII Errol Rizzuto Leads Longest SD Parade in History, *Ambush Magazine,* September 17–30, 1999.

8. Rip and Marsha Naquin-Delain, "Southern Decadence XXIX," *Ambush Magazine,* September 1–14, 2000.

9. Rip and Marsha Naquin-Delain, "Southern Decadence XXX," *Ambush Magazine,* September 14–27, 2001.

10. Rip and Marsha Naquin-Delain, "100,000 Revelers Expected for Southern Decadence," *Ambush Magazine,* August 30–September 19, 2002; Rip and Marsha Naquin-Delain, "Mayor Welcomes Southern Decadence Visitors," *Ambush Magazine,* August 30–September 19, 2002.

11. Bruce Nolan, "Local Pastor Is Targeting Decadence—Leaders of Gay Community Blast 'Strictly Homophobic Campaign,'" *New Orleans Times-Picayune,* October 10, 2002.

12. Bruce Nolan, "Eye of the Storm," *New Orleans Times-Picayune,* August 30, 2003.

13. Lili LeGardeur, "Decadence Videotape Raises Questions—Officials' Goal Is to Protect, Enforce," *New Orleans Times-Picayune,* September 19, 2002; Grant Storms, "Not Just Inappropriate: Illegal," *New Orleans Times-Picayune,* October 12, 2002.

14. Frank Perez, "Louisiana Lesbian and Gay Political Action Caucus (LAGPAC)," *Ambush Magazine,* May 5–18, 2015.

15. Daniel Martiny, "Anything-Goes Mentality," *New Orleans Times-Picayune,* September 29, 2002.

16. "'Christian Patriot' Targets Gay Mardi Gras," October 6, 2003, abcnews.go.com.

17. Susan Mole Shelley, "Editorial," *New Orleans Times-Picayune,* October 5, 2002.

18. Steve Teeter, "It's Not His Business," *New Orleans Times-Picayune,* October 15, 2002; Mark A. Stafford, "Everyone Cuts Loose in Quarter," *New Orleans Times-Picayune,* October 12, 2002.

19. Michael Franklin, "What About Decadence All the Rest of the Year?" *New Orleans Times-Picayune,* October 1, 2002.

20. "Conservative Christians, Gays to Share Quarter," *WDSU News,* updated February 28, 2011, www.wdsu.com/article/conservative-christians-gays-to-share-quarter/3353015 (accessed November 20, 2016).

21. "Archbishop Blasts Gay Celebration—But Backer Says Fest Not Centered on Sex," *New Orleans Times-Picayune,* August 15, 2003.

22. Nikki Usher, "Gay Celebration Stirs Controversy—Promoters Warn Against Public Sex," *New Orleans Times-Picayune,* August 28, 2003.

23. Lily LeGardeur, "Decadence Fans Set to Welcome Protesters," *New Orleans Times-Picayune,* August 28, 2003.

24. "'Christian Patriot' Targets Gay Mardi Gras," October 6, 2003, abcnews.go.com.

25. Aesha Rasheed, "Protesters, Festival-Goers Meet in the French Quarter—Police Keep Groups Separate and Calm," *New Orleans Times-Picayune,* September 1, 2003.

26. Rip and Marsha Naquin-Delain, "It's Official—Rusty LaRoux Will Lead the 32nd Official Southern Decadence Celebration," *Ambush Magazine,* July 29–August 1, 2003.

27. Rip and Marsha Naquin-Delain, "What's Hot," *Ambush Magazine,* September 9–22, 2003.

28. Phyllis Denmark, "The Big Diva," *Ambush Magazine,* September 9–22, 2003.

29. Michelle Hunter, "Anti-Gay Pastor Booked with Obscenity—Storms Arrested Near Playground," *New Orleans Times-Picayune,* March 1, 2011.

30. Michelle Hunter, "Southern Decadence Protest Leader Booked with Masturbating at Metairie Park," *New Orleans Times-Picayune,* February 28, 2011.

31. Phyllis Denmark, "The Big Diva," *Ambush Magazine,* August 31–September 13, 2004.

32. Buzzy's Boys and Girls, www.facebook.com/buzzys.boysandgirls.

33. Perez and Palmquist, *In Exile,* 156.

34. Brian Tashman, "Joyner: Hurricane Katrina Was God's Judgment For Homosexuality," www.rightwingwatch.org/post/joyner-hurricane-katrina-was-gods-judgment-for-homosexuality.

35. Karl Lueger, commenting on the stormfront.org website, which promotes itself as White Pride World Wide, September 1, 2008.

36. Chris Rose, "Meet the Co-Grand Marshal of the 37th Annual Southern Decadence Celebration," *Times-Picayune,* August 29, 2008.

37. Ibid.

38. Martha Carr, "Southern Decadence in New Orleans in Full Swing," *Times-Picayune,* September 4, 2009.

39. Dykeadence, www.autostraddle.com/celebrate-labor-day-and-homosexuality-at-dyke adence-in-new-orleans-105991.

40. Maggie Migliozzi, "Southern Decadence for Women, Too," September 2, 2011, www.nola .com/nolavie/index.ssf/2011/09/southern_decadence_for_women.html; Heather Cassell, "Dykeadence Steams Up New Orleans," July 6, 2012, girlsthatroam.com/dykeadence-steams-orleans; grrlspot.com; fonseca, "Dykeadence: Southern Hospitality with a Side of Debauchery," August 23, 2012, www.autostraddle.com/dykeadence-southern-hospitality-with-a-side-of-debauch ery-144513.

41. Rip and Marsha Naquin-Delain, "Hurricane Issac [*sic*] Dampens Attendance at 41st Southern Decadence Estimated to be 25–30,000," *Ambush Magazine*, September 11–24, 2012.

42. Rip Naquin, interview by Frank Perez, October 2016.

43. Frank Perez reached out to Conard via Facebook and initially agreed to an interview in 2016. The interview was never done because Conard backed out at the last minute.

44. Rip and Marsha Naquin-Delain, "Hurricane Issac [*sic*] Dampens Attendance at 41st Southern Decadence."

45. Katherine Fretland, "Nine preachers arrested at Southern Decadence," *Times-Picayune,* September 2, 2012; updated June 2, 2016, www.nola.com/crime/index.ssf/2012/09/nine_preachers _arrested_at_sou.html.

46. Rip and Marsha Naquin-Delain, "Southern Decadence Grand Marshals XXXIX Tami Tarmac & Venus Santiago Raise over $4,000 for Belle Reve," *Ambush Magazine*, September 10–23, 2013.

47. Greg Manogue (Miss Love), interview by Frank Perez and Jeffrey Palmquist, 2017.

48. Rip and Marsha Naquin-Delain, "44th Southern Decadence Gears Up for More Than 160,000 Revelers; 41st Southern Decadence Grand Marshals Raise over $30,000 for Charity," *Ambush Magazine*, September 1–14, 2015.

49. Frank Perez, "An Interview with the Southern Decadence Grand Marshals," *Ambush*, September 1–14, 2015.

Chapter Ten

1. Publicity text explaining Southern Decadence, southerndecadence.com (accessed September 5, 2014).

2. Michel Foucault, *The Use of Pleasure: The History of Sexuality*, trans. R. Hurley (Paris: Vintage, 1990), 10.

3. Frank Perez, "Pop-Up Lesbians: GrrlSpot," *Ambush Magazine*, October 7, 2014.

4. GrrlSpot, grrlspot.com/fleurt-southern-decadence (accessed September 1, 2017).

5. Doug McCash, "Check out the steamy Southern Decadence Grand Marshal's Parade 2017," *Times-Picayune* (accessed October 22, 2017).

6. Edward P. McDaniel, "NOLA LGBT Fundraising: Charity or Business?" April 20, 2017, *Squirrel News*, squirrelnews.net/my-blog/nola-lgbt-fundraising-charity-or-business (accessed July 7, 2017).

7. James Garner, interview by Frank Perez, October 2017.

8. David Lee Simmons, "As Southern Decadence Takes the World, 10 Keys to Global Dominance," *New Orleans Advocate*, September 1, 2016.

9. Leo Watermeier, "Hate Preacher Arrested at Southern Decadence," joemygod.com, September 4, 2017 (accessed October 22, 2017).

Appendix: Early Southern Decadence Invitations

1. Brant and Johnny Hart Parker, *The Wondrous Wizard of Id* (New York: Fawcett Gold Medal, 1970).

2. Robert Laurent, interview by Howard Philips Smith, September 2016.

3. Letter from Robert Laurent to Howard Philips Smith, dated October 2017, Tulane University, Special Collections, Southern Decadence Archive.

4. Email from Robert Laurent to Howard Philips Smith, dated October 22, 2017.

INDEX

Italicized page numbers indicate illustrations

A Confederacy of Dunces (Toole), 18–19
A Streetcar Named Desire (Williams), 43, 47, 118
absinthe, 105
Adams, Regina, 33, 133, 137–38
AIDS epidemic/crisis, 80, 85, 89, 92, 97, 114–18, 123, 140, 182, 184, 194, 197, 210–11; fundraising (*see* NO/AIDS Task Force); Robert H. (patient), 116
Aizpurua, Drew (Persana Shoulders), 35–36, 162, *166*
Alotta Mulatta, 83, 113
Ambush Magazine, 39, 77, 103, 119, 122–23, 125–27, 132, 136, 218–21, 243
Ambush Mansion, 35, 39, 222, 243
Amon-Ra, Krewe of, 35, 85, 102–3, 201, 244
And Tell Sad Stories of the Deaths of Queens (Williams), 19
Anderson, Sherwood, 69, 105
Anger, Kenneth, 14
Animal Rescue New Orleans (ARNO), 27, 40
Antill, William, *24,* 28, 31, 37, *142*
Ates, Misti, 25, 29, 33, 36, 138, 140
Bagneris, Larry, 121, 127, 137, *146,* 208–9, 214, 216
Bailey, Lee, 71
Batson, Roberts, *165,* 206
Bead Toss, 2, 38–39, 123, 125–26, 156, 222
Beaumann, Lisa, 33, 133, 192, 220
Belle Rêve, xii–xiii, 15, 43–55, 57–58, 61, 63, 79–80, 82–83, 95, 162, 184, 188–91, 225, 228; AIDS hospice (*see* Belle Reve [AIDS hospice]); incorrect French, 47–48
Belle Reve (AIDS hospice) 118, 123, 132, 136, 220, 244
Bennet, Wilhemina, 23, 30, *111*
Bernard, Lou (Lucille), Jr., 35, *84,* 85, 87, 96, 110, 174, 194–200, 203
Bernhardt, Earl, 132
Big Easy Sisters of Perpetual Indulgence, *147*
Big Marshal's Shalimar Club, 57, 190, *234*
Block, Charlie, *42,* 43, 46, *52,* 63, 65–66, 79, 184, 186–87, 189–90, 193
Block, Maureen, *42,* 43, 46–47, 50, 55, 63, 65–66, 79, 184, 186–90, 193, 207; Mother of Southern Decadence, 171–72, 228
Boggs, Luther, 73
Bongé, Dusti, 71
Book of Secrets, 33

Boudreaux, Andy, 123, 206, 209
Bourbon House Bar and Restaurant, 107–8
Bourbon Pub and Parade Discothèque, 27, 34, 56, 113–14, 119, 123, 127, *165*, 183, 218
Bourbon Street Awards, 181, 201
Bourgeois, Douglas, 59
bourré (Cajun card game), 48, 53, 58, 63, 188, 190–91, 211
Boutte, Chad, 138
Bouvier, Elizabeth, 29, 36
Brady, John, 4
Brady's Bar, 113
Brasseaux, Lee "Bunny," 31, 36, *150*
Bryant, Aletha, 204
Bryant, Anita, 76–77
Buster Holmes Restaurant, 11, 199, 205
Buzzards Walking Club, 100
Buzzie's Boys and Girls, 132, 244

Café Lafitte in Exile (Lafitte's), 9–10, 23, 26, 28, 33–34, 38, 56, 102, 106, *107*, 111, 114, 123, 125–27, 201–3, 244
Capote, Truman, 71
Carnival, 4, 98; Gay Carnival, 81, 98, 102–13, 181; gay krewes, 102; walking clubs, 100–102
Carter, Troy, 121–22, 208–9
Cazenave, Arnaud, 67–68
Chelsea Girls, 16
Chase, Michael, 204
Chi Chi LaRue, 35
Clay, Gary (Ms. White Lightning), 81, 86, 179
Clover Grill, 93, 96, 127
Club My-O-My, 106–7, 113
Club Rendezvous, 106
Cockettes, 17
Coffee Pot Restaurant, 11, 86
Cole, Myron, 182
Coleridge, Samuel Taylor, 1, 2, 20, 47
Conard, T. J., 136, 215, 219–20
Congo Square, 45, 127
Conlon, Kathleen, 33, 36, 85–87
Connick, Harry, Sr., 55, 120, 210
Corner Club, 101
Corner Pocket, 32, 34, 38–39, 114, 125–26, 192, 204–5
Cossitt, George Marney, 87, 92, *111*
cross-dressing. *See* drag/drag queen
Crowley, Aleister, 105
Crutchfield, Finis, 74

Daisy Mae (Kenneth Toncrcy), 10, 13
Danna, Samuel Colby, *24*, 28, *148*
Dayrides, Provosty A., 108
Decadent Ducks, 35
Decadents, xii, 4, 20, 43, 45–49, 51, 54, 57, 59, 61, 63, 94, 104, 119, 131, 160, 165, 174, 184, 190, 223–26, 228
DeLong-Church, Barrett, 27, 36, *169*
DeLong-Church, Braddsten "Beaux," 36, *169*
Demented Women, 81, 174, 181, 183
Devine, Dennis, 61
Divine (Glenn Milstead), 16–17, *17*
Dixie's Bar of Music, 106, 108
Dixie's Land, 60, 226
dog days, 4, 45
Donovan, Nick, 110, 174, 196, 203
Double Dealer journal, 68
Double Play Bar, 26, 31, 34, 38–39, 187, 202
Doucet, Walter, 203
Douglas, Reba, 138, *145*
drag/drag queen, 2, 11–12, 15–17, 19, 25–28, 30–32, 34–35, 37, 50, 52–53, 57–60, 62, 75, 81–87, 89–90, 93–95, 99, 103, 106, 108, 112–14, 127, 132, 160, 162, 172, 181–83, 190, 195, 199–200, 203, 207, 210, 212, 213–14, 218

Dream Palace, 182
Dunbar, George, *70*, 71
Dykeadence, 135, 161, 222
Dykes on Bikes, 135

Eggleston, William, 18, 235
Electra City, 25, 33, 36, 103, 134
Emerold, John, 9–10, 12
Emmett, Daniel Decatur, 60
Eros, Krewe of, 78
Eureeka Starfish, 36
Evers, Michael, *42*, 43, 45, 52, 184–85, 187–89, 191
Ezell, Donnie, 81–82, 117, 179, 181, 184

Fairmont Hotel, 19, 86, 182
Fanning, William J. "Buzzy," 132
Fatted Calf Restaurant, 73
Flamingo's Restaurant and Bar, 199
Faulkner, William, 47, 68–69
Feastherston, Lee (Ms. Fly), 39, 94, 102, 118, 122–23, 204–5, 207–8, 211–12, 221–22
Fellini Satyricon, 14, *15*
Fields, Flo, 67
Finale Bar, 9–10
Flaming Creatures, 15–16, *16*
Flot, Kevin, 60
Fontenot, Adam, 73
Foster, Richard R., 108
Four Seasons Restaurant and Bar, 25, 34
Frankie Fierce, 25, 33, 36, 138
French Opera House, 99
Friendly Bar, 30, 37, 195
Funky Butts, 56, 58

Gaither, Catherine, 29
Gallatin Street, 54, 99
Galley House, 11
Gallmeyer, Ann, 76
Garner, James, 28, 136, 163, 217, 220
gay liberation, 72, 74, 77, 182
Gay Liberation Front, 72
Gay Easter Parade, 204, 244
Gayfest, 73, 201
Gay People's Coalition (GPC), 75
Gay Pride Festival, 201
Genet, Jean, 16
Gertrude Stein Society, 73, 76
Gil, Mickey, 201
Golden Lantern, 28, 34–35, 37, 39–40, 55–56, 80–84, 86, 93, 102, 110, 114, 123, 125, 127, 133, 136, 163, 174, 179–83, 194–95, 198–99, 201, 203, 206, 217, 220
Goode, George, 90–91, *91*, 196–98
Gore, Robert, 43, 52, 185, 187, 189
Graham, Larry, 32, 197
GrandPre, Ken, 29
GrandPre Bar, 26, 29, 31, 34, 38–39, 215
GrrlSpot, 135, 161

Hachard, Sister Marie, 120
Half-Fast Walking Club, 101
Hall, William Weeks, 69
Harris, Bruce 43, 62, *64*, 184, 190, 228
Harris, George Edgerly (Hibiscus), III, 17–18
Haylock, Roy (Bianca Del Rio), 103, 127, 209
Haywood, Robbie (Ruby), 92, 117, 196
Hearn, Lafcadio, 3, 7–8
Hemmings, Preston, 43, 57–58, 62–63, 66, 184, 190
Hickerson, Michael (Fish), 85, 87, 92, 102, *111*, 122, 137, 204, 208, 212, 214–15
Hickman, Travis, 113
Hughes, Alfred, 130
Human Equal Rights for Everyone (HERE), 76–77

Hurricane Isaac, 135, 220
Hurricane Katrina, 118, 133–34, 164, 192, 196–97, 210, 220
Hurricane Gustav, 134

Inauguration of the Pleasure Dome, 14
International Imperial Court, 243
Ishtar, Krewe of, 78, 102, 201

Jackson, Rachel, 5
Jackson Square, 11, 63, 65, 72, 77, 130, 228
James, Donald (Donnie Jay), 113, 132, 210
Jax Brewery, 62, 72
Jethro Tull (*Thick as a Brick*), 54
Jewel's Tavern, 55–56, 81–82, 113, *113,* 179, 184, 196
Jindal, Bobby, 135
Jim Crow South, 43, 56, 227
Johnson, Christine, 135
Jolly, David, 81, 179
Joyner, Rick, 135

Kavanaugh, Kathleen, 43, 46, 62–63, *64,* 125, 175, 184, 191
Kerouac, Jack, 9
krewes. *See* Carnival
King, Robert, 43, *51,* 52, 57, 62–63, 66, 79–81, 125, 184, 188–91, 193, 204, 218, 227–28
Knights d'Orléans, 81, 111
Knights of Decadence 34, 216, 222
Koch, Richard, 68–69
Krevitt, Zachary "Zak" Mason, 143–44

Landry, Tilden, *70*
Langlinais, Tony, 125–27, 201, 203, 205
LaRoux, Rusty, 130–31, 214
Laughlin, Clarence John, 6–7
Laurent, Robert, *42,* 43–61, 63–65, *65,* 79, 81, 95, 120, 137, 161, 164, 184–93, 202, 204, 207, 210, 215, 223–28, 235
Lefort, Tony, 34, 137, 216, 222
Leggio, Anthony, *22,* 23, 25–27, 29, 36, *146, 151*
Legume, Jerome, 87, *88,* 89, 92
LGBT+ Archives Project of Louisiana, 38, 118, 138, 174, 221, 244
Long, Huey P., 59
Lords of Leather (Krewe of), 34–35, 78, 94, 102, 111
Louisiana Lesbian and Gay Political Action Caucus (LAGPAC), 77–78
Lucille's and Friend bar, 85, 87, 90, *110,* 174, 194–95, 198–99, 203
Lucille's Golden Lantern. *See* Golden Lantern
Lucille's Weenie Women Café, 199

McArdle, Pat (Miss Hope), 136–37, 214, 219–20
Mahaffey, Ted, 39
Malta, Robin, 102, 123, 164, 201–4, 208–10, 212, 217, 244
Maniaci, Charles, 9–13
Manogue, Greg (Miss Love), 23, 29, 33, 118, 121–23, *121,* 137–38, 193, 195, 202, 204, 206–18
Marcel, Marcy, 200, 244
Martiny, Daniel, 128–29
Marti's Restaurant, 56–57
Matassa, Cosimo, 48–49, 55
Matassa, Johnny, 48
Matassa, Louis, 49, 187
Matassa's Bar, (Johnny), *48,* 48–49, *55,* 60, 63, *64,* 80, 86, 110, 180–81, 183–84, 187, 190, 201, *234*
Maxime's Supper Club, 68
Melton, Jeffrey (Olive), 87, 90, 92, 204, 218
Menefee, Jerry, 198

Mercer, Bob, 193
Merry Antoinettes, The, 162
Mesa, Coca (Josh Mesa), *22, 24,* 28, 30, 33, *149,* 162, *167*
Metropolitan Community Church (MCC), 73–74
Miller, Blake, 136, 220
Mint Bar, 192, 196
Miss Do, 187
Miss Jasmin, 11
Montez, Maria, 59
Montez, Mario, 16
Mora, Steven, 25, 33, 37, 138, 140
Morlet, Emile, 106
Morning Call Restaurant, 11, 72
Morris, Major Henry, 74
Morrison, Chep, 109
Moyer, Michael (Raven), 204
Murphy, Thom "Smurf," 125–27, 205
Mwindo, Krewe of, 30, 34

Nagin, Ray, 127–28, 134
Naquin-Delain, Rip and Marsha, *24,* 25, 28–29, 33, 35, 37, 39, 103, 119, 130, 132, 136–38, 163–64, 217, 218–22, 243–44
New Orleans Advocates of GLBT Elders (NO-AGE), 27, 40, 221, 244
New Orleans Southern Decadence Inc., 137–38, 163, 220, 244
New Orleans Gay Men's Chorus, 78
Newlin, Jon, 187
Nin, Anaïs, 13
NO/AIDS Task Force, 78, 92, 116–17, 132, 244
nondiscrimination ordinance, 78
Norton, Edward (Miss Blanche), *80,* 81–83, 95–96, 112, 174, 179–85, 198–99, 201, 207, 209, 218
Nunez, Roger Dale, 74

Odiorne, William "Cicero," 69
Old Absinthe House, 56, 85, 105
Olympus, Krewe of, 84, 102, 174, 194, 196, 203
Oncle, Gerard, 120, 217
One-Eyed Jacks Bar, 35
Overland, Paul (Miss Helga), 202
Owens, Chris, 57–58, 226
Oz Bar, 113–14, 123, 125, 127

Page Bar, 30, 38–39
Pair-O-Dice Tumblers, 63, *64,* 65, 165
Palmquist, Jeffrey, *22,* 23, *24,* 25–30, 33, 36–39, 103, *142, 146, 151–52,* 163, 175
Parents and Friends of Lesbians and Gays (PFLAG), 77–78, 95, 221
Parrish, Leonard, *70,* 71
Pawell, Father Bob, 116
Penton-Robicheaux, Derek, *22,* 23, 25, 27–30, 36–37, *146, 151*
Perez, Frank, *24,* 28, 31–32, 37–38, 144, *170*
Perry, Troy Rev., 74
Persana Shoulders. *See* Aizpurua, Drew
Phillips, Felicia (Philip Anthony), *22,* 23, 25, 27–32, 36, *146, 150, 151, 153*
Phoenix bar, 32, 34–35, 40, 82, 85, 87, 90, 92, 94, 102, 110–112, 114, 222; police raid, 111–12
Pink Flamingos, 16, *17*
pleasure dome, 1, 2
Plessy, Homer (*Plessy v. Ferguson*), 45
Plundering Purple Pirates, 36
Poché, Paul, 101
Polyphemus, Krewe of, 78, 85, 102
Powers, Terry, 199
Princess Stephaney. *See* Starnes, Danny
Project Lazarus/Lazarus House, 78, 116–18

Quartermaster (Nellie) Deli, 27
Queer space, 161–62

Quistadors, 19, 23, *24,* 28, 31–33, 36–37

Radical Faeries, 34
Randolph, David, 43–45, *49,* 49–50, 52, 57, 187–90
Rawhide Bar, 32, 34, 123, 127
Rasmussen, Buddy, 73
Rechy, John, 107
Red, David, 43, *49,* 63, 79, 161, 184, 186, 188, 190–91, 228
Red Party, 123, 244
Redd, Rikki, 39
Rednour, Clifford, 113
Regent's Row, 9–10, 12, 113
religious conservatives/protesters, 38, 62, 164
Ritter, Pat "Estelle," 127
Rizzuto, Errol, *24,* 28, 33, 103, 123–25, *124,* 137, 164, 200–205, 207, 214, 244
Robinson, Alan, 76–77
Robinson, Chuck, 132
Robinson, Jack, 71
Robinson, William (*The Diary of a Samaritan*), 3
Roger, Arthur, 117
Rocking Times Bar. *See* Dixie's Bar of Music
Rowena (Roy Hermann), 83, 113
Rubyfruit Jungle Restaurant/Bar, 125, 203
RuPaul, 94, 127
Rushton, William, 75–77
Russell, Randy, 199
Ruthy the Duck Lady, 10, 56, *65,* 190

Safari House Bar, 11, 56, 113
Santiago, Venus, 33, 136, *145, 154,* 215
Satyricon, Mystic Krewe of, 103, 127
Saxon, Lyle, 68–69
Schindler, Henri, 101
Schneider, Charlene, 73, 92, 112, 201
Scott, Barbara, 73
Seale, Ed, 43, 184, 188, 190
Seidenberg, Jean, *70,* 71
Shadows-on-the-Teche, 69
Shapiro, Judith, 43, *52,* 79, 188, 190
Sheehan, "Irish" Mike, 127, 137, 210, 214, 217
Sherman, Harry (Rhie), 94
Shoulders, Persana (Drew Aizpurua), 35–36, 162, *166*
Simard, Alain (Miss Alain), 95, 207
Simpson, Russell (Lady Russell), *18,* 59–60, *61,* 161
Smith, Jack, 15–16, 59
Smith, Ron, 61–62, 77
Smoky Mary's Restaurant, 92
Société de Sainte Anne, La, 101–2
Southern decadence: definition, 5, 8; general, 19, 21, 23, 78; nonprofit organization 501(c)(3), 136–38, 163, 216–17, 220
Southern Decadence Security Team, 130
Spires, Adolphus (Mumbo), 39, *84,* 85, 92, *111,* 183, 193–94, 197–98, 201, 207–8, 212, 218
Spratling, William, 68–69, 71
St. Claire, Adrian, 75, 113
Starlet Lounge, 109
Starnes, Danny (Princess Stephaney), 36, 162, *168,* 212–13
Stephan, Tommy (Miss Cakie-Tee), *80,* 81–82
Storms, Grant, 127–32, 210
Stormwatchers, 130
Stranded in Canton, 18, 18, 235
Sulpizi, Adikus, 32, 36, *148, 153*
Superdome, 57, 225–26
Survivors' Bar Crawl, 39–40
Synclaire, Aubrey, 33, 103, 138, *145*
Synclair-Kennedy, Monica, 28, 36–37, *157*

Talsman, William (*The Gaudy Image*), 19
Tami Tarmac, 103, 136–37, *154*, 215–17, 220
Tangerine Queens, 201
Tau House, 116–17
Temple, Jamie, 87, 92–94, 102, 110, *111*, 112, 201, 211–12
Theriot, Martha and Becky, 59, 191–92, 228
Thomas, Ricky, 127
Tippin, Tom, 43, *51*, 45, 63–65, *64–65*, 183–84, 189, 218, 224, 227
Tittie Toulouse, 25, 103, 134
Tony Bacino's Bar, 109, 111
Toole, John Kennedy, *18*, 19
Tour of Tours, 53
Train Wreck, 26
Travis's Bar, 75, 113, 132, 203
Tremé (Faubourg Tremé), 2, 15, 20, 43, 45, 184, 187–88, 190
Tremé, Claude, 45
Tressner, William (*Queens of the Quarter*), 19
Trévigne, Paul, 45
Twain, Mark, 105

Up Stairs Lounge, 11, 73–75, 113, 210
Utley, Samson (Paloma), 33, 134

Verona, Jay, 196, 198–99

Walking Clubs. *See* Carnival
Wanda's Bar, 56, *65*, 65, 113
Warhol, Andy, 16
Watergate Hotel, 41
Waters, John, 16
Werlein, Elizabeth, 67
White, Jack, 81, 179
White, Wayne, 96, 201, 204, 207–8, 211
Whitesell, Joseph Woodson "Pops," 69
Whitman, Walt, 105
Wolfendale's Bar, 206
Wonder Bar. *See* Club My-O-My
Wood, Tom, 96, 111, 217
Woodard, Earl, 198
Wilde, Oscar, 105
Williams, Jerome "Pickle," 43, *49*, 57–58, 81, 184, 188, 190, 226
Williams, Tennessee, xi, 19, 47, 71, 106, 199
Wilson, Danny, 81, 83–86, *84*, 179–80, 183, 194, 199
Wright, Frederick Douglas, *42*, 43, 46, 48, 54–57, *55*, *61*, 63, *65*, 79, 95, 120, 137, 184–87, 189, 193, 200–202, 207, 210, *234*